Praise for *Men Still at Work*

"Should you work beyond 'normal' retirement age? *Men Still at Work* answers important questions and offers encouragement for people who want to remain in the workforce for years . . . or decades." —**Douglas Goldstein**, Profile Investment Services

"I, like many elders I know, am still working because I love what I do and I feel I have knowledge and experience to offer anyone interested. It's a beautiful thing to be a musician still able to perform, compose, and educate at the age of eighty-seven. This is a must-read for someone looking for a road map." —**Jimmy Heath**, professor emeritus, Queens College; jazz saxophonist, composer, and arranger

"We will need to know more about the labor force involvement of Americans over age sixty-five—because this segment of the population will continue to grow, because this stage will represent a greater portion of our lives, and because this group will increasingly impact our economy and culture. Elizabeth Fideler offers us engaging and highly readable stories of men who continue to work while the majority of their cohort has retired, which complements her earlier study of working women in this age group. These accounts remind us of the importance of meaning and engagement at work, and not just for the elderly." —**Jerry A. Jacobs**, University of Pennsylvania

Men Still at Work

Professionals over Sixty and on the Job

ELIZABETH F. FIDELER

ROWMAN & LITTLEFIELD
Lanham • Boulder • New York • Toronto • Plymouth, UK

Grateful acknowledgment is made for permission to reprint excerpts from the following copyrighted works:

From AGING WELL by George E. Vaillant, M.D. Copyright © 2002 by George E. Vaillant, M.D. Used by permission of Little, Brown and Company. All rights reserved.
From BORN TO RUN: A HIDDEN TRIBE, SUPERATHLETES, AND THE GREATEST RACE THE WORLD HAS NEVER SEEN by Christopher McDougall. Courtesy of Random House.
From TOWNIE: A MEMOIR by Andre Dubus III. Courtesy of W. W. Norton Company.

Published by Rowman & Littlefield
4501 Forbes Boulevard, Suite 200, Lanham, Maryland 20706
www.rowman.com

10 Thornbury Road, Plymouth PL6 7PP, United Kingdom

Copyright © 2014 by Rowman & Littlefield

British Library Cataloguing in Publication Information Available

Library of Congress Cataloging-in-Publication Data

Fideler, Elizabeth F.
  Men still at work : professionals over sixty and on the job / Elizabeth F. Fideler.
    pages cm
  Includes bibliographical references and index.
  ISBN 978-1-4422-2275-5 (cloth : alk. paper) — ISBN 978-1-4422-2276-2 (electronic)
  1. Older men—Employment—United States. 2. Professional employees—United States.
  3. Retirement age—United States. 4. Age and employment—United States. I. Title.
  HD6280.F53 2014
  331.3'980973—dc23

                                                                        2013040402

♾™ The paper used in this publication meets the minimum requirements of American National Standard for Information Sciences—Permanence of Paper for Printed Library Materials, ANSI/NISO Z39.48-1992.

Printed in the United States of America

Contents

Acknowledgments

I am very grateful to all 156 professionals who completed my survey, especially the thirty-three men who so generously gave their time for in-depth interviews and profile editing as well as those who forwarded the survey on my behalf to older working men around the country.

Many other people offered strong encouragement for the project and helped to recruit survey participants, including: Charles V. Willie, Mary Coleman, Barbara Resnek, Carolyn Kiradjieff, Allan Shedlin, Sam Klaidman, Richard Winslow, Henry Field, John Willett, Jeremy Freund, Richard Eisenberg, Ruth Winett, Ann Kaganoff, Sharon Caballero, Gayle Rich, Judith Zorfass, Vernise Cardillo, Elise Savage, Maxine Greenwald, Ann Arvedon, Esther Novak, Ann Chuk, Linda Nilson, Barbara Millis, Diane Sasson, Judith Stames-Hamilton, Nancy Weibust, Katherine Eyre, Elaine Cooke, Mary Antes, Jean Canellos, Judith Mir, Patricia Hartney, Lisa Shapiro, Lila Packer, Richard Pomerance, Tom Lazarus, Andrew Fogelson, and Louis Nemser.

Research progressed faster with help from the Sloan Center on Aging and Work at Boston College and John Collins III and Marcella Flaherty at Harvard's Gutman Library.

Sarah Stanton, Kathryn Knigge, Lisa McAllister, and colleagues at Rowman & Littlefield worked their publishing magic.

My husband, Paul, gave up his home office and moved to the dining room (my office) so I could finish the book. For that sacrifice and for his unwavering support, I am forever thankful.

1

Introduction

Real success is finding your lifework in the work that you love.
—David McCullough, Historian

Wall Street is said to be buoyant. Corporate profits as a share of national income are at a record high last seen in 1950. At the same time, job growth remains stalled and 700,000 layoffs are anticipated as $85 billion in automatic cuts to the federal budget ("sequestration") kick in.[1] In this thorny context, it is remarkable that labor force growth rates for older men and older women, taken separately or combined, are greater than for any of the younger groups participating in or endeavoring to participate in the US workforce. This phenomenon can be explained only partially by Americans' greater longevity and by the arrival of the leading edge of the baby boomer cohort in the senior ranks. There is far more to it.

Men Still at Work: Professionals over Sixty and on the Job shows how older men are prospering in the paid workforce, particularly those who are well educated and in professional jobs, despite the recession of 2007–9 and the economic downturn that has persisted in its wake. (The recession may have ended and the stock market appears to have recovered, yet employment has not rebounded to former levels, home foreclosures are still numerous, and credit remains extremely tight.) Older men are the *second*-fastest growing segment of the US labor force because the participation rate of older females is even higher. This book highlights important factors that are sparking this phenomenon and influencing the timing of retirement for older men. It uncovers their reasons for opting to work well past conventional retirement age, for example, contributing experience, know-how, and institutional knowledge, not just making money (which some excel at doing)—and tells how they balance the demands of work, family, and the wider community with personal interests and needs. And, throughout, it makes a special point of comparing the genders on such measures as career field, length of career, time out for caregiving, employment status, and earning power. It identifies similarities and differences in the careers of older men and women—in particular, who and what influenced or encouraged them along the way and what motivates them to continue working. In so doing, it continues the narrative presented in *Women Still at Work: Professionals over Sixty and on the Job.*[2]

Many well-known American men work past conventional retirement age. Composer Elliott Carter, who died recently at 103, worked almost to the very end of his life. Seth Glickenhaus, a ninety-eight-year-old money manager who started his career on Wall Street as a messenger, is in the process of selling his advisory firm to a firm led by retirement money manager Marvin Schwartz, who is a mere seventy-two. Tom and Ray Magliozzi of *Car Talk* and *Good News Garage* fame are seventy-six and sixty-four, respectively, and still working even though they are not making new radio shows. Framingham's Danforth Museum of Art recently featured the work of ninety-year-old Bostonian John Wilson, the sculptor whose bronze bust of Martin Luther King Jr. stands in the Rotunda of the US Capitol. (On Inauguration Day, President Obama paused in the Capitol Rotunda in front of Wilson's dignified bust of Dr. King.) More than half of the members of the US Senate are in their sixties, seventies, and eighties, including Chuck Grassley, eighty, and Carl Levin, seventy-nine. Forty-seven of the senators age sixty or older are men and twelve are women.

A completely random list of prominent older working men might well include: novelist Herman Wouk, ninety-eight; architect I. M. Pei, ninety-six; folksinger, songwriter, and environmental activist Pete Seeger, ninety-four; former POTUS, Nobel Peace Prize winner, and human rights advocate Jimmy Carter, eighty-eight; economist Paul Volcker, eighty-six; pop and jazz singer Tony Bennett, eighty-seven; business magnate Warren Buffett, eighty-three; stage, television and film actor James Earl Jones, eighty-two; author, historian, narrator, and lecturer David McCullough, eighty; country music singer-songwriter and film actor Willie Nelson, eighty; neurologist and author Oliver Sacks, eighty; economist, author, and Nobel Prize winner Daniel Kahneman, seventy-nine; journalist, commentator Bill Moyers, seventy-nine; chef, television personality, and author Jacques Pepin, seventy-seven; blues singer and guitarist Bobby Rush, seventy-seven; actor, director, screenwriter, and author Alan Alda, seventy-seven; associate justices of the US Supreme Court Antonin Scalia and Anthony Kennedy, both seventy-seven; bandleader and jazz pianist Eddie Palmieri, seventy-six; columnist and political commentator Mark Shields, seventy-six; sportswriter and novelist Frank Deford, seventy-four; professional football and soccer team owner Robert Kraft, seventy-two; Vice President of the United States Joseph Biden Jr., seventy; Mayor of New York City Michael R. Bloomberg, seventy-one; political commentator David Gergen, seventy-one; humorist, author, storyteller, and radio personality Garrison Keillor, seventy-one; and violinist Itzhak Perlman, sixty-eight.

Less well known but equally impressive are the men who bypass retirement simply because they enjoy their jobs and want to keep working full time or part time. Income is certainly important to them, but they believe that there is more to life than making money. Or they agree with the late Pulitzer Prize–winning editor and columnist Eugene Patterson, who lived to age eighty-nine according to his personal edict: "Don't just make a living. Make a mark."[3]

Each individual has his own reasons for continuing to work, whether driven by financial or familial circumstances, or dreading what will happen if he stops—perhaps long-term unemployment or permanent joblessness, perhaps unrelieved lassitude. Here is what keeps Marc Mosko on the job. Mosko, a teacher of graduate courses in business management, marketing, creativity and design who also has a start-up company, told his daughter: "I work at age seventy-four because I don't know how to stop, and I don't like being too tight with money. Social Security does not start to cover the bills. But most important, work (if you are doing what you like to do) is very satisfying. So I continue teaching and am working hard at building an eBay business from home. This year it is starting to pay off as I am gathering a following of customers and learning how to buy better."

Then there is ninety-three-year-old Newt Wallace of Winters, California, who published the local weekly, *The Winters Express*, from 1946 until 1983 when he passed the baton to his son. After that, Newt Wallace wrote columns for a time and began delivering the newspaper in the Winters business district. He has been delivering the paper ever since because he enjoys connecting with people he knows and, in the words of the March 3, 2013, *New York Times* feature story about his long tenure, "keeping a finger on the pulse of a town after a life in journalism."

The longest-serving state legislator in Wisconsin is eighty-five-year-old Fred Risser, who has been in politics nearly sixty years. He was one of the seniors interviewed by Ina Jaffe for National Public Radio's "Working Late" series in February 2013 to emphasize a point: the paycheck is welcome, but their real reason for working is *they want to and they can*. Working past retirement age has become "the new reality."[4]

Even before *Women Still at Work* was published in June 2012, I had been contemplating a companion volume that would be about older men choosing to continue working. Then, at a book party thrown by my husband and children to celebrate *Women Still at Work*, several men in their seventies challenged me to write about them. "What about me? I'm still working," was the refrain. It didn't take arm twisting to get me started. By July I was in the first phase of data collection. To ensure comparability, I revised only a few items from my survey of women to facilitate the change to men. I circulated it via e-mail and regular mail to colleagues and friends and to the women who had responded to the original survey, asking my contacts to complete the survey (if sixty or older, male, and still working for pay) or to refer or recruit other men who might be interested in participating in the project. Again, the survey snowballed and responses came from all over the country. This methodology, known as "snowball sampling" for obvious reasons, produced 156 respondents. Virtually all professionals, they are well-educated high achievers still working and still enjoying good health and abundant energy. Notably, these older men are quite similar demographically to the 155 older women identified by the earlier survey.

With most of the surveys in hand, I completed the second phase of data collection in the fall and winter of 2012–13 by conducting hour-long interviews (mostly by telephone and some in person) of a subset of thirty-three men, or 21 percent of the survey respondents. To ensure comparability of interview data, the questions for men were essentially unchanged from the protocol I had used for interviewing women. The individual profiles based on those interviews serve to put a face on the statistics about older workers;

achieving that goal is the primary purpose of both books. With increasing numbers of older workers delaying retirement and remaining in the paid workforce—the share of employed Americans past sixty years of age is over 10 percent and climbing[5]—it is important to learn not only the dimensions of this "new reality" but also what forces are driving the trend and what gets factored into the older worker's decision-making process.

A few caveats about the study are in order. First, and most obvious, my focus is on *men*. Naturally, women often come into the picture, for example, when discussing national and population and labor market trends, calling on the retirement research literature, and comparing findings about older working men with findings drawn from my research on older working women.

The second caveat concerns age—here it is sixty and older. While it is not at all unusual for men who are sixty to sixty-four to be working, I recruited them for the survey to include the oldest of the baby boomers (who have just started to reach retirement age). And, again, I needed to use the age parameters that I had chosen for my study of older women to obtain comparable data. (A longer discussion of what "older" means follows in chapter 2.)

Third, respondents for this study had to be in the *paid* workforce. Men who were doing volunteer jobs (unless they also held a paid position) were not eligible. This is not meant to slight volunteerism. Far from it. My fellow trustees on the board of the Framingham Public Library and I (as board chair) devote countless hours to civic improvement, and as I have discovered, many of the surveyed men contribute their time and energy as volunteers in their communities, too. Sociologists draw the distinction between *work*—expending mental and physical effort to perform a task—and *occupation*—performing a job in exchange for a wage or salary. The point being that work can occur outside of formal employment and without remuneration, for example, on behalf of the family or the community. Having stated the technical distinction, however, I will blur the two definitions by referring to that sort of unpaid work as volunteering and rely on the popular connotation of *work* to describe a job performed in exchange for a wage or salary.

Fourth, the findings discussed in *Men Still at Work* do not represent and cannot be generalized to the population of all older male workers. This is due to the chief drawback of snowball sampling: the survey does not reach all socioeconomic groups. As sociologist Sarah Willie acknowledges, snowball sampling fails to attain diversity when a survey circulates among people who share many characteristics, such as education level, jobs, race or ethnicity, religious affiliation, and so on.[6] My survey identified older men engaged in a broad spectrum of occupations, living in different geographical regions, and having different religious affiliations, who nonetheless tended to be white men with similar socioeconomic status. To be sure, the respondents from minority groups (8 percent of the total of 156 survey respondents) share impressive advanced degrees and professional status with their white counterparts. The populations not represented in this book are poorly educated men, employed in low-wage, low-skill, high-turnover jobs, who are often obliged to continue working when they are older out of economic *necessity*. In contrast, my survey respondents are all at least above average financially after many years on the job and fortunate to be in a position to *choose* whether to retire or continue working.

Sarah Willie's study of the college experiences of alumni—all black males and females, who attended either Howard University or Northwestern University and had similar experiences to her own—raised the question: would subjects be more forthcoming with an interviewer of similar race or ethnicity? Willie found that she needed to send potential interviewees letters of introduction explaining her qualifications and her intentions. She found that "their willingness to proceed with the interview and their candor during the interview were in very large part based on whether they believed I was trustworthy and empathetic, and those characteristics were connected to the knowledge that we shared a similar racial experience." Willie's reflections made me wonder whether potential respondents would be suspicious of a researcher whose race, ethnicity, or gender differed from their own. Fortunately, in addition to the letters of introduction I myself sent out, several friends (who are mentioned in the acknowledgments) ran interference for me, calling or writing to potential survey respondents and interviewees they knew well and reassuring them about the soundness of both the researcher and the research. This helped greatly in obtaining participation.

Fifth, while the question of whether to retire comes up throughout the stories in this book, *Men Still at Work* is neither a book about retirement nor a guide to decision making in the senior years. I acknowledge that retirement is a long-desired choice for many people, for there are many, many valid reasons to exit the workforce—such as physical, economic, or personal reasons—as well as numerous alternative ways to find enjoyment in one's senior years. With that in mind, let me point out that the purported lure of retirement is precisely what makes the phenomenon of men and women choosing to delay it and continue working so intriguing. Among the options available to a senior male who wants to remain engaged and productive, how viable is the *worker* role? The next chapter contains an array of perspectives on aging and work to help answer that question.

2

Perspectives on Aging and Work

Quarante ans, c'est la vieillesse de la jeunesse, mais cinquante ans, c'est la jeunesse de la vieillesse. [Forty years is the old age of youth, but fifty years, it is the youth of old age.]—Victor Hugo

Census data indicate that the US population is growing bigger, older, and more racially and ethnically diverse.[1] The population age sixty-five and older is singled out for the fastest increase as a percentage of the total US population during the one hundred years from 1950 to 2050 (projected): 8.1 percent of the total in 1950, 12.8 percent in 2009, and 20.2 percent in 2050. Based on projections, one out of every five persons (or 88.5 million) will be sixty-five or older in 2050.[2] Ten years later, this age group will total 92 million, and for the first time ever, will outnumber people younger than eighteen in the United States.[3]

At a recent meeting organized by the Economic Development Authority of Fairfax County, Virginia, the head of the Chamber of Commerce described the demographic shift to an older workforce as the "Silver Tsunami."[4] Another speaker at that meeting, John Martin, author of *Boomer Consumer*, noted that the traditional population "age pyramid" featuring youth at the wide bottom and elders at the narrow peak is turning into an "age rectangle" with nearly equal numbers distributed at the young, middle, and older levels. In the relatively brief period from December 2007 to March 2012, an increase of 14 percent in the fifty-five and older population (from 69.6 million to 79.5 million) occurred.[5] Economists and gerontologists are watching these demographic shifts closely, as are business leaders, human resources managers, financial advisors, insurance companies, government officials, journalists, ad agencies, and others.

Figure 2.1 shows the growth of the population age sixty-five and over and age eighty-five and over from 1900 to 2010 and their projected growth from 2020 to 2050.[6]

However, it seems to me that the shape of the population distribution one draws depends on how one defines and views aging and the "older" person. A recent MetLife study of baby boomers determined that men consider themselves old at seventy-seven on average and women say they are not old until eighty.[7] To confuse matters, it has become a cliché to say eighty is the new seventy, seventy is the new sixty, sixty is the new fifty, and so on. Plenty of evidence supports that claim—seniors enjoying greater health, longevity, well-being, and vigor—yet for researchers it lacks precision. Fortunately, economists and other researchers at the US Bureau of Labor Statistics have a

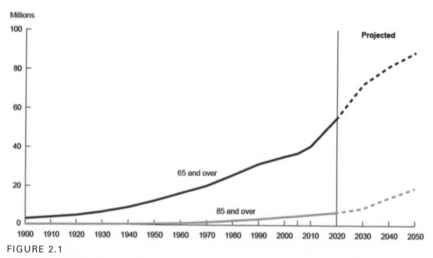

FIGURE 2.1
Number of Older Americans

Source: US Census Bureau, 1900–1940, 1970, and 1980, US Census Bureau, 1983, Table 42; 1950, US Census Bureau, 1953, Table 38; 1960, US Census Bureau, 1964, Table 155; 1990, US Census Bureau, 1991, 1990 Summary Table File; 2000, US Census Bureau, 2001, *Census 2000 Summary File 1*; US Census Bureau, Table 1: Intercensal Estimates of the Resident Population by Sex and Age for the US; April 1, 2000 to July 1, 2010 (US-EST00INT-01); US Census Bureau, 2011, *2010 Census Summary File 1*; US Census Bureau, Table 2: Projections of the Population by Selected Age Groups and Sex for the United States: 2010–2050 (NP2008-t2).

sure grasp of demographic changes, but even they categorize "older" workers as sixty-five in some reports and fifty-five and up in others.

Employers are known to acknowledge that older workers can make good employees and still refuse to hire them. Opinions regarding the desirability of hiring older workers run the gamut. At one end of the opinion spectrum lie negative stereotypes:

- Older workers are considered less productive and more expensive.
- They are resistant to change.
- Their skills and knowledge are not cutting edge.
- If not outright Luddites, they cannot get the hang of new technologies.
- Hiring and training them is a waste of time and money because they will have costly health problems or decide to quit.

Toward the other end of the opinion spectrum are the superlatives about older workers:

- They bring valuable skills, expertise, and experience to the workplace.
- They are known for reliability: consistent day-to-day performance, low absenteeism, and commitment to the job.
- They are conscientious and display good work habits, such as thoroughness and a low error rate.
- Their maturity sets an example for younger workers.

Employees of the Vita Needle Factory have plenty of each quality on the list of superlatives. At Vita, founded in 1932 in Needham, Massachusetts, and run today by the fourth generation of the same family, the median age of employees is seventy-four. About half are over sixty-five and most are part-timers. Vita employs about forty-nine men and women in production, packaging, and shipping of reusable and disposable stainless steel needles, syringes, tubing, wire, and custom-fabricated parts for industry and retail. Having worked for years at other jobs, they bring knowledge, skills, experience, and an outstanding work ethic.

As reported this year by Paul Solman for the *PBS NewsHour*, the oldest member of Vita's geriatric labor force is one-hundred-year-old Rosa Finnegan, a retired waitress who has worked at Vita for sixteen years. Next oldest is Bill Ferson, age ninety-four, who originally thought he would work at Vita for five or six months, and that was twenty-four years ago. Workers interviewed by Solman say they are not there for the money so much as for the camaraderie among coworkers and knowing they are being of use. Bill Ferson says it keeps his "upstairs" going. Many of his friends have passed away or are in tough shape, and he doesn't want to get that way. Because of Vita's "unique model for doing business," Solman observes, "age discrimination means the older the better."[8]

When pondering attitudes about older men and women in relationship to work, it is interesting to compare contemporary thinking with notions that were widely accepted nearly half a century ago. For example, we can go back to October 19, 1970, when anthropologist Margaret Mead spoke at the Community Forum on Social Change in Framingham, Massachusetts. Her topic, "Marriage in an Age of Social Change," elicited a host of questions from the audience on gender roles and behavioral differences. The original tapes (now CDs) of her presentation reveal that some of her observations were light-hearted and most were absolutely serious.

In the question-and-answer portion of the program, Dr. Mead compared the behavior of older men and women, "older" to her meaning *fifty* years of age. She observed, for example, that most men have gone as far as they can go by the time they reach fifty. Aside from a handful of older men who continue career building to the highest positions, the average man who is a second vice president is stuck at that level and a man who is the principal of a small high school is not going to run the New York City schools. A fifty-year-old man may work another fifteen years, then he will retire to a life of quiet and fishing. Just at that moment, his fifty-year-old wife is full of beans and she isn't fit to have around the house. She has postmenopausal zest and is looking forward to the best years of her active life. This can be the time when her husband replaces her with a new, typically younger wife. (I am not sure whether Dr. Mead meant that to be funny or serious.) According to Dr. Mead, a compensatory factor has been around since primitive times. A great invention of human biology makes it possible for men to father children after fifty but prevents women from further childbearing. What made this arrangement fair, at least historically, is that it saved women's lives and kept them around to help the family and tell people where their forebears found food during a famine in earlier times. There was no way to save men;

they, unfortunately, drowned when they went over the reef or were clawed to death by a lion, as Dr. Mead tells it.

Thirty-five years ago, David Hackett Fischer's *Growing Old in America* provided a comprehensive history of aging in America.[9] In the eighteenth and nineteenth centuries, life expectancy was much shorter and people often had to labor into old age, most working until they were worn out. By the early twentieth century, Americans began to think of old age in a new way. Fischer cites a 1903 *Cosmopolitan* magazine article by Edward Everett Hale (then in his eighties and still working as chaplain to the US Senate) worrying that there was "no place in our working order for older men." Forced retirement had become common. Children were supposed to support aged parents. Hale drew attention to the plight of poor elderly, and following the recession of 1908, awareness of their plight began to grow. Fischer tells us that 1909 saw the first public commission on aging appointed in Massachusetts, the first federal old age pension bill proposed in Washington, and a new discipline named "geriatrics" invented in New York City; 1915 saw the first state old age pension system established in Arizona; 1935 saw enactment of the Social Security system; and 1965 brought the Older Americans Act to provide social services, as well as the Medicare and Medicaid programs.

Fischer acknowledges that the majority of Americans dislike their jobs and retire as soon as they can. "For others," he says "the right to work is central to life itself." Thus, in his view, forced retirement at age sixty-five is arbitrary; a person should be judged according to individual merit and competence, not the chronological age group to which he belongs; and he should be free to choose whether to work or not.

Also appearing in the mid-1970s was *Why Survive? Being Old in America*, written by Robert N. Butler, the inaugural director of the National Institute on Aging (NIA), as an exposé and critique. Like Edward Everett Hale nearly three-quarters of a century before him, Butler decries the denial of work to older people who need to earn a living and who derive satisfaction and a sense of purpose from work, as well as the associated loss to society of their skills, knowledge, insights, and experience.[10]

More recent books pick up the thread of the argument. Shea and Haasen's *The Older Worker Advantage* describes older workers as a valuable resource whose capabilities and talents are increasingly important to workplaces and society.[11] Since, as they say, we are increasingly dependent on older workers to produce for, and help manage, our society, we should reject false assumptions about older workers that are merely "insulting myths" and "damaging stereotypes."

Helen Harkness, too, disputes the myths of aging, particularly "the myth that growing up means running down," "the myth of the shrinking brain," and "the myth of wilting originality," especially as they apply to the "career clock."[12] To Harkness, elderly means age ninety and older, but she prefers to focus on *functional age*, not chronology. Functional age "combines and integrates the biological, social, and psychological measures into one active package," and focuses instead on how well we "act, perform, execute, move, think, feel" in our various roles. "For a full life," she concludes, "aging and working are tied together."

False assumptions and myths about aging bring to mind what happened to my mother, a psychotherapist of high intelligence and zest for life, when she became very ill on a trip around the world. The ship's medical officer suspected the worst and advised her to fly home from Hong Kong immediately. Upon her return, she went to her local doctor, who examined her and said dismissively, "You're eighty-six. What do you expect?" (Fortunately, I scheduled an appointment for her at Massachusetts General Hospital where she was diagnosed with late-stage ovarian cancer and treated. She benefited from most of the chemotherapy she and her doctor were willing to try and lived another two and a half years.)

Whether depicted in a disparaging or a flattering light, the senior years have been receiving greater attention of late. Popular designations are "Prime Time," "The Second Half," "The Third Chapter," and "The Third Age." Often authors use such terms to refer to activities following exit from one's career job.[13] Marc Freedman urges men and women to transform what it means to age by dedicating their "prime time" to civic engagement and volunteering, thus balancing personal fulfillment with responsibility to others.[14] One "encore careerist" friend fits the bill perfectly. After a career as a chemical engineer at Polaroid, Fred Wallace taught chemistry part time at Framingham State University for several years until vision problems made him give up lab work. He then revved up his longtime interest in and talent for genealogy and local history and became the (unpaid) town historian and author of a book about a Civil War general from Framingham.

Yet another encore careerist is Sanford Moss, the tour guide I met at the New Bedford Whaling Museum where a group from the Framingham Library visited as part of our "one book, one community" initiative, Framingham Reads Together. (FRT 2013 featured Nathaniel Philbrick's *In the Heart of the Sea: The Tragedy of the Whaleship* Essex, hence the trip to the whaling museum and "The City That Lit the World" in the mid-nineteenth century.) Sandy, a retired marine biologist who volunteers at the museum, enthusiastically shared his extensive knowledge of cetaceans, whaling, and scrimshaw. His baseball cap caught my attention, too, with its wry humor: "In Dog Years I'm Dead." Sandy also shared some information with me about his background:

> First, let me say that I greatly enjoyed the group of people that you brought to the New Bedford Whaling Museum last Sunday. It is always refreshing to engage folks who are interested in things nautical and who are smart and ask good questions. It is nice that you have such an interesting topic—older men still at work—to write about. I have no objection to your using either a description of your visit to the museum or my name in your book. After all, we geezers have to reach for every opportunity to grab a little bit of immortality!
>
> In that vein, here is a little background information for you. I'm seventy-four (as of yesterday) and have been retired from university teaching (University of Massachusetts at Dartmouth, Yale, and Cornell) for about eleven years. Having been a marine biologist (shark and fish biology), I made a near-complete break with that background upon retirement due to a host of developing interests. The first of these was the operation of a small antiques business dealing originally with old hand tools. This preyed on my innate interests in history and my hobby of making furniture with hand tools.
>
> About six years ago my wife, Barbara, and I took the docent training course at the museum. About 85 percent of the trainees from that program participate in directing tours of school-age children through the museum. Having interacted only with university students for forty years, I eschewed the school tours and opted to interpret the museum displays for mostly adults and adult tour groups on weekends (usually Sunday mornings). I also have worked extensively with the Museum Registrar, assisting in maintaining the order of the collections, and participating in installing new exhibits and tearing down the old ones. Finally, I spend one day a week (usually Thursday) participating in a "Scrimshaw Forensic Group" that is under the direction of Senior Curator

Emeritus, Stuart Frank. About six or seven of us gather to examine items of scrimshaw that have been submitted for verification and analysis. This is a very interesting (and educational) exercise, and I look forward to it each week.

Altogether this volunteer work is pretty extensive, and the recordkeeping at the museum has me credited for between three hundred and five hundred volunteer hours each year. But I thoroughly enjoy it, especially since it gives me and my wife (who does her volunteering at the museum library) the opportunity to make new friends among the volunteers and museum staff, as well as to meet many interesting folks who visit the museum.

Returning to the discussion of aging and working, we find many different points of view. For sociologist William Sadler, Third Age refers to the maturing worker's productive years after *forty*.[15] But productivity does not always mean employment. Gerontologists Dawn Carr and Kathrin Komp credit Peter Laslett with popularizing the term Third Age to describe "active engagement" during later life.[16] Yet, among the gerontologists represented in their edited volume, there is little agreement as to (a) what it means to be old, (b) when the Third Age begins, and (c) what active engagement entails. Phyllis Moen, for one, says the Third Age starts after retirement from the career job. She posits a life-course approach: once retired, men and women choose pathways, but their choices remain gendered—women responsible for hearth and home, men responsible for the family economy and "more apt than women in the Third Age to work for pay"—as well as subject to inequities based on race and class differences.[17]

Acknowledging that the territory of the Third Age is "largely uncharted" and "not easily defined," Graham Rowles' and Lydia Manning's chapter in the Carr-Komp volume lists multiple ways to demonstrate one's "new, early late-life identity," for example, through creative pursuits, lifelong learning, spiritual development, or expanded leisure activities. However, *participation in the workforce is not among them*.[18]

In contrast, in discussing the ways society provides opportunities for older people to remain engaged and productive, a chapter by gerontologist Scott Bass lauds seniors' capacity for *both* employment and volunteer activity. He mentions the 1986 amendments to the 1967 Age Discrimination in Employment Act[19] that eliminated mandatory retirement for the vast majority of American workers as well as a set chronological age as a criterion for exiting the workforce. Pointing again to the pioneering work of Robert Butler (the NIA director mentioned earlier) who introduced the term "productive aging" (later amended to "productive engagement," a more inclusive term that views older people as "assets and contributors"), Bass concedes that today, nearly four decades later, "we may not be much farther along in our discourse about significant roles for the aged."[20]

Psychiatrist George Vaillant is convinced that "successful aging is not an oxymoron."[21] In *Aging Well*, he identifies seven major factors or "guideposts to a happier life" that predict healthy aging (from retirement to past eighty)—mature adaptations, education, a stable marriage, not smoking, not abusing alcohol, some exercise, and maintaining a healthy weight. Also important are relationships to other people, preferably warm connections.[22] Vaillant extrapolated his findings about what is needed for healthy adjustment in the senior years from the comprehensive Harvard Study of Adult Development, which he directed for many years.[23] In 1967, he took over a longitudinal research project called the Grant Study that had been following 268 Harvard undergraduates from the 1930s. He then merged the study of the Grant men with the Gluek study of inner-city nondelinquent males that began in 1939 and with a study of gifted females, known as the Terman women, from the 1920s. This yielded a cohort of more than eight hundred men and women for the Harvard Study of Adult Development, as the project was subsequently renamed.

Several of Vaillant's discoveries about the Harvard men who survived into old age are particularly applicable to the professional men in my study, notably the following: by age seventy-five, one Harvard man in twelve was still working. Of the twenty men still working for full salary at that age, most were self-employed—six lawyers, four doctors, and five CEOs of small businesses.[24] Vaillant's opinion of retirement is unequivocal: "Retirement should be voluntary. If work is more fun, keep on doing it."[25]

Of course, gerontologists and psychiatrists are not the only ones with valuable insights into aging and work. Bill Bailey, one of my survey respondents, shared his thoughts on the subject with me. Bill is a longtime lawyer in private practice and now full-time law school faculty member and writer. "I had been teaching law part time at the University of Washington for thirty years when the dean asked me to teach full time. I was by then in a solid enough financial position to be able to absorb the substantial income loss. There is more to life than money." Bill also wonders where the years have gone: "It is such an odd disconnect to be turning sixty-four. I remember vividly when my college roommate brought the *Sgt. Pepper* album back to our dorm room and played it in the spring of 1967. I laughed then at the ironic quaintness of Paul McCartney's song, 'When I'm Sixty-four,' thinking that people at that age were only a short step from the grave. I have a far different take on this song now. As my ninety-one-year-old mother continues to demonstrate, successful aging requires a sense of humor, humility, and finding meaning in the simple events of everyday life. The humility piece is a real challenge to the younger self within, who beholds the appearance in the mirror and says, 'Dude, what happened?'"

Even nearly half a century after Margaret Mead's pronouncements about gender roles and aging, some things have not changed all that much. Many people still consider fifty to be "older," and few would contest Dr. Mead's point that most men have gone as far as they can go with respect to career building by the time they reach fifty. Conventional wisdom also says that fifty-year-old men want to work until they are sixty-five, whereupon they retire to a life of quiet and fishing.

Except, that is, for men who most assuredly do *not* hold those views. Take sociologist Richard O. Hope, age seventy-three, as an example. After many years of university teaching and administering Woodrow Wilson National Fellowship Programs that train students for careers in public policy, international affairs, and foreign service, he is now drawing on his extensive knowledge of intercultural, interracial, and gender relations to assist Department of Defense efforts to expand diversity programs, as well as consulting on international affairs. His reaction to a question about retirement is this: "If you mean sitting in a rocking chair, watching television, and nodding off—no way!"

PROFILE: RICHARD O. HOPE

A professional career path might have seemed foreordained for Richard Hope. After all, his grandfather, John Hope, was the first black president of Morehouse College in Atlanta (the historian John Hope Franklin was named after him). Richard's father, an economist, taught at Spelman College in Atlanta and at Fisk University in Tennessee, and his mother was a college teacher, too. But the early years were not entirely easy. The esteemed patriarch of the family believed that his children and grandchildren deserved no special treatment, so they all went to public school in the projects of Atlanta and Nashville.

While at Morehouse College in the late 1950s, Richard participated in Crossroads Africa, a precursor to the Peace Corps, that gave him a taste of international work. While completing his bachelor's degree, Richard became active in the civil rights movement. He helped to start a chapter of the Student Non-violent Coordinating Committee (SNCC) in Atlanta with Julian Bond, participated in sit-ins, and was jailed. After several years of civil rights activities, he decided to go to graduate school, and by 1968, he earned a doctorate in sociology from the Maxwell School at Syracuse University.

Richard taught sociology in such schools as Brooklyn College, Morgan State University, Indiana University, and MIT. Soon he was teaching at Princeton and was involved in investigating interracial conflict on military bases and carriers around the world. Cognizant of lessons learned from the civil rights movement, he convinced military leaders to understand that working together across racial lines was not only the right thing to do, but also was essential to military readiness. Richard was asked to lead an interservice taskforce charged with studying causes and possible cures of conflicts within the military. This led to the establishment of the Defense Race Relations Institute (DRRI) in 1971 at Patrick Air Force Base in Florida. The DRRI, renamed the Defense Equal Opportunity Management Institute (or DEOMI), has trained more than forty thousand reserve and active duty military members and civilian employees of the American armed forces since its creation. The name change reflects the growing array of issues included in DEOMI courses, including the study of racism, sexual harassment, sexism, extremism, religious accommodation, and anti-Semitism. Richard's book on the subject, *Racial Strife in the U.S. Military*, was published in 1979. In recognition of his work, Patrick Air Force Base dedicated a building to him in 2011, called the Richard Oliver Hope Research Center.

The largest portion of Richard's fifty-eight-year career in sociology, public policy, and the academy has been spent at the Woodrow Wilson National Fellowship Foundation (WWNFF), based in Princeton, New Jersey. Although he retired in 2010 after twenty years as vice president of higher education fellowships at WWNFF, he remains with the foundation as a senior fellow. A major thrust of the fellowship programs is strengthening the capacity of underrepresented minorities and women to pursue international service careers as public policy analysts and leaders. In his presentation at a UCLA conference, Richard challenged the country "to examine and renew its commitment to preparing the most talented students for the global economic and international affairs responsibilities that will occupy center stage in the coming decades. While efforts have been under way in recent years to educate a cadre of minority policy professionals in the international sphere, statistics indicate that minorities still remain greatly underrepresented at the highest levels of the international affairs hierarchy. A new public/private partnership is required that will promote international career opportunities for talented students of color." He went on to describe WWNFF's programs that promote diversity for the twenty-first century and that can serve as models for expanding international affairs opportunities.

One of the programs he administered, the Pickering Foreign Affairs Fellowship Program (named for Career Ambassador Thomas R. Pickering), has produced more than six hundred foreign service officers, including a number of ambassadors, most of whom are women and minorities. In 1990, when President Nelson Mandela heard about the Pickering program, the US State Department established the Public Policy Partnership in South Africa. Each year, these fellowships support two hundred undergraduate students through the master's degree program, training them at universities in Cape Town, Natal, and (in this country) at Georgetown and George Washington Universities, for government positions in public policy.

Another initiative, the Career Enhancement Program, aims to expand the number of minorities and women in the academy, providing them with mentors and funding them for a year while they prepare for tenure. Some seven hundred faculty have received such assistance to date.

"Why did you step down from the WWNFF?" I asked Richard. "Twenty years is enough," he pronounced. "And, there is an excellent staff in place to continue the programs." His current focus is heading up a new foundation for the US Department of Defense that will support and expand diversity programs. He serves on the board of the Andrew Young Center for International Affairs in Atlanta. He may also become involved as a consultant to USAFRI-

COM, one of nine Unified Combatant Commands of the US armed forces, which is responsible for promoting a stable and secure African environment in support of US foreign policy.

Richard also wants to make more time for family—his wife, Alice, a retired schoolteacher, and their two grown children, Leah, a news anchor in Chicago, and Rick, an artist trained at the School of the Art Institute of Chicago who teaches in Palm Springs, California, where Richard and Alice also have a house. The magnet is their grandchild. "Our three-year-old grandson has re-ordered my life and given me new priorities, such as making time to Skype with him," Richard confesses with a chuckle.

Will he retire fully? "If you mean sitting in a rocking chair, watching television, and nodding off—no way. I talk about it with Alice and take her counsel very seriously, yet I will probably work forever. I have no plans to stop. First of all, it's fun. While it is extremely gratifying to see younger people carrying on with this important work, I want to continue doing what I can to expand horizons and improve intercultural, interracial, and gender relations. It is important to contribute to society, even when you're ninety, and I am only seventy-three."

With that, Richard is off to a meeting of the Council on Foreign Relations and to wish Hillary Clinton well in her retirement.

Of course, professionals like Dr. Hope and the other men in this book are lucky to choose between retiring or continuing to work. Many older men who would prefer to retire at sixty-five or earlier have to keep working for a variety of reasons, usually financial in nature, whether they like it or not. As we shall see in the next chapter, landing on the desired career path and finding job satisfaction and personal satisfaction over the years can be a real challenge for any man.

3

A Man's World

I had run with him once before when I was eight years old. . . . I'd run two miles and when I stepped inside our cool, dark house, I yelled up the stairs to Mom, "I ran two miles with Daddy, Mom! I'm strong. I'm *strong!*"
—Andre Dubus III, *Townie: A Memoir*

Many an adult male can recall a father or grandfather who set an example that influenced his understanding of manhood and a grown man's responsibilities, including the career he would choose (or reject) and how long he would keep working. For the quintessential all-American boy coming-of-age story, consider Gay Talese's *New Yorker* profile of Joe Girardi, forty-nine-year-old former Major League Baseball (MLB) catcher and current manager of the New York Yankees. Read about Girardi's Midwestern roots, religious training, devotion to family, education, love of sports, especially baseball (he played catcher in high school and college and in the major leagues for fifteen years), competitiveness, and close relationship with his father. Mr. Girardi was a bricklayer on weekends, bartender at night, and during the week a traveling salesman for a gypsum manufacturing company. According to the profile, young Joe tagged along on road trips and helped his dad on bricklaying jobs, building muscle in the process. In turn, his dad was the one who played catch in the backyard with Joe and took him to Cubs games. Girardi says his dad was always there for him, and he never wanted to let his dad down.[1]

Joe Girardi was fortunate to have two parents who set positive examples in so many important ways, not only as paradigms of hard work but also of nurturance, guidance, and constancy. Many men in their sixties, seventies, and eighties today learned from their fathers about work and the economic responsibilities of a family man but were shortchanged when it came to paternal nurturance, guidance, and constancy. In the words of legendary UCLA basketball coach John Wooden: "Being a role model is the most powerful form of educating . . . too often fathers neglect it because they get so caught up in making a living they forget to make a life."[2]

As Wooden well knew, mentors and role models can play an important part in career decision making of both professional men and professional women with respect to *career choice, conduct,* and *duration.* There is a difference: a mentor serves as an advocate, and a role model is one whose behavior is imitated. For instance, if your parent was a doctor who worked well into the senior years, chances are you will aspire to follow in his footsteps. Nearly three-quarters of the older men in my study reported having one or more mentors or role models at some point in their careers. Forty-three percent said their father or other male relative, such as a grandfather, uncle, or brother, set an example or was the primary source of support and encouragement. Twenty-seven percent cited a boss, supervisor, or employer, and twenty-five percent cited a teacher, professor, or college/university dean as positive role models or mentors. Other admired mentors or role models included respected doctors, wives, Woody Guthrie, Red Auerbach, Red Skelton, John Fitzgerald Kennedy, Tom Hayden, Perry Mason, Harold "Doc" Howe, and Marian Wright Edelman. One wag said the "fear of poverty" motivated him to excel.

For Larry Lucchino, president and CEO of the Boston Red Sox, older brother Frank showed the path to higher education and his mentor, the hard-charging, high-profile Washington attorney Edward Bennett Williams, opened the door to the world of professional sports. Now sixty-seven, he is still trying to balance a twenty-four/seven job with the rest of his life.

PROFILE: LARRY LUCCHINO

Larry Lucchino, president and CEO of the Boston Red Sox, cites two people who had the greatest influence on his career—his older brother by six years,

Frank, and Edward Bennett Williams, founder and senior partner at Williams & Connolly in Washington, DC. "My brother was the first in our family to complete college. Williams opened the doors to the sports world for me and had a profoundly positive influence on my career."

Larry describes himself as a "transitional man." He came from a working-class family in Pittsburgh and attended Princeton University on scholarship where he excelled academically and on the basketball court. (He was on the team led by Hall-of-Famer Bill Bradley that made it to the Final Four of the 1965 NCAA Men's Division 1 Basketball Tournament.) Despite Princeton's elite reputation, it proved to be a meritocracy in which Larry thrived. After Princeton, he earned a JD from Yale Law School and became a specialist in sports law and litigation at Williams & Connolly. Edward Bennett Williams, defender of high-profile clients and owner of two professional sports teams, the Baltimore Orioles and the Washington Redskins, was his role model and mentor at the firm. (Williams was a workaholic who, despite undergoing seven cancer operations, never quit working until his death in 1988.) Under Williams, Larry prospered. By 1979 he was vice president and general counsel for the Baltimore Orioles and the Washington Redskins. In 1983 he acquired his first World Series ring when the Orioles won the championship. Five years later, Williams appointed Larry to his position as president of the Orioles; and, after Williams's death in 1988, he became an owner and continued to lead the process of building the acclaimed new-but-old-fashioned Camden Yards ballpark, for which he had the original vision. In 1994 he became an owner of the San Diego Padres as well as president and CEO and again led a successful effort to fund, design, and build a new stadium. He left the Padres in 2001 to join the new baseball ownership team in Boston.

In December of that year, John Henry, Tom Werner, Larry Lucchino, and a group of investors successfully outbid several competitors to purchase the Red Sox, Fenway Park, and 80 percent of the New England Sports Network. MLB approved the sale early in 2002. Henry became principal owner of the club, Werner the chairman, and Lucchino was named president and CEO. (Like Larry, John Henry and Tom Werner had experience in MLB before becoming stewards of the Red Sox.) Each has a seat at the table for all major baseball decisions, including acquisition of managers and players. Larry oversees the "superstructure" of on-field and off-field operations in all major departments, a staff of several hundred, and "a whole panoply of services."

He feels blessed to have such an interesting career filled with hard work and the adrenaline rush that comes from "contest living," a term coined by his mentor, Edward Bennett Williams. An intensely competitive person, Larry channels his energies in the sports management field. "A strong work ethic is part of my DNA," he remarks. Equally satisfying is the knowledge that his work generates good feelings, not only for Red Sox fans but also in the Boston community.

In a *Boston Magazine* article in 2006, writer John Wolfson quoted Larry as saying that he "makes his living in the toy store of life." Although that sounds frivolous, nothing could be farther from the truth: he is a hard-charging and serious person who is known for getting the facts straight. It just so happens that MLB is conducive to blurring the line between work and play.

Larry told me that he is proudest of four achievements over his career:

- Breaking the "Curse of the Bambino" in 2004 after an eighty-six-year drought. "It was poetry, really. We came back from being down 3-0 Yankees to win the pennant in a historic manner, then rolled over the Cardinals to win the Series."
- Camden Yards—the design and building of Oriole Park that set the mark for ballparks. "It produced a sea change in ballpark architecture. After we built a traditional old-fashioned ballpark with modern amenities in Baltimore, twenty-one other ballparks adopted the formula." And writer George Will, who identified baseball's three most important achievements in the second half of the twentieth century as Jackie Robinson, free agency, and Camden Yards, seems to agree.
- Preservation and renovation of Fenway Park, and his contribution to the pride, excitement and enjoyment of the everyday people who belong to Red Sox Nation.
- Corporate social responsibility—the Red Sox' owners using their franchise for charitable purposes, especially in support of the newly created Red Sox Foundation and the Jimmy Fund at Dana-Farber Cancer Institute in Boston.

Now sixty-seven years old, Larry thinks that the days of "the proud workaholic" may be behind him. In part this may result from his relatively new status as a family man. He was a confirmed bachelor until 2002, when he married Stacey and became stepfather to her two children. After the Lucchinos moved to Brookline, Massachusetts, Stacey, a former teacher in California, became very involved in community and charitable work on behalf of health and mental health and inner-city schools. Larry is equally committed to community service, particularly expanding and deepening the Red Sox' ties to the Jimmy Fund. "Dana-Farber Cancer Institute saved my life, and Stacey and I love the Jimmy Fund."

Versatile as he is, Larry admits that he does not always maintain a good balance between work and the rest of his life. "I've been grappling with that my entire career. I have a twenty-four/seven job that I love, and I love my family and friends. It's harder than ever to sit still and focus because I am pulled in so many directions. Private life comes in bites and interludes." As a result, Larry is trying to delegate more. Fortunately, a cadre of very loyal people has been working with him since the Orioles and Padres days. When I suggest that such loyalty is a compliment to him personally, he deflects the compliment by saying, "Baseball is a glamorous business that offers attractive opportunities to people, and Boston is Mecca."

To answer my question regarding thoughts of retirement, Larry points to MLB Commissioner Bud Selig, who is seventy-nine and still on the job.[3] Similarly, retirement is not presently in the cards for Larry. "I have high standards for myself. I like a bold way of living. If I just sat around, I would probably have little or no energy. My mother, who lived to be ninety-four, taught me that the secrets to a good life are staying active and continuing to grow. If and when to retire are the proverbial $64,000 questions."

Jim Levinson can trace his fifty-year career in international development (nutrition and public health) to the influence of numerous heroes, role models, and mentors. Heroes included Mahatma Gandhi, Mother Teresa, Rabindranath Tagore, Martin Luther King Jr., and Dorothy Day.

Role models included activist Father Daniel Berrigan and Catholic Worker leaders. Under their influence, Jim moved with his young family to Haley House, the Catholic Worker house in Boston, where he and his wife provided food and hospitality to homeless people and the elderly. Two years later, the family was living communally at Catholic Worker's Noonday Farm in Winchendon, Massachusetts; they farmed there for ten years. Through the Catholic Worker community, Jim also met Quakers, Protestants, Buddhists, and a mentor, a young rabbi who rekindled Jim's interest in his Jewish heritage, coached Jim in the oral tradition, and taught him to lead religious services. At seventy, he continues as a consultant on nutrition in Pakistan and Afghanistan, officiates at weddings, and conducts religious services, in part because the work is so satisfying and in part to pay for home improvements and for his daughter's wedding.

PROFILE: F. JAMES LEVINSON

Jim Levinson was one of many people in or near their seventies who responded to *New York Times* columnist David Brooks's invitation in October 2011 to write a brief autobiographical essay on their lives to that point, an evaluation describing what they did well and not so well and what they learned along the way. Brooks suggested several categories of modern adulthood, such as career, family, faith, community, and self-knowledge, and asked respondents to grade themselves in each area. He thought that engaging in self-appraisal would be salutary as well as potentially useful to younger persons who could benefit from their elders' life experience. Although Brooks did not publish Jim's "life report," writing it helped Jim to crystallize his current thinking, especially about work and retirement.

Jim has long subscribed to the idea that life is circular, that the first half of the circle is for *becoming, doing, acquiring,* while the second half is for *being, giving, divesting.* Turning the "wheel" to make a circle takes conscious effort and hard work; modestly, Jim doesn't claim to be doing that as well as he might. To the despair of his family who beg him not to take on an additional endeavor unless he drops two, he seems to add instead of cutting back. Still, at age seventy, what remains most important to him is living consistently with the values he has honed over a fifty-year career in international development (nutrition and public health). As he wrote in his life report, "Despite the infighting, the nutrition work, mostly in South Asia and Africa, plus university teaching, has been deeply rewarding and makes me feel like a citizen of something larger than a single nation."

Jim lives in a house in the woods near Marlboro College in Vermont, the summer home of the Marlboro Music Festival. He plays the piano and sings, goes canoeing with his wife, and is still consulting part time on malnutrition and poverty in Asian and African countries, which requires extensive travel. He would like to be doing the tough but personally rewarding hands-on work that junior staffers do, but has resigned himself to writing government policy and preparing agency documents. He also teaches an online course on international nutrition to students located all over the world. He is nearly fluent in Urdu and Hindi and can sing in those languages, which, sad to say, often makes the Pakistanis and Afghans he meets doubt that he's an American.

If a picture is worth a thousand words, the Heroes Wall in his office clearly shows who and what Jim values most. There are photographs of Gandhi and Nehru, Vinoba Bhave, Mother Teresa, Rabindranath Tagore, Martin Luther King Jr., Paul Robeson, Jackie Robinson, Dorothy Day, esteemed philosophers, singers, musicians, and more. There is also a framed question posed by his older daughter Mira when she was a little girl to remind him of his calling: "How come you aren't talking about the hungry children?"

It all started after Harvard, when Jim led the Krokodiloes, the college's a cappella singing group, on a 1964 trip to India. There he became fascinated by the Gandhian movement and its offshoots, especially their commitment to social justice, economic opportunity, and sustainable agriculture. He was supposed to go to law school after college but "jumped ship" and took a job with the United States Agency for International Development (USAID) instead. For the next five years he worked on a project in India to reduce child and maternal malnutrition. Then, he headed to Cornell for his doctorate in agricultural economics and nutrition with a focus on policy and planning.

In 1972, when he was just thirty years old, Jim was invited to head a new program in international nutrition planning at MIT. His first marriage (to Mira's mother, Sati) having ended, Jim met and married Louise Cochran, who went on to a divinity degree, a fascination with Eastern religions, and team building counseling using the Enneagram, a personality assessment tool. Altogether, he has three grown children in what he considers his "joint family." All three work in the public health field.

After four years at MIT, he went to Washington, DC, to head USAID's worldwide office of nutrition. This was when Henry Kissinger was departing as secretary of state and Jimmy Carter had become president. Shortly thereafter, he was posted to Bangladesh to work on nutrition for two years. Bangladesh, in Jim's estimation, proved to be an unhealthy working situation, one that brought out the worst in people. That posting led to what he experienced as a midlife crisis, one reinforced by an evaluation finding that USAID's development program in Bangladesh had the net effect of *widening* not narrowing the gap between the haves and have-nots, an assessment that gave no major USAID program in the country a grade better than "D." Shortly afterward, an assignment in the Philippines only reinforced this sense of disillusionment: our government seemed to be more eager to support President Ferdinand Marcos than the desperate people who needed help to escape poverty. Jim concluded, "I'm on the wrong side!"

Small wonder that Jim soon came under the influence of activist Father Daniel Berrigan and Catholic Worker leaders Dorothy Day and Peter Maurin. He moved with his young family to Haley House, the Catholic Worker house in Boston, where he and his wife joined other activists in providing food and hospitality to homeless people and the elderly.

Jim and Louise also performed acts of civil disobedience that landed them in jail, such as protesting the nuclear arms race and South Africa's apartheid. Ironically, Jim's father, who ran a steel company in Pittsburgh and had been in the forefront of civil rights struggles in that city, was at the time serving on the board of a company seeking to export nuclear technology to South Africa. Father and son, who had been unusually close in earlier years, clearly did not see eye to eye on this one.

In 1982, after two years at Haley House, the family, along with two other families and several individuals, created Catholic Worker's Noonday Farm in Winchendon, Massachusetts, where they farmed organically, supplied soup kitchens and shelters, and lived as a community for ten years. Jim also resumed nutrition work for the World Bank in Africa, which allowed him to contribute financially to the farm.

Because the Catholic Worker communities were interfaith, Jim also met Quakers, Protestants, and Buddhists who quickly became kindred spirits. He also met, while living at the farm, a young rabbi who rekindled Jim's interest in his Jewish heritage—he's descended from a long line of rabbis and cantors in Poland and Russia. The rabbi coached Jim in the oral tradition and taught him to lead religious services.

Although Jim was not ordained, he became a "Sh'liach Tzibur" or "Messenger of the People," the spiritual leader of synagogues in Athol, Massachusetts, and Brattleboro, Vermont, for the next twenty years. This was in addition to his government work and, beginning in 1994, a long stint teaching nutrition policy and planning at Tufts University. Dubbed the "Activist Academic" in a laudatory article in the spring 2007 magazine of Tufts' Friedman School of Nutrition Science and Policy, Jim expanded the reach and effectiveness of the nutrition program by securing internships for students and introducing a PhD seminar. In the article a former student commented that he was known to teach more than international nutrition, monitoring, and evaluation; his true subjects, she said, were peace and goodwill.

Jim expected to continue in the Sh'liach Tzibur role after retirement. However, when contract renewal time rolled around in 2009, Jim's nonconformist attitude didn't sit well with some members of the synagogue board. They objected to several things: the amount of time he spent on interfaith activities, such as organizing Jewish-Muslim interfaith services; his willingness to officiate at weddings and funerals and do pastoral counseling for people who were not paid members of the congregation; and his questioning of Israeli government policies.

No longer leading a congregation, Jim continues to officiate at weddings with his wife, is actively involved in Brattleboro's Interfaith Initiative, and participates in leading Jewish High Holiday services in Athol. He and Louise are members of a spiritual group of a few families that meets regularly for deep sharing. They plan to participate in a new, collaboratively designed interfaith evening service at the old Marlboro Meetinghouse (established 1776) just down the road from their house.

Jim told me that the most satisfying aspect of his core work is seeing what his nutrition strategy efforts accomplish in countries like Pakistan and Afghanistan. However, as he gets older he finds that his energy level isn't what it used to be. Getting up early and staying up late to meet a writing deadline are taxing. Whenever he can afford to step back from the consulting work—right now he is paying for weddings and home improvements—he would like to concentrate on what most nourishes body and soul and sustains the richness and fullness of life. Family, friends, spirituality, and music head the list.

Although Jim recently admitted failure in a valiant effort to learn ice skating, he has other projects up his sleeve and possibly a book or two in the years ahead. Additionally, he is committed to helping with his son's project, Calcutta Kids, seeking to improve the health of mothers and young children in India's slums. But Jim also is fascinated by a Hindu teaching about stages of life that has, as its penultimate stage, that of "forest dweller," meaning a gradual withdrawal into nature and contemplation. He and Louise already have their dream house in the woods; they just need more time for the contemplation.

Role models and mentors were also very important to oncologist Bruce Chabner, director of clinical research at Massachusetts General Hospital's Cancer Center in Boston. Early career influences started with his dad, a physician, and continued in the laboratories of top cancer researchers. Today a highly respected leader in his field at seventy-two, he considers it part of his job to mentor younger staff members and share his excitement over breakthroughs in cancer research.

PROFILE: BRUCE A. CHABNER
Bruce's roots run deep in Shelbyville, Illinois, where his father was a highly respected physician and a man of great integrity. Bruce is still very fond of the Shelbyville friends he grew up with in the 1940s and 1950s. "We were kids together in that little town in the middle of nowhere. After more than seventy years, we remain very close friends, and despite living all over the country, we get together once a year, often in Shelbyville."

Google Bruce and you learn that the mayor declared April 7, 1995, "Bruce A. Chabner Day" in honor of Shelbyville's native son and his contributions to cancer drug discovery and development. You also find out that he is director of clinical research at Massachusetts General Hospital's (MGH) Cancer Center in Boston and professor in the Department of Medicine at Harvard Medical School. He is a coleader of the Dana-Farber/Harvard Cancer Center's (DF/HCC) Translational Pharmacology and Early Therapeutic Trials. He is the editor of the professional journal *The Oncologist*, and he serves on advisory boards. For example, for the past two years he chaired the National Cancer Advisory Board, the group of experts that sets research policy for the

National Cancer Institute (NCI). He is also a member of the Cancer Center Scientific Council at the DF/HCC.

"I love what I do, every aspect of my work—the intellectual challenges, the emotional challenges, and the clinical environment itself. I can't imagine sitting home doing nothing. I will continue to work, as long as I can do useful things. The field of cancer research is dynamic and, even after forty-seven years, I find each day very exciting."

Sharing his excitement over breakthroughs in the pharmacology of anticancer drugs, Bruce recently wrote an article titled "Not Your Father's Chemo: Targeted Therapies and 'Personalized Medicine' for Cancer Patients." In it he explains how advancement in understanding the genetic basis of cancer has led to the development of drugs that are specifically targeted to block the errant genes that drive cancer cell growth and survival. The article, which he wrote for his daughter's website (http://www.bfflco.com offers cancer care and maternity merchandise), conveys his excitement over new technologies that are revolutionizing the approach to treatment of patients with leukemia, lung cancer, breast cancer, and melanoma.

What is hardest about Bruce's job are the long hours he must devote to the considerable volume of work in the hospital and outside, as well. "There is a misperception that older people give up lots of things and lighten their load. Actually, I have taken on new responsibilities as I've gotten older, while still trying to maintain some of the older interests. True, my workload has changed: I do less administration and less patient care than in the past, and do more advising, consulting, and mentoring." Bruce may be doing less patient care, but he gives 100 percent to those patients he does see. And when he can report a successful outcome of treatment, he is likely to choke up with emotion. (I have witnessed this myself.)

Here is Bruce's background. After graduating from Yale University in 1961, Bruce headed for Harvard Medical School. In 1964 he married Davi-Ellen, my friend from high school and one of the women I profiled in *Women Still at Work: Professionals over Sixty and on the Job*. The following year, they both graduated—he with an MD from Harvard Medical School and Davi with a master's degree from the Harvard Graduate School of Education. Bruce did his residencies at Brigham and Women's Hospital in Boston and at Yale-New Haven Hospital, and they raised two kids. It was during the second residency that he worked in the laboratory of Joe Bertino and was mentored by him as well as by other colleagues. "Joe was a great cancer researcher who became my lifelong friend and golf buddy."

After the Yale-New Haven residency, the Chabners moved to Maryland where Bruce worked at the National Institutes of Health's (NIH) NCI for the next twenty-four years. From the 1970s to the mid-1990s, he held progressively higher positions in cancer pharmacology, culminating as director of the division of cancer treatment at the NCI. During this period, early reports about unusual cases of what came to be known as AIDS caught the attention of Bruce and other top-level NCI administrators. In 1981, they organized and sponsored the first scientific workshop about AIDS that was held in this country. Once AIDS was determined to be an infectious disease and not a malignancy, that is, it was not clearly within the mandate of NCI, another institute within the NIH took the lead in directing the research effort. But Bruce's division was responsible for the first isolation of the virus (Bob Gallo's laboratory) and discovery and testing of the first anti-AIDS drugs (Sam Broder).

Having experienced mentoring by some of the top researchers in the field, it was only natural that Bruce would take mentoring seriously. At NIH/NCI he directed fellowship programs in medical, pediatric, radiation, and surgical oncology. One mentee was a doctor from Amsterdam named Bob Pinedo, who came to Bruce's lab in 1975 and went on to be influential in cancer research in the Netherlands. In gratitude for Bruce's mentoring and friendship, Bob gave the Chabners a cherry tree to plant near their house in Maryland, telling them that the tree was fruitful year-round, just like Bruce. The tree flourished, as did Bruce's career. In 1995 he joined the MGH staff as clinical director of its cancer center and chief of hematology and oncology, and not long after also headed up clinical sciences for the partnership among Boston hospitals that became the Dana-Farber/Harvard Cancer Center.

In Boston Bruce has continued to mentor younger staff members of whom he is extremely proud. "I am happy to watch the success of outstanding men and women at MGH and elsewhere in the field. I see them advancing, taking good care of patients. I have known them since their residencies and fellowships, and I have offered them their first faculty positions. It is reassuring to know that such capable young people are coming along to move our field forward."

Bruce and Davi have achieved a harmonious rhythm to their busy lives in Boston. Davi insists that Bruce stay out of the house from 9:00 a.m. to 5:00

p.m., so she can concentrate on writing her books on medical terminology. "She has many projects, commitments, and interests. I am always wondering what she will come up with next!" (I cannot help remarking that this observation comes from someone who is totally dedicated to saving as many lives as possible, one patient at a time, one "smart" drug and clinical trial at a time.) He continues, "Davi is busy with her own projects and doesn't really mind the traveling that I do. She does like to accompany me when we can see friends in other countries." The couple also has a long list of new places they would like to visit, including, for Davi, Burma, and for both of them, Poland (where their families came from). Above all, they look forward to vacations on Nantucket with their children and five active grandchildren.

What delights Bruce the most—after his family—are his cocker spaniels, Greta and Owen. "They keep me young by lowering my blood pressure and providing an emotional outlet after a tough day at the hospital. Greta is almost a person to me. She may even be a reincarnation of someone from the past." Hmmm, is this a scientist speaking?

Sometimes a role model exerts a negative influence on a young man or woman. The role model could be a parent who had followed a path his son or daughter decides *not* to emulate. Andrew Fogelson, who has worked with and for the major film studios since 1970 in film marketing and distribution, knew early on that he was willing to take risks his risk-averse father would never take.

PROFILE: ANDREW FOGELSON

Andrew Fogelson has been in film marketing and distribution since 1970, working both *with* and *for* the major film studios, including Warner Bros., Columbia Pictures, and United Artists (UA). At Warner he launched the *Superman* film series. A senior manager with whom Andrew worked at that studio knew innovation when he saw it, trusted Andrew, and became a "way paver" when Andrew was persuading the studio to make its first-ever network television buy. At UA he had the misfortune to introduce Timothy Dalton as the next James Bond. He also produced six movies, about which he wise-cracks, "Three of them were actually seen."

His choice of career was somewhat influenced by his dad, who was in retail advertising, but the similarities stop there. His dad was risk averse and remained with the same department store chain for years, berating himself in his later years for not taking chances. In contrast, Andrew has had a new job every two years, except for one four-year stint. "Couldn't keep a job! When I finally realized that I was the world's worst employee, I opened my own film consulting business, AFA Co."

That was in 1988. In the mid-1990s, PolyGram, then the world's largest record label, wanted to get a foothold in the North American movie business by investing in a lot of movies and building a film library that would make big money for the company. PolyGram hired Andrew to start the business and build it up in North America. After four years as president of PolyGram Filmed Entertainment Distribution, Andrew returned to consulting, getting films to movie theaters and promoting them.

More recently, Andrew conceived of a new business model that would enable producers to take advantage of digital production and marketing capabilities. With the advent of social media, he saw that the new technologies were forcing change, not only in how movies are made but also in how they are distributed. "The public can comment on and critique a film almost instantaneously. Opinions spread virally. It's a game changer that is costing the studios a lot of money, and it has certainly changed my approach to the business as well." Entrepreneurial as ever, Andrew is three years into his newest venture—TODPix.com, a twenty-first-century digital distribution entertainment platform. He and his son, Noah, have built an innovative start-up company that markets and distributes movies predominantly through social media and mobile applications for on-demand film programming in the global theatrical market. Targeted or niche films are new studio and independent titles as well as studio "back catalog" selections.

Andrew's talent is inventing new and different strategies for changing the entertainment environment. He also knows what he is not very good at doing. "My memory has always been poor," he admits. "I put stickies on my dashboard, tie strings on my fingers, my wife reminds me . . . and I still forget!" He describes himself as a "good" manager who cares about people who work with and for him. A great manager, though, is detail-oriented, and he is just not.

Andrew's family has always been the top priority. He and his wife, Susan, have two sons and four grandchildren. All the Fogelsons live in southern California. Susan is one of the women who participated in my survey for *Women Still at Work* and remains a close friend since high school. She is an educational therapist with a thriving private practice. She sees K–12 students and some postsecondary students, assessing and treating their struggles with learning disabilities and other learning challenges, teaching testing skills and study skills, and consulting on individualized education programs. Andrew describes Susan's work in four words: "She saves kids' lives." Susan has co-authored a book on educational therapy, is active in the Association of Educational Therapists, and has no intention of retiring.

Andrew, however, has mixed feelings about retirement. Aside from the satisfaction he gets from the challenges of starting a new business and the opportunity to change the entertainment environment once again, he has another even more pressing reason for continuing to work. Owing to the recession and economic downturn, he and his wife are worried about managing the expense of her rare progressive disease going forward.

Nevertheless, Andrew dreams of not having to work every day and taking time to be by himself, perhaps write a book, and (definitely) play golf. "Just me, with my laptop and golf clubs, driving a Volvo station wagon." And playing golf for a month in Ireland or Scotland! Like most dreams, however, these are not particularly practical. For one thing, there is his wife's health. For another, Andrew has gained so much weight since surgery and dropping a smoking habit eleven years ago that he can no longer walk the golf course.

Now that he is seventy, he finds that he thinks about mortality and has become preoccupied with ensuring the quality of his remaining years. "I don't have a plan per se. Anyway, it's all subject to the Queen, i.e., my wife! I'd like to move out of Los Angeles, at least part time, but she doesn't want to budge. Her profession, our family, our roots are here. I understand how important that is to someone who experienced many upheavals in her childhood."

According to Andrew, retirement is different in the movie business, where people, particularly creative people, do not retire; they *get retired*. Ageism sometimes is part of it, too. Retirement, in his opinion, is "not conceptually valid. Other than in jobs requiring a great deal of physical output, there is simply no need for retirement. Today, with technology, you can reach out and connect with the world. You can easily stay connected to your interests and your colleagues without going to an office. You can earn or attempt to earn a pretty good living, until the time comes that you can't or don't want to do any more." Andrew says he is "monumentally" looking forward to that time.

Meanwhile, TODPix.com is reinventing the model once again, and it's too soon to tell whether it will meet expectations. If it doesn't, Andrew has his laptop and golf clubs ready.

What if a boy's father is absent or deceased? Who guides him through young manhood and teaches him about a grown man's responsibilities? When Paul Fideler's father, Arthur, a Wall Street bond broker, died of tuberculosis (TB) in Saranac Lake, New York's Trudeau Sanitarium at age forty-seven, Paul was ten and had few close interactions with his dad. Fearful of spreading the disease to his wife and two children, Arthur confined himself to his room as much as possible when living at home or was completely inaccessible when living in the sanitarium. Nevertheless, Paul was fortunate to rely on his loving mother and older sister and family friends for support and guidance, among them a physician and infectious diseases researcher, Emanuel Wolinsky, himself recovering from TB, and a former US ambassador to Peru and Guinea, James I. Loeb, who published the local newspaper, *The Adirondack Daily Enterprise*. Compelling history and literature teachers in high school and his Catholic faith were additional important early influences on the future professor of history and humanities, as later were generous scholars in his chosen research field of British social welfare history and historiography. Paul also benefited a great deal from his two years of active duty in the US Army as the executive officer of an artillery battery following his graduation from St. Lawrence University in 1958, having majored in history and government. Upon the completion of his military service, he undertook doctoral studies in the History of Ideas program at Brandeis University and embarked on a career in academe. Paul's profile clearly spells out his reasons for staying on the job.

PROFILE: PAUL A. FIDELER
"At this juncture in my seventies, I continue to feel healthy, enjoy my teaching and scholarship, and am challenged by both. I am contributing to the enlight-

enment of my students and to the knowledge base and integrity of British studies." So states Paul A. Fideler, professor of history and humanities at Lesley University in Cambridge, Massachusetts, and a publishing historian of early modern and modern British social welfare. Yes, he is my septuagenarian husband who recently accepted another multiyear contract from the university. What can I say? As a champion of older men (and women) continuing to work, I can only weigh the pros and cons of retirement with him. The long and often tiring commute, the not infrequent late-night course preparations and manuscript or review deadlines, and so on. However, he has made it clear that the attraction of his work is much stronger than the pull of retirement.

He has many good reasons for his decision. He enjoys interacting with his students and is convinced that his senior status gives him an unusually positive influence on them. He remains interested and involved in shaping the curriculum, particularly the ways the humanities and social sciences are promoted and taught. His wide interdisciplinary interests also give him many opportunities to interact with and mentor younger colleagues across fields.

Paul's participation in academic culture beyond his university continues to be another lure to keep working. He is a past president of both the New England Historical Association (NEHA) and the North East Conference on British Studies (NECBS). He is a regular book and manuscript reviewer for the prominent journals is his field and continues to present his work at local, national, and international meetings. For example, he assembled a panel on images of the poor across five centuries for the 2014 European Social Science History Conference (ESSHC) that will convene in Vienna. The presenters include two historians from Australia, one from Scotland, and two from the United States. He is working on his third book, *Manchester in the Time of Cholera*, in which he explores the efforts of civil society volunteers and the government to remediate the appalling spread of poverty and disease in early Victorian Manchester by combining the emerging sciences of statistics and epidemiology with visiting the poor to encourage their edification.

Paul admits that another reason for continuing to work is financial: he enjoys earning a salary that makes our traveling possible and allows us to help our two children and five grandchildren when necessary. He also admits that he probably spends too much time on his work and claims that he is learning to make more time for family and leisure. For sure, staying fit is part of his daily routine, as are reading, enjoying music, and, in season, pruning and maintaining the superabundant shrubbery on our property. After a lifetime of road running, he has the bad knees to show for it. This one-time Northern Adirondack Water-Skiing Champion has lost some mobility and flexibility; most days he walks or rides his bike—at a moderate pace—and every morning faithfully does stretching and weight lifting.

Ever since his antiwar activism and support for Eugene McCarthy's presidential bid in the 1960s and 1970s, a continuing interest for Paul has been current events and the probity of the media in covering the news. He and I gravitated toward Unitarianism in the late 1960s in part because ours was a "mixed marriage" (no longer the big deal it was then to our Catholic and Jewish parents), in part because our immediate family grew with the arrivals of our daughter and son, and in part for the affinity we sought with other social activists. During our more than forty-five years of participation in the First Parish Unitarian-Universalist in Framingham, we both have served on the church's Board of Assessors, and Paul served twice as chair of the Social Concerns Council and was named an "Outstanding Parishioner."

We were well into the interview process when Paul shared his most personal reason for continuing to work: one thing that drives him to keep going is to do what his father did not have a chance to do. When his father died after a long battle with TB, Paul was only ten. "My dad's family life and his professional life were cut short. Even before he died, I was aware of the desperate struggle my parents were mounting in those pre-antibiotic years to find the right 'climate cure' for him, first in Tucson, Arizona, then Waukegan, Illinois, and finally Saranac Lake, New York. Ever since my father's death, whenever I have faced a seemingly daunting challenge, recalling what he and my mother were facing in those years quickly puts matters in their proper perspective."

When we return to the retirement conversation, Paul concedes that *my* well-being is a central consideration. But, since I am busy researching and writing books, he feels free to go on with his work. Like many of the older men and women I interviewed, Paul thinks "you should work if you're feeling healthy and still enjoying it." He sees the "boundary" between work and retirement evolving into more of a threshold or transition. Individuals are defining their own life cycles, subject to changing expectations and conditions, for example, health and the economy. "Retirement is no longer an automatic next stage toward which we march in lock step. Of course, this applies to people who are fortunate enough to have a choice in the matter."

What if a man doesn't know how to parent? (Sorry about using a noun as a verb, but that is the correct term.) Educator and author Allan Shedlin has dedicated his life's work to researching and writing about parenting and developing programs to foster positive engagement between fathers and their children. He is especially grateful to two men who helped him develop his own special gift for working with children. Now seventy-one, he wouldn't dream of retiring because he loves his work and "So much still needs to get done."

PROFILE: ALLAN SHEDLIN

In the belief that "A father is not something you are, but something you do," Allan Shedlin coined the term "daddying" in 1994 to connote where fatherhood and nurturing merge. At the time, many people told him that the term was too wimpy and that men would never speak it; however, some dozen or so years later, "daddying" began to appear (unattributed) on Hallmark cards. Allan's friends and colleagues suggested he sue Hallmark, but he was delighted to see the word gaining wider usage. In 2003 he founded DADS Unlimited as a vehicle for strengthening men's parenting skills. In 2008 Allan invited two colleagues to join him—a documentary filmmaker and a clinical social worker/narrative therapist—to create REEL FATHERS, an initiative that "inspires and supports men to build loving, committed relationships with their children by using film as a touchstone for reflective dialogue, by teaching key skills, and by elevating the cultural perception of fathers."

Through his commentaries in the popular press, by 2009–10 Allan attracted the attention of the White House Office of Faith-based and Neighborhood Partnerships. This office invited Allan to offer the new administration suggestions on how the president could lead a fatherhood movement. After many years of researching and writing about parenting and developing programs to foster positive engagement between fathers and their children, Allan was excited about this possibility. After hearing what the White House was already planning, he offered two specific suggestions: first, raising the bar of expectations and signaling that by replacing the tired phrase of "encouraging responsible fatherhood" with something more compelling, the president would encourage fathers to reach higher. Suspecting that the administration might not embrace calling for "exuberant daddying," he was willing to settle for "vibrant father engagement."

His second suggestion was that the White House sponsor one of its three planned 2010 "Fatherhood Forums" in New Mexico where REEL FATHERS conducted its programs. He pointed out that the state's demographics foretold future changes in the rest of the country and that New Mexico was chronically one of the bottom three states on almost every measure of social well-being. Allan then led a mobilization of forces in the state to create the New Mexico Alliance for Fathers and Families (NMAFF), which successfully persuaded the White House to cosponsor with the United States Department of Agriculture (USDA) and NMAFF a Fatherhood Forum in August 2010. NMAFF's comprehensive report to the cosponsors (the only forum to issue a report) secured participation by the White House and USDA in another Fatherhood Forum two years later. New Mexico was the only state to hold a second forum.

Using a combination of film and video, expressive arts projects, and facilitated dialogue, between 2009 and 2012 REEL FATHERS provided thirty-seven programs for New Mexico organizations directly serving fathers. Partners included Head Start centers, public schools, Big Brother/Big Sister, Gear Up, the State Corrections Department, and various parenting, youth development, violence prevention, and family services organizations.

Allan's background includes a master's degree in elementary and special education from Columbia University's Teachers College and ten years of experience teaching special education and regular education classes. He went on to become an elementary school principal, the founding executive director of the National Elementary School Center, an advisor to a US Secretary of Education, an education writer, and a parenting consultant.

Two men had a particularly strong influence on Allan's career choices and the type of man he is. Allan stayed in touch over the years with both of them until they died. One was a fifth grade teacher who, Allan realized only later, presented a different male role model from other men he knew as a kid; and the other was a psychology professor and the director of the summer camp for emotionally disturbed children where Allan, as a high school senior, had his first job working with children. The director highly praised Allan's ability to work with severely disturbed kids. "Until I realized the gratification of

helping these children and was told I had a 'special gift,' I thought I was pre-
determined to go into my father's business after college. It was the first time
I realized I actually had a choice about my life's work."

Between 1976 and 1983 Allan served as principal of the Ethical Culture
School in New York City. It is one of the largest co-ed independent elementary schools in the country. His next endeavor was leading a study group
of independent school educators, a college dean, and a clinical psychologist
with a shared vision of (a) highlighting the importance of the early school
years and (b) having professionals with different training work together
across traditional professional boundaries. This study group became the
National Elementary School Center (NESC), which he directed from 1984 to
1994. NESC promoted the idea that *schools serve as a locus of child advocacy*
because, logically, that's where the kids are. He also made time for freelance
writing on education and parenting as well as serving as a parenting coach.

Allan has written widely in the popular and professional press based on
his focus group interviews with children and youth in the United States, the
United Kingdom, and Switzerland, as well as his 128 face-to-face daddying
interviews with fathers, grandfathers, and great-grandfathers. One interview
was with his own eighty-seven-year-old father, a highly successful businessman whom Allan admired as one of "the titans" of his childhood, yet a man
who was not around very much. As a result, Allan was determined to be a
nurturing and attentive father to his own children. Sometimes wondering
whether he was born with an extra nurturing gene, Allan is gratified that
many of the young men he associates with refer to him as "Dad." For example,
a young Native American father from the Taos Pueblo asked Allan to become
his father and they informally agreed to become father and son.

Allan draws immense satisfaction from bringing attention to a fundamentally important set of social and educational issues and getting people to
think differently about being a dad and more broadly about the changing role
of men. Nevertheless, his modest income from this work couldn't keep pace
with the rising cost of health insurance. The solution was to take another job
that offers health insurance benefits if he works an annual average of at least
twenty hours per week.

Initially, Allan's three grown daughters were shocked at his decision to do
work that seemed "menial" and made no use of his professional training and
experience, and they were worried that the physical challenges might be too

great. But after seven and a half years as a "crew member" at a Trader Joe's store, the job is no longer a source of contention within the family. And he has been explicit in pointing out that sometimes one makes these kinds of life decisions to pursue a higher calling. The store is so close to his home in Chevy Chase, Maryland, that his commute is a mere ten-minute walk. "Walking to and from the store and doing the physical work required is like going to the gym. The work is fun, I meet very interesting customers, and I have a group of wonderful coworkers who are very different from others I've ever worked with. I enjoy it, and I never have to take my job home with me." His colleagues call him "The Mayor of Trader Joe's" and tell him, "For an old guy you're in pretty good shape!" They can't believe that he's seventy-one; some have even insisted on seeing an ID to prove his age.

When I asked Allan how long he expects to continue working at his main job, REEL FATHERS, he replied that "retirement" doesn't even enter his thoughts. "So much still needs to get done. People are beginning to pay attention to *daddying* and the work of REEL FATHERS, its mission and its programs. My work is incredibly gratifying and my schedule also enables me to make time to spend with my eight grandchildren. Why would I ever consider stopping?"

In fact, Allan thinks he might be more productive now than ever before as this combination of professional and family commitments seems finally to bring together the sum total of his life's work and those things that are most important to him personally. *Mothering Magazine* apparently agrees: the June 2008 issue featured him as a "Living Treasure."

While leisure time is almost nonexistent, one thing Allan remembers to do for himself is to take an annual solitary retreat in a cabin in the Eastern Sierra Mountains of California. Last year he went for a ten-day retreat and produced "Seventy Thoughts . . . and Then Some" as well as "The Adventures of Daddy Appleseed." Both were written to share "points picked-up" with his children and his grandchildren. This year he went for eight days to work on other writings. Next year he plans a twelve-day stay to adapt some of these thoughts and points picked up for sharing more publicly. One piece of advice will be, "Don't allow your intellect to bully your intuition." Another will capture the essence of a George Bernard Shaw quotation from *Man and Superman* (1905) that Allan has lived by for years:

This is the true joy in life, being used for a purpose recognized by yourself as a mighty one. Being a force of nature instead of a feverish, selfish little clod of ailments and grievances complaining that the world will not devote itself to making you happy. I am of the opinion that my life belongs to the whole community and as I live it is my privilege—my privilege—to do for it whatever I can. I want to be thoroughly used up when I die, for the harder I work the more I love. I rejoice in life for its own sake. Life is no brief candle to me; it is a sort of splendid torch which I've got a hold of for the moment and I want to make it burn as brightly as possible before handing it on to future generations.

Without reviewing the history of marriage and family, let's hark back to the decades when my survey respondents were coming of age, finishing college or graduate school, marrying, raising families, and building their careers. For some, this was in the 1950s, for most it was in the 1960s and 1970s. It was commonly accepted then (and to some extent still is) that men defined themselves in terms of their work, gauging themselves and being gauged by their ability to be good providers. Barbara Ehrenreich put it more crudely in 1983: "God gave women uteruses and men wallets."[4] That was twenty years after Betty Friedan's *The Feminine Mystique* appeared and women were supposed to be liberated, but Ehrenreich saw that they were still to a large extent economically dependent on men. The adult male was still expected to shoulder the responsibility of supporting a wife and family. A man who took pride in his wife not having to work might feel inadequate if she did have to get a job. (I know this from my own experience. When both of our children were in elementary school and I broached the subject of getting a job, my husband's initial reaction was negative. Couldn't I be content to play tennis and do other things while the kids were in school? Fortunately, this line of thinking was momentary. College teaching was paying him considerably less than a decent salary, and we clearly needed the second income.)

A few years earlier, Erik Erikson's stage theory of adult development helped to shape the seminal work of psychologist Daniel Levinson and colleagues, who described overlapping eras in a man's development and the characteristics of each.[5] Within the life cycle they found that "A man's work is the primary base for his life in society. Through it he is 'plugged into' an occupational structure and a cultural, class and social matrix. Work is also of great psychological importance; it is a vehicle for the fulfillment or negation of central aspects of the self."[6] In a parallel study of female development conducted with his wife, Levinson found "gender splitting" in many forms, for example, "the Traditional Marriage Enterprise, with its distinction between the male husband/father/provisioner and the female wife/mother/ homemaker; the linkage between masculinity and authority, which makes it 'natural' that the man be head of household, executive and leader within the occupational domain and predominant in a patriarchal social structure."[7] Although Levinson noted that the traditional patterns were already changing and eroding at the time of the second study, he felt that satisfactory new ones were not yet available to replace them.

Levinson and his fellow researchers did not study men (or women) beyond the middle years, however. Thus, they could only speculate about later and late-late adulthood, believing the senior years were often characterized by a man's bodily decline, responsibilities reduced, recognition lessened, and authority and power diminished in both the family and work settings. They did not hesitate to declare that "there will be serious difficulties if a man holds a position of formal authority beyond age sixty-five or seventy. If he does so, he is 'out of phase' with his own generation and he is in conflict with the generation in middle adulthood who need to assume greater responsibilities."[8] That opinion from thirty-five years ago still has some traction today among employers and among younger workers who think older workers are clogging up the pipeline.

Sociologists have been studying social relations in the workplace, the organization of work, and the role of the work experience in daily life, ever since a trio of classical sociological theorists—Marx, Durkheim, and Weber—developed interest in the field. As one contemporary sociologist explains, "Work is perhaps the most important way in which society impacts our social experiences and life chances."[9] Evidence of changing attitudes toward employment comes from the Sloan Center on Aging and Work's Generations of Talent survey.[10] Sloan researchers studied attitudes toward gender roles in work and family held by employees of diverse ages working for multinational companies located in the United States, Brazil, China, India, Japan, the Netherlands, and the United Kingdom. "Traditional" gender perspectives encouraged a division of labor in which a married woman raised the children while her husband worked full time. The husband's career came first, and the wife was expected to forgo or at least delay her academic and career aspirations and opportunities. Reflecting newer thinking, Generations of Talent survey responses fell into two main areas: (1) men and women should put in the same amount of time but have different roles and responsibilities (labeled "equal time/specialized roles"), and (2) men and women should share all responsibilities, such as caring for family members and earning money (labeled "equal responsibilities"). While Sloan researchers found that education and income levels were somewhat associated with respondents' approval or disapproval of gender parity, *gender* proved the single most important variable associated with the "equal responsibilities" perspective—both men and women favored equal responsibilities, but women did so more strongly than men. In addition, differences in gender role perspectives were not attributable to a country's level of economic development (as determined by per capita national income). Differences were associated with national culture: participants from "the conventionally masculine societies" of China and Japan favored the "equal time/specialized roles" perspective.[11]

American men and women raising families today may in principle favor sharing responsibility for family care and for earning money, but their good intentions are often thwarted by practicalities beyond their control. Anne-Marie Slaughter's *Atlantic Magazine* essay, "Why Women Still Can't Have It All," makes it clear that even a high-powered woman who can afford help with child care and domestic chores will experience "unsolvable tensions between family and career" if she cannot control her schedule.[12] (Critics were quick to point out that the parenting problem belongs to *both* men and women.) Companies that were allowing employees to work from home for part or all of the five-day week or considering telecommuting's merits will be revisiting their policies now that Yahoo!'s CEO, Marissa Mayer, has summoned employees back to the office where face-to-face interactions can take place and (presumably) stimulate productivity and innovation. Stymied by family-*un*friendly workplace policies and lack of accommodations, couples with young children are reluctantly concluding that the spouse with the smaller income (usually but not necessarily the wife) should give up full-time work or leave the workforce altogether. As Stephanie Coontz recently observed on the fiftieth anniversary of the publication of *The Feminine Mystique*, the gender revolution has "hit a wall."[13]

At the same time, the flagging economy and the loss of millions of jobs have put men, particularly lower and middle-class men, at a distinct disadvantage. Hanna Rosin's *The End of Men and the Rise of Women*[14] describes how newly unemployed or underemployed men who define themselves by the old "macho" rules and roles are unexpectedly having to depend on the women in their lives for support, resilient women who are more readily adapting to the changing economy, getting retrained, going back to college, finding new careers. These recent socioeconomic changes make it difficult to know whether and to what degree the once-inviolable "masculinity rules" still have meaning for men in the senior years.

For instance, a comparison between older men's and older women's responses to my survey question about mentors/role models reveals an intriguing difference. As stated earlier, nearly three-quarters of the older men in my study reported having one or more mentors or role models at some point in their careers. Even more of the women—more than three-quarters—had one or more mentors or role models, among them a list of supportive family members, employers, and educators that was similar to the men's list. Yet the women included two groups scarcely mentioned by the men: colleagues and friends. One can only speculate that men launching careers in the 1950s, 1960s, and 1970s had less need to depend on colleagues and friends for help than women did.

That explanation is far more palatable than John Gray's stereotypical observations in *Men Are from Mars, Women Are from Venus*.[15] For Venusians, said Gray, it's all about sharing feelings and the quality of relationships, about supporting, helping, and nurturing. "Relationships [to Venusians] are more important than work or technology. . . . To share their personal feelings is much more important than achieving goals and success."[16] Martians, in contrast, are more interested in objects and things than people and feelings. "Martians value power, competency, efficiency, and achievement. They are always doing things to prove themselves and develop their power and skills. Their sense of self is defined through their ability to achieve results. They experience fulfillment primarily through success and accomplishment."[17]

Gray's portrayals of gender differences, once all the rage, are no longer valid insofar as they completely underestimate twenty-first-century women's commitment to their careers and their striving for success, as well as men's greater willingness to share in parenting and be more communicative. Still, for better or worse, there is at least a small kernel of truth in the rest of his analysis. It is still hard for men to ask for help. And, true to form, relationships are extremely important to women: they are still more likely than men to cite positive connections with coworkers or managers as reasons for staying with their current employers.[18] (These workplace networking kinds of relationships differ from close male friendships with buddies, also known as male bonding, that can involve "arguing, competing, or doing nothing much at all"[19] and can last for years.)

How are men reacting to changing concepts of masculinity? Robert Bly's *Iron John* told us that "The Fifties man was supposed to like football, be aggressive, stick up for the United States, never cry, and always provide."[20] Later on, after the feminist movement urged men to be "softer" and more "receptive," Bly found that men were no happier. Thus, according to Bly, for a young man to transfer from the mother's influence to the father's and enter into adulthood, he needs to "find the father" (who may be absent or remote) and do the hard work of connecting with "the deep masculine" within himself.

An outgrowth of the contemporary men's movement is the Mankind Project (MKP), inspired by mythopoetics like Robert Bly, Joseph Campbell, John Lee, and others. The MKP helps men face challenges and heal emotionally and supports their further growth and development. Ed Barton, the subject of the next profile, serves as a leader and an elder in the MKP, internationally and in this country, in addition to his day job. Being an elder has nothing to do with being elderly, he assures me. He plans on working for another ten years.

PROFILE: EDWARD BARTON

Ed Barton was comfortable talking about a series of midlife crises he suffered—Chapter 11 bankruptcy reorganization in the mid-1980s; the suspension of his law license in 1990, followed by the dissolution of his marriage; several years spent agonizing over coming out as a gay man; and, nine years ago, triple bypass surgery. Now in his midseventies, he has managed to put all that behind him or grow through them, thanks in large part to MKP, his other mythopoetic men's emotional healing activities, and a little therapy.

The MKP is a global nonprofit organization "that conducts challenging and highly rewarding training for men at every stage of life." MKP "helps men through any transition, men at all levels of success, men facing almost any challenge." The MKP's flagship training, called the New Warrior Training Adventure (NWTA), stresses initiation, accountability, intention, commitment, and emotional intelligence. The MKP also sponsors peer-facilitated men's support groups (called I-Groups), which teach *emotional authenticity, personal responsibility, leadership mastery, empowered mission,* and *supportive community.* In short, the MKP encourages men to self-reflect, grow, and move forward. While the MKP is composed largely of heterosexual men, it holds special "gateway" weekends to initiate gays into the organization and has an annual Rainbow Warrior Gathering for gay men of the MKP and their allies.

Ed told me that he earned a JD from Cornell in 1964, passed the bar the next year, and practiced law for twenty-five years. He lost his law license for three years after he "went too far for a client" by committing perjury, a felony offense. He pleaded guilty and was sentenced to two years of probation. He paid all the fines and court costs assigned to him, never missing a payment, in fact paying them off early, and earning an early release. Ed has been asked why he went so far for a client. His explanation: "I think I subconsciously knew I had to do something to get off the treadmill, and that's what allowed me to start on a more healing and spiritual journey."

By the time the suspension of his license had expired, however, Ed knew he didn't want to return to the high-pressure legal arena and he didn't want the hassle of applying for reinstatement. To keep his mind active, he took some part-time paralegal jobs, such as doing collections work for an attorney (pursuing overdue payments was an area in which he had years of experience) and reviewing and editing legal documents. He chose not to do legal research (tasks that he never liked and that required computer skills that he lacked).

He also began working on a doctorate at Michigan State University in Family and Child Ecology, which is the study of the family as an ecological system. He completed his PhD in 2003. With men's support groups having been so important in Ed's emotional growth and development, he wrote his dissertation on men's support groups.[21] Then sixty-five, he began looking for a faculty position. When interviews with a few college departments didn't pan out, he suspected that they were unwilling to hire someone his age. Consequently, he continued doing part-time paralegal work, convinced that, "If I tried to land a full-time paralegal job, I would again encounter age discrimination."

Ed still owns the family farm where he grew up outside of Kalamazoo, Michigan, but he has been leasing the land and buildings. Until his marriage and his livelihood began to fall apart, he, his wife, and stepchildren raised purebred sheep on the farm with the help of a hired hand. Meanwhile, Ed operated his law office full time as a sole practitioner with four full-time secretaries. His former wife waited until Ed had been sentenced by the court, and finally she moved out.[22]

Realizing that he needed help after the separation, Ed sought out a counselor. Ed knew it was important to answer his counselor's questions honestly: "I couldn't fudge, couldn't gloss over the truth." The first thing the counselor asked after Ed had completed an inventory was, "You are gay, aren't you?" Ed's reply was, "Gulp, gulp, gulp. Yes."[23]

Later Ed joined the counselor and a half dozen other men in starting a men's peer support group in Kalamazoo. Emotional authenticity, personal responsibility, empowerment or no, it took Ed (as a gay man) two and a half years to come out to his Kalamazoo support group of mainly nongay men. "If they had been gay guys, it wouldn't have taken me so long."

Even many years later, Ed found coming out publicly was still a struggle. As an example, when he attended his fifty-fifth high school reunion in 2011, he waffled about disclosing that he was a gay man. "I decided to go for it and came out as gay to my classmates. One classmate said that she already knew. I asked her how she knew and she said, 'Because you never hit on us gals like the other guys did.'" And as he expected, the extremely religious classmates didn't stop to talk to him after the reunion was over.

Ed has been very involved in the MKP, serving as a staff member for fifty-three NWTA trainings to date, taking advanced MKP trainings, Shadow Healing trainings, and undertaking many leadership roles. He is the research coordinator for MKP International (MKPI), secretary to MKP-USA, and is centre elder in the Windsor-Detroit MKP Centre. To Ed, the MKP means community and inclusivity. "I am accepted both as a gay man and in a general sense. My skills and contributions are appreciated, in particular my legal skills and understanding of governance. I'm an elder holding *elder energy*, and that has become part of my identity.[24] I hope you understand that elder energy is not at all the same as being 'elderly.' Elderly is old, like the stereotype: retirees go off to Florida or Arizona to vegetate in a retirement village. That's definitely not elderhood or positive elder energy; elderly is not who I am!"

Ed explained that the MKP belongs to a division of the contemporary men's movement known as the "mythopoetic" branch. Inspired by the work of poet Robert Bly, mythologist Joseph Campbell, John Lee,[25] and others, mythopoetics engage in meaningful men's initiation, spiritual rituals, and psychological self-help workshops aimed at helping men reclaim and restore their "deep masculine" natures that have been lost due to modern lifestyles and consumerism. Among Ed's own contributions to the men's movement is an anthology he edited, titled *Mythopoetic Perspectives of Men's Healing Work: An Anthology for Therapists and Others.*[26] In addition, he coaches two or three *warrior* brothers who phone him on a regular basis about their own midlife crises, and he attends a local co-ed support group once a month.

When I asked Ed whether he thinks men and women differ in terms of career choice and ambition, his first response was that men seemed more focused and goal oriented than women. Then he quickly reconsidered. "If we're talking about *older* people, elders, I've seen women who were primarily nurturers for years turn into *warriors/crones* once their kids left 'the nest,' while men who have been on point in the 'provider role' for years often look to their softer side, their feminine side, as they get to midlife and beyond."

Ed has also devoted countless volunteer hours as Curator of the Changing Men Collections (CMC) in Special Collections of the Michigan State University (MSU) Libraries.[27] The MSU Libraries have the largest collection of men's movement materials in North America and possibly the world. For example, there are newsletters from groups of all branches of the contemporary men's movement—profeminist, fathers' rights, men's rights, Promise Keepers (a Christian men's group), the mythopoetic, African American men, Jewish men, Moslem men, and gay-lesbian-bisexual-transgender (GLBT) organizations. In the CMC there are nearly four hundred different men's movement newsletters from around the world that have been cataloged and another four hundred remaining to be cataloged. He seeks materials at conferences and requests other donations such as the archives of the Mid-South Men's Center and the Ithaca Men's Center.

Looking ahead, Ed expects to keep working as a paralegal for perhaps ten more years to supplement his Social Security benefits, provided his health holds up—his cardiologist says Ed is doing well and is cutting Ed's medications in half. "My job gets me up and out of here in the morning. I could stay home and read all day, but that would not be healthy for me either, mentally or physically." Ed thinks he will probably cut back his volunteer hours at the library. "I am getting burned out on the collection and would really like to find something else to be passionate about. Remember Joseph Campbell's advice? Campbell famously said 'Follow your bliss,' find something you really enjoy doing that nurtures your soul, and make it work for you emotionally and physically to restore passion in your life. That's what I intend to do!"[28]

When it comes to masculinity, the military is one institution that holds a prominent place in the public's mind as the bailiwick of powerful men. Military service has historically been synonymous with patriotism, courage, might, *and* masculinity. The father of the next man you will read about embodied all those qualities. Chris Walsh's father was an admiral in the US Navy who commanded a squadron of nuclear missile submarines. According to Chris, his father's powerful aura affected all three of his children, and it wasn't until Chris was fifty that his father let him know how proud he was of Chris's accomplishments. Chris, now sixty-one, is an architect serving his second term in the state legislature. Retirement is nowhere on his radar screen; he has too many other plans.

PROFILE: JOHN CHRISTOPHER WALSH

Chris Walsh's father, a highly successful naval officer and a hard worker, was a big influence on his son's early years. Graduating from the Naval Academy at the close of World War II, Jack Walsh worked in naval intelligence and commanded several submarines, eventually commanding a squadron of nuclear missile submarines and achieving the rank of admiral. It is hard for Chris to believe that his father, now eighty-nine, is prey for Internet and telephone scammers who take advantage of and abuse the elderly. "Part of elder caregiving," according to Chris, "is morning coffee with my dad and keeping a step ahead of the scammers. I systematically delete junk from my dad's computer so he doesn't see it, and try to intercept any checks he writes to suspicious groups. I also had to make the decision to stop him from driving." Chris sees caregiving as a learning experience. "With our children we go from heavy involvement to lesser involvement over the years; with our parents we reverse that and go from lesser to heavy involvement. It's hard to watch a man who was in charge of submarines be frustrated by his checkbook."

Shelia Walsh, Chris's mother, influenced him in a different fashion. As was typical in the 1950s and 1960s, she was the primary caregiver and, in a military family, often functioned as a single parent for long stints. "My mother was the creative personality with the big and interesting ideas; she was mercurial but very nurturing." Beset with many years of health issues, including strokes and near total blindness, there is very little left of the élan that was her hallmark, explains Chris. Sadly, it is sometimes a struggle to remember her former personality.

As the son of a navy man, Chris experienced frequent moves around the country while he was growing up. His college years were equally checkerboarded: he enrolled in and dropped out of one school after another, with stints as a waiter, bartender, salesman, and delivery van driver along the way; always, however, taking night classes in diverse subjects, such as linguistics, welding, botany, and Chinese poetry. In retrospect, the van-driving job was fortuitous: it was for an architecture firm where Chris interacted with some of the world's leading architects. In a bizarre and almost comical set of circumstances, his causing an extensive ten-car, slow-speed accident prompted the architects to invite him to "turn in the keys," come inside, and *draw*, at which point he began to take architecture night classes. He later completed his degree in the five-year architecture program at the Rhode Island School of Design (RISD) and there he met his future wife, Cindy.

Architecture being a somewhat nomadic profession for a young man, Chris moved from Manhattan to Dallas and eventually to Massachusetts where he, Cindy, and their two small children relocated so Chris could open his own architecture firm. They temporarily moved into his parents' spacious antique house in Framingham to get a better sense of where in New England they wanted to settle down. Some twenty-six years later, there they remain. As his dad and mom aged, it became clear that the home they loved was becoming dangerous and they were at risk of injury on the rickety staircases. To prolong the ability of his parents to live at home, Chris designed and had built an extension onto the house with a handicapped-accessible suite of rooms for them.

Four years ago when Chris was fifty-seven, he made a career move that he had been contemplating for some time: a run for state representative. The incumbent won that 2008 race, but Chris came close, losing by one hundred votes. Emboldened rather than discouraged, he ran against the incumbent again in 2010 and won. A Democrat, he represents the Sixth Middlesex District, encompassing some forty thousand people or close to two-thirds of Framingham, the largest *town* in Massachusetts. He serves on three House committees: Children, Families and Persons with Disabilities; Tourism, Arts and Cultural Development; and Transportation.

In Massachusetts, state representatives have to run for reelection every two years; and in 2012 Chris was elected to a second term. He is the only architect serving in the State House. "The last time there was an architect in the State House was in 1886," he tells me. "One of my goals is to encourage more architects to run for the legislature. People trained in design are good at conceptualizing; they tend to be good at redefining a problem or reframing a question so it can be solved." He points, as one example, to the popular shopping malls on busy Route 9 that drained business away from downtown Framingham. "Downtown is no longer a retail center, so what is it? How can it be transformed? I see that as a design problem."

When I asked Chris to talk about his career change, he surprised me by insisting it was *not* a career change. First of all, he still considers himself an architect. Then too, in his view, architecture and serving in the state legislature are quite similar. "Both require you to be interested in the quality of the environment, be able to listen well to your clients/constituents, understand how things work or not work, and figure out which pieces affect a situation so you can solve a problem and make things better."

He explained that his decision to close down his architecture practice was driven in part by the high cost of liability insurance, especially for a sole practitioner. A legislator can influence local and state affairs without carrying liability insurance. He also realized that he needed a bigger playing field to get things done, that is, the leverage a seat in the legislature affords. "I suppose if

I had been fabulously famous as a sole practitioner, it would have been harder to close up shop. Given the recession and the continuing economic slump, however, it was a good decision.

"My current job and my interests match up well. It meets my need to tinker—with things, with ideas about improving the quality of life not only in our community but also more broadly, attending to the environment, education, transportation, and being a caring society. That's what is important. On the downside, it doesn't pay all that well, so I am less successful in a monetary sense. When one hops around over the years career-wise as I have, it's hard to amass a fortune."

Chris's wife, Cindy, runs her own business called Red Rover Clothing. She designs and manufactures women's outerwear and accessories, including jackets, pullovers, and capes made of Polartec, scarves and baby gifts. Her studio is located in a nineteenth-century clapboard building adjoining Framingham's historic town common. "Cindy's business is amazingly time-consuming. She works intensely, sewing most of the goods herself," Chris says admiringly. "Aside from the fact that she's always doing something, always on the go, the family depends on her and the business that she has created from scratch."

When I asked Chris whether Cindy agreed with his career move, he said that she was not overly enthusiastic about his run for state representative the first time because she dislikes politics in general and campaigning in particular. When he ran again, she was not happy. "Making a major move at my age was tricky for both of us. However, I visualized it, I went for it, and once I won, she relaxed or at least became resigned to it. I do my thing, she does hers, but we continue to do a lot of things together." They also enjoy sailing, camping, reading, gardening, and travel, activities that "fit into small crevices" of time. "Cindy and I are both workers, so down time has become incredibly important."

It is clear that Chris knows himself well. "I'm a joiner. Being a state rep fits my personality. I enjoy campaigning, listening to people (complaints and all) and attending dinners. I try to work smarter, not harder. Still, I admit to being tightly wound and driven by fear—a fear of being unsuccessful drives me to try harder. Actually, what I am really looking for is *respect* for what I accomplish. You might say that my father's aura got to all three of his children." Chris reveals that his sister, a talented playwright, shares a similar fear; and his brother, also an architect, was laid off during the recession and has not worked for several years. "I think it wasn't until I was fifty that my dad let me know how proud he was of me. All this introspection may come across as narcissism, or, in a better light, it may simply be what prods me to try to accomplish more."

Does Chris aspire to higher office? "Not really. As a state legislator I have more potential influence for those community quality-of-life issues than I ever did as an architect. If I became state senator, I might have even more leverage, but a move like that would depend on a lot of reshuffling. In the game of politics the ball can bounce erratically. If it falls into your hands, you run with it. It can just as easily bounce crazily away. There are many, many moving parts."

Chris would like to remain in office for at least a few more sessions. "I've just gotten started and I really believe my best work is yet to come," he tells me. After that, there could be yet another career move, perhaps into teaching. Meanwhile, he is thinking about taking a master's degree in public administration. Being one of the older House members, he is aware that he perhaps sees things a bit differently than other reps. He often reminds himself not to be "delusional," that is, so attached to his own ideas that he cannot hear other people, other ideas or other alternatives. He cites a Zen koan: "The finger is not the moon." This, in his view, means that pointing at something, naming it, defining it or putting his own expectations on it, does not necessarily make it so and says more about him than about the world.

Thoughts about masculinity and the military bring up gender issues. In January 2013 Secretary of Defense Leon E. Panetta and the Joint Chiefs of Staff announced the end of the military's ban on female troops engaging in combat. Secretary Panetta and the chiefs said not everyone is going to be a combat soldier, but everyone is entitled to the opportunity, if qualified. It made many observers wonder whether the new policy of equality in combat operations is an important breakthrough for soldiers of either gender. While we cannot know how Dr. Mead would have responded were she here today, I can report some things she said about men and the often unforeseen consequences of women's lib: On the one hand, a woman should be allowed to have children *and* do other things and have a style of life that doesn't demand that she stay at home day in and day out waiting for the plumber to show up. On the other hand (she reminded us), we've forgotten that for every woman who is boxed up in the suburbs *there's a man boxed up in a job*. Women's lib forgets that *men's* lives can be just as ruined by children as women's! Following that rather daring remark, Dr. Mead next responded to a question about role reversal, that is, the man becoming a house-husband and the woman going off to the office: A man who can cook better than his wife should do the cooking. And if he is better at nursing the children when they are sick, he should be the nurse. However, in her candid assessment, "We haven't gotten there yet."

Can the idea that men suffer from being boxed up in their jobs be reconciled with John Gray's picture of men (Martians) always doing things to prove themselves and develop their power and skills, defining their sense of self through their ability to achieve results, and experiencing fulfillment primarily through success and accomplishment? Wouldn't a man who feels trapped in his job eagerly look forward to retiring as soon as possible? Or would a powerful need to prove himself keep him on the job and trying to achieve results? It turns out that reality is not so black and white. If it is "axiomatic that a man's professional identity or work role fundamentally shapes the organization of his life,"[29] there are many things to consider carefully when that professional identity or work role nears its end. In the next chapter we will look at today's economic environment and the factors that are most likely to influence a man's decision to retire or stay on the job.

The Employment Situation for Adult Workers in the United States

---

Retirement should be voluntary. If work is more fun, keep on doing it.
—George E. Vaillant, *Aging Well*

Let's review an essential part of the context for men staying on the job—the employment situation for adult workers in the United States. For that, statistics are in order. This chapter presents the current picture of labor force participation, including long-term unemployment, part-time versus full-time work, and other US labor market conditions, plus up-to-date information on a range of issues related to age and gender, work and retirement.

Labor force participation by older age groups, that is, people age fifty-five and over who are working or looking for work, has been escalating, according to the US Bureau of Labor Statistics (BLS). What's more, a larger share of people *sixty-five and older* is staying in or returning to the labor force. People in this age group comprised 16.2 percent of the labor force in 2011 (up from 12.1 percent in 1990) and they numbered over 6.5 million (up from 3.8 million in 1990).[1] Figure 4.1 shows the steady rise in participation rates of older worker cohorts over the past twenty years. If it is unremarkable that two-thirds of Americans ages fifty-five to sixty-four are in the labor force today, what surely is attention-grabbing are the labor force participation rates of even older age groups, particularly those seventy and older.

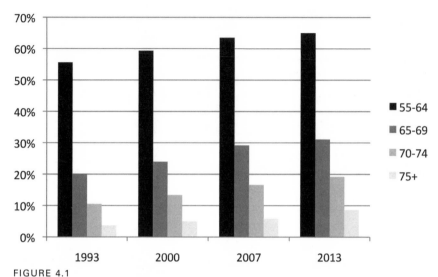

FIGURE 4.1

Labor Force Participation Rates by Age Group, January 1993–January 2013, Selected Years Only (in percentages)

Source: US Bureau of Labor Statistics, Current Population Survey. Adapted from Sara E. Rix, "The Employment Situation, January 2013: Jobs Added to the Economy but Unemployment for Older Workers Holds Fast," AARP Public Policy Institute, Fact Sheet 277 (February 2013). Washington, DC. Retrieved February 28, 2013, from http://www.aarp.org/research.

There are many possible explanations for these escalating rates of labor force participation by mature workers. First and foremost, the US population is aging. According to the Heldrich Center for Workforce Development, "Demographic trends predict a US population that is made up of a much greater proportion of older adults than in the population today, thanks largely to the size of the baby boom generation—those individuals born between 1946 and 1964—relative to younger cohorts. According to the 2010 US Census, 13 percent of the US population in 2010 was sixty-five or older. By 2030, the Census Bureau projects that the percentage of the population sixty-five or older will have risen to 19.3 percent—or nearly one in five individuals."[2] And this and other demographic trends are reconfiguring the composition of the workforce.

In 2010 the labor force held 30 million workers who were *fifty-five years and older* (19.3 percent of the total). By 2020, the BLS foresees 41.4 million workers fifty-five and older in the labor force (25.2 percent of the total, or one in four workers). In 2011 there were nearly 7 million people *sixty-five or older* in the labor force; by 2050, the number is projected to be nearly three times that, or 19.6 million. In a much shorter time span (by 2022), the number of men and women in the labor force sixty-five years or older will grow by 75 percent, compared to the number of prime-age workers (ages twenty-five to fifty-four), which will grow just 2 percent.[3]

The labor force is becoming more diverse, as well. The *growth rate* of women in the labor force, which has been "significantly higher" than that of men, is projected to slow by 2020, and the growth rates for men and women will be similar for the 2020–50 period.[4] Older men will continue to outnumber older women in the workforce, as they have historically, but the gap will be much narrower. Figure 4.2 compares labor force participation rates by age (fifty-five and older) and gender for selected years.

Whites are the largest group in the workforce but their population growth rate is slower than other racial and ethnic groups: Asians (the fastest-growing population) are expected to more than double their portion of the labor force (adding close to 9 million) by 2050; blacks will add 6.4 million, owing to high participation rates of black women; and Hispanics will add 37.7 million (almost 80 percent of labor force growth). In this decade alone, participation of

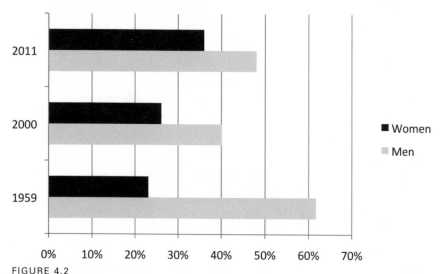

FIGURE 4.2
Labor Force Participation Rate, by Age and Gender, 1959–2011, Selected Years Only (in percentages).

Source: US Bureau of Labor Statistics, Current Population Survey. Adapted from Economic Policy Institute, "Labor Force Participation Rate, by Age and Gender, 1959–2011," *The State of Working America*, 12th ed. (Washington, DC: Economic Policy Institute, 2012). Retrieved February 11, 2013, from http://www.stateofworkingamerica.org/jobs/figure5L.

older Hispanics in the civilian labor force is projected to increase at a faster rate than any other Hispanic age group.[5]

There are many and varied reasons for older workers staying on the job. When the American Psychological Association conducted a Workforce Retention Survey to find out why working Americans stay with their current employers, "work-life fit" and "enjoying what they do" topped pay and benefits across all age groups.[6] For adults age fifty-five and older, eight out of ten cited "enjoying the work," more than three-quarters cited "work-life fit," nearly two-thirds said "feeling connected to the organization," and more than half said "having an opportunity to make a difference." (My respondents' reasons are discussed at length in chapter 7.)

The BLS highlights several reasons for the significant increases in labor force participation rates among older Americans:

- Longer and healthier life spans are enabling additional years of earned income.
- Availability of employer-based health insurance is keeping people in the labor force.
- Hikes in eligibility for collecting Social Security benefits are encouraging delayed retirement and rewarding older workers for each additional year of employment.[7]
- The shift from defined benefit to defined contribution pension plans (i.e., from employer "pay out" to employee "pay in") means benefits accrue with additional years of work.
- The Age Discrimination in Employment Act (ADEA) has eliminated most mandatory retirement ages.
- Labor market participation rates are higher among better educated citizens.
- Negative consequences of the financial crisis induce older workers to remain in the labor market.[8]

For an older adult nearing retirement age, such as a baby boomer, those negative consequences of the financial crisis might include: wage or salary stagnation, the loss of value in his home (or loss of the home through foreclosure), and diminished investments and savings, coupled with responsibility for a growing share of health-care costs. Although economic factors loom large, they are not the only drivers of working in the later years. Another array of influences on the retirement decision partially overlaps the previously referenced BLS list and adds the following: incentives, such as employers offering phased retirement options or reduced hours; status of physical and cognitive health (one's own and one's family's); availability of disability and unemployment insurance programs; and individual preference for leisure versus employment.[9]

An increasing number of even younger boomers have lost confidence in their ability to retire with sufficient financial security, and they, too, are opting to delay retirement. A 2012 Conference Board survey of 15,000 individuals found nearly two-thirds of Americans between the ages of forty-five and sixty saying they plan to delay retirement, and this was more than 20 percent higher than the response to the same survey item in 2010.[10] Similarly, MetLife's 2012 study of boomer attitudes regarding retirement found them "wearily eyeing working beyond the age of sixty-five."[11] (Despite their professed intention to delay retirement, it is entirely possible for boomers to change their mind when decision time arrives, as Sloan Center economist Kevin Cahill and other researchers point out.)[12]

A 2012 retirement readiness survey by the Aegon Group of nine thousand current workers in the United States, France, Germany, Hungary, the Netherlands, Poland, Spain, Sweden, and the United Kingdom found only 15 percent of respondents were confident that they are "on course to achieve the retirement income they need." Sixty percent expect to keep working in some manner beyond their retirement age. They did not want a traditional "retirement cliff" experience (i.e., going straight from working life into full retirement), a retirement cliff apparently having as little appeal as a "fiscal cliff." Across all nine countries participating in the Aegon survey, some form of *phased* retirement was preferred, such as changing to part-time status for a little while or changing to part-time status and continuing to work longer, or starting one's own business. Aegon sees phased retirement becoming the norm because people are living longer yet are less prepared for retirement financially.[13]

Retirement researchers Alicia Munnell and Steven Sass address the economic arguments for continuing to work past the traditional retirement age, asserting that "the economic dynamics currently in play . . . are unlikely to provide today's workers with economic security in their old age." With Social Security's retirement age for collecting full benefits moving from sixty-five to sixty-seven, higher health-care costs, rising tax rates, and weak-to-nonexistent retirement savings, they advise older workers who are healthy and willing to stay in the labor force, add to 401(k) accumulations, decrease the projected years in retirement, and leave more income for later years.[14] *New York Times* economic reporter Eduardo Porter also makes the case for delaying retirement for at least a few years. Doing so would not only increase one's income in retirement—annual Social Security benefits would increase along with each additional year in the workforce—the income taxes paid would also augment and take some strain off the government's social insurance programs. Porter points out that lower-wage workers would have the most to gain from additional years of work (although it has been shown that low-wage earners tend to exit the labor force earlier than higher-wage workers). Continued participation in the workforce would also help to offset slow growth in the labor supply, which the Congressional Budget Office expects to contract even more in the coming decade.[15]

To be sure, the United States is not alone when it comes to a shrinking supply of younger workers. With longevity increasing apace in Japan, a government report warns the country "to harness the skills of its graying workers," for "the nation's economic prospects depend on making them productive."[16] Promoting employment of mature workers is also a priority for European Union member countries. As Netherlands professor Annet de Lange reports, in the twenty-seven countries in the European Union as a whole, the rate of participation in the labor force for the population age fifty-five to sixty-four was 47.4 percent in 2011. Rates of participation by that age group vary widely from country to country in Europe. At one end of the spectrum is Sweden's high rate of 72.3 percent, with Germany, the Netherlands, and the United Kingdom close behind, and at the other is Belgium's rate of 38.7 percent the same year.[17]

In Germany, one of the European countries experiencing marked population declines, the government is inducing older workers to postpone retirement by raising the retirement age gradually from sixty-five to sixty-seven, and companies are offering flexible hours and redesigning assembly lines to minimize bending and lifting.[18] Luxembourg's National Employment Administration is considering a national policy to extend the careers of older persons—both by keeping them employed and by facilitating "reinsertion" (or reentry) into the workforce—through personnel training and guidance geared to job market requirements and favorable working conditions. The European Social Fund and the Ministry of Labour in Luxembourg are supporting the development of a "scorecard" intended to change the image of workers age fifty and older so companies won't be so quick to lay them off when they turn fifty-five.[19] In Australia, too, the government is urging employment of "mature age" workers and encouraging them to prolong their work lives by raising the eligibility age for the Age Pension and promoting tax-based incentives for employers and employees to contribute to retirement funds.[20]

Although hiring in this country has picked up somewhat—nearly every industry except state government added jobs—most of the gains are coming via low-wage and part-time jobs.[21] The economy is still not generating enough jobs to replace what was lost in the Great Recession.[22] Some states, such as Nevada, California, Michigan, North Carolina, and Florida, have been especially hard hit by unemployment. Although the majority of jobs lost in the downturn were middle-income jobs, highly educated, salaried professionals (who supposedly have an advantage over people who lack college degrees and hold midskilled jobs) are by no means immune to layoffs. The BLS Current Population Survey provides a comparison of unemployment rates in 2000 and 2011, by *gender* and *educational attainment*, illustrating the worsening employment picture for well-educated men and women alike.[23] As shown in figure 4.3, between 2000 and 2011, the percentage of unemployed men with college degrees jumped from 1.8 to 5.2 percent, and the percentage of unemployed men with advanced degrees went from 1.4 to 3.25 percent. In the same period, the percentage of unemployed women with college degrees jumped from 2.2 to 5.1 percent, and the percentage of unemployed women with advanced degrees went from 1.5 to 3.4 percent.

Unemployment data from the same source sorted by *education, race,* and *ethnicity* reveal additional evidence of disparate impacts.[24] As shown in figure 4.4, between 2000 and 2011, the unemployment rate among white college graduates grew 2.7 percent; among Hispanic college graduates it grew 4.4 percent; among Asian college graduates it increased 4.3 percent; among black college graduates the increase was an even greater 5.4 percent. In the same time period, advanced degree holders fared somewhat better: unemployment grew 1.7 percent among whites, 2 percent among both Hispanics and Asians, and 3.6 percent among blacks with advanced degrees.

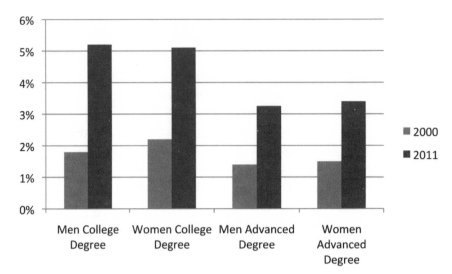

FIGURE 4.3

Unemployment Rate, by Gender and Education, 2000–2011, Selected Years and Education Levels Only (in percentages)

Source: US Bureau of Labor Statistics, Current Population Survey. Adapted from Economic Policy Institute, "Unemployment Rate, by Gender and Education, 2000–2011." *The State of Working America*, 12th ed. (Washington, DC: Economic Policy Institute, 2012). Retrieved February 11, 2013, from http://www. stateofworkingamerica.org/jobs/table5.4.

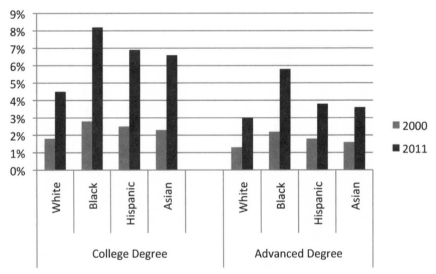

FIGURE 4.4

Unemployment Rate, by Education, Race, and Ethnicity, 2000–2011, Selected Years and Education Levels Only (in percentages)

Source: US Bureau of Labor Statistics, Current Population Survey. Adapted from Economic Policy Institute, "Unemployment Rate, by Education, Race and Ethnicity, 2000–2011." *The State of Working America*, 12th ed. (Washington, DC: Economic Policy Institute, 2012). Retrieved February 11, 2013, from http://www.stateofworkingamerica.org/jobs/table5.3.

Prior to the federal ADEA of 1967 employers could justify establishing a termination policy based on older worker age, productivity, cost, and the need for an objective process. The ADEA not only prohibits discrimination against workers age forty and older in hiring, promotions, wages, or termination of employment and layoffs, as of 1978 it raised the protected age to seventy and in 1986 it also abolished most mandatory retirement, with the exception of certain employment categories. Some types of employment can terminate early due to physical requirements in job performance (constituting a bona fide occupational qualification, or BFOQ, usually involving safety), such as police work, firefighting, and commercial airplane piloting. Another exception applies to top (highly compensated) executives who are at least sixty-five and entitled to a company retirement benefit, that is, a plan or plans equal in the aggregate to at least $44,000 per year. Meeting those criteria, law firms and some other sectors of the corporate world have made it a practice to mandate retirement when an executive attains a designated age. In the process, they are putting out to pasture highly educated and experienced professionals. Somewhat to my surprise, one fellow, a self-employed long-term care advisor, told me that he favors mandatory retirement. He states a popular argument for mandatory retirement, along with a caveat that suggests why he is nonetheless still working at age sixty-nine: "I feel that it is not in the best interest of seniors to hold jobs that should be filled by younger people. I am in favor of a mandatory retirement age. However, unless the social contract is improved, I am engaged in wishful thinking."

Some professionals turn to consulting work after mandatory retirement. For example, a sixty-five-year-old former executive at Ernst and Young is now a consultant and expert witness for accounting and auditing matters. Another man, Walter Arensberg, whom you will read about next, was only sixty-two when the Inter-American Development Bank's mandatory retirement policy ended his job as chief of the Environmental Division at the bank. Since he wanted and needed to keep working—he was still putting two children through school—he began consulting. Three years later, he landed a full-time position in social risk management for the Social Capital Group of Peru. Now seventy-three, he divides his time between Washington, DC, and Latin America. Thanks to the Great Recession, he expects to keep working for another five years or so.

PROFILE: WALTER WHITMAN ARENSBERG

When the Inter-American Development Bank's mandatory retirement policy kicked in for Walter Arensberg in 2003, he was only sixty-two. "It was too early to be retired, and I was still putting two children through school," he recalls. Determined to keep working, Walter took up independent consulting in his area of expertise—complex public and private sector programs and projects involving environmental planning and management, program evaluation, policy development, and institutional capacity building and community engagement. After three years of freelancing and what he describes as "constant scrambling," he wanted to find something that would be more stable. In 2006 Walter joined Social Capital Group (SCG) of Peru as a managing director.

SCG was founded in 2000 to address complex social issues associated with extractive industries and large-scale infrastructure projects. With more than one hundred professionals in its offices in Peru, Brazil, and Colombia, SCG works with private and public sector clients engaged in exploration, development, and operation of oil and gas projects, mining, industrial enterprises, hydropower, large-scale infrastructure development, and regional and watershed management programs. While the majority of SCG's clients are private companies, the firm has also worked with the World Bank, the International Finance Corporation, and the Inter-American Development Bank.

In addition to running SCG's North American office in Washington, DC, Walter oversees projects in Colombia and Panama and markets SCG's social risk management and due diligence services to international financial institutions interested in investing in Latin America. He helped open SCG's Colombian office about two years ago and travels there every month or so for four to five days to oversee its work. "I meet with clients and visit communities, going into the field to observe and evaluate the potential social impacts of a potential mining operation or a hydro-electric dam, for instance. In Peru, our firm is involved in resettling some two thousand families from a truly Dickensian mining town to a brand-new settlement for workers and their families. They will have new houses, schools, and other essential facilities, partially funded by the Peruvian government. It took nearly two years of discussion for our team to earn the community's trust and obtain its consent for the resettlement process."

Now seventy-three, Walter lives in two separate worlds and is comfortable in both. His home base and office are located in Washington, DC, but he works primarily in Latin America, and enjoys switching into another culture and speaking Spanish all day long. The language comes easily to him because he moved from Pittsburgh to Havana at the age of six and lived there steadily until he was fifteen and was shipped off to boarding school in Exeter, New Hampshire. "My father came back from wartime naval service in the South Pacific in 1946 and took a job in Cuba. I learned Spanish playing with my friends in the streets and attending a bilingual school. Our family relocated to Washington, DC, in the fall of 1960 after the new Castro government took over the school where my mother worked," he explains. "I felt fortunate to grow up in Cuba even though I was really an outsider—a blond American kid transplanted from Pittsburgh to a Latin country in the Caribbean. Among other things, it taught me, an American, that I wasn't the center of the universe."

While still an undergraduate studying political science at Harvard College, Walter became a contract interpreter for the State Department. The job involved showing foreign visitors around town and serving as their interpreter. "I learned to deal with a wide variety of people and I began to develop some of the core listening and communication skills I still call upon in my current work for SCG." After graduation in 1962, Walter had an Inter-American Cultural Convention Fellowship that took him to Colombia for a year of study where he attended the University of the Andes and made many friends. Those connections are still useful today when he is knocking on the doors of Colombian government and business contacts.

From 1966 to 1969 he had what he considered the perfect job as an evaluation officer for the Peace Corps. He assessed Peace Corps programs firsthand in Honduras, Ecuador, Venezuela, Chile, and Panama, as well as volunteer training programs in eastern Kentucky and the Dominican Republic. "This was a truly formative experience: the evaluation process required extensive field interviewing, building trust, researching and analyzing programs, and writing critical reports—all skills that I have used ever since."

For a brief time Walter worked with John Gardner's National Urban Coalition as a community organizer before landing a more permanent position with the international architectural and planning firm Skidmore, Owings and Merrill in 1970. With the passage of the National Environmental Policy Act, the firm, which had become involved in urban land use, transportation, and redevelopment projects, needed staff who could work with urban communities on environmental and social impact assessments. Some of these projects included a highway on the West Side of New York City, the Big Dig in Boston, the Northeast Corridor High Speed Rail Improvement Project, and housing master plans in Ecuador and Chile. During a paid leave, Walter took a master's degree in urban planning at Harvard and became a partner in the firm in 1978. While in Cambridge, he met and married his wife and the couple returned to Washington, DC.

By 1987, Walter had moved on to the World Resources Institute (WRI) as deputy director for WRI's Center for International Development and Environment. Then, nine years later and still in Washington, he became chief of the Environmental Division at the Inter-American Development Bank, the primary multilateral lender to Latin America and the Caribbean. His career was interrupted when the bank's mandatory retirement policy forced him to leave after seven years. "That was nine years ago. I definitely wanted and needed to keep working, so I tried consulting and finally landed the SCG job."

Now that his children are out on their own, Walter has mixed feelings about continuing to work. "If we won the lottery, I'd love to travel with my wife or write a book instead of writing proposals, policy papers, and official reports. But right now, after the Great Recession, I've got to keep working and probably will continue to do so, as long as I stay healthy and still enjoy the work. I've had a couple of bouts with cancer, but so far, so good; so we'll see how it goes for another five years or so. We are a two-income family, so whatever I do will be a joint decision for me and my wife."

In his twenty-four years in intellectual property law with Weil, Gotshal and Manges LLP, Steve Kahn had plenty of time to plan for mandatory retirement at age sixty-nine. He had been working pro bono for Save the Children-USA for several years, so becoming part-time general counsel there seemed a good fit and a logical next step. Until it wasn't. After a few months, Steve and the CEO realized that the organization really needed a full-time general counsel, so he stepped down. He soon was in discussion with another organization that needs his expertise. If it is stimulating and useful work, that's for him.

PROFILE: STEPHEN D. KAHN

Scarcely twenty-four hours elapsed between Steve Kahn's retirement from Weil, Gotshal and Manges LLP, the large Manhattan-based international law firm where he had worked as an intellectual property/litigation partner for twenty-four years, and the phone call inviting him to become general counsel for Save the Children-USA. Fully aware that Weil, like most law firms, enforces a mandatory retirement policy at the end of the year a lawyer turns sixty-nine, unless he is still actively involved in a case, Steve had been preparing for retirement by gradually cutting back on his workload. And the call from Save the Children did not come out of the blue, since Steve had already been working pro bono for that not-for-profit organization for several years in addition to his main responsibilities. Pro bono service was part of the culture at Weil—the firm has a pro bono counsel and Weil lawyers are expected to provide at least fifty hours of pro bono service per year. Yale Law School, where Steve got his degree in 1968, had also encouraged pro bono service, and he has always enjoyed it along with intellectual property law.

"I was lucky in choosing IP as my area early on. I know many lawyers working in less interesting areas who are bored. The significant difference between IP law and older areas is that IP law deals with subject matter that is constantly new, so the law itself is always in flux and is useful in advancing many aspects of our lives." Steve offers two good examples. The first is the sudden explosion of computer software as a core technology in the 1970s. No existing body of law instructed courts in the United States as to how they should protect the assemblages of ones and zeros against blatant copying, semi-blatant copying, or outright theft—misappropriation—of the ideas they contained or the way they were written. Biotechnology, another rapidly developing field with which the courts were unfamiliar, came into being about a decade after software. The law is still trying to determine appropriate protections for developments in that industry. Through the 1980s and 1990s, judges struggled to make sense out of such emerging technologies and to encourage creativity and the growth of computer science without allowing industrial competition to run amok. Steve was immersed in and fascinated by issues of technology-related public policy and copyright, trade secret and patent law. "If you enjoy dealing with developments in science and technology and public policy, as I do, it's hard to imagine a more interesting career. When I had a patent case involving the technology of a wastewater treatment plant, I had to learn enough about that industry to run the plant if I had to! I have also taught IP law for the last few years, and for the same reasons find that great fun."

One of the cases for which Steve was lead counsel became famous: *Computer Associates International, Inc. v. Altai, Inc.*, which was the first to determine the extent to which nonliteral elements of software (e.g., the structure, sequence, and organization of a program) are protected by copyright. (Previously, judges did not know how to rule regarding copyright infringement of software because it was so new.) Known for the "Altai Test" which was developed and applied by the US Court of Appeals for the Second Circuit in its 1992 decision, the landmark case is still taught in law schools today and applied by courts in the United States. Prior case law said that all aspects of a computer program except the highest-level abstraction of the idea underlying it were protectable. The Second Circuit, however, deemed that too broad a test for evaluating the protection to which a program was entitled and for determining the degree of similarity between protectable aspects of programs. To replace prior law, the court devised the three-step process that is still applied today. Once defendant Altai's computer program was separated into its constituent parts using the three-step test, it was found to have infringed on plaintiff Computer Associates' program to a lesser degree than would have been true under the facts when measured against the former test. Thus, though Computer Associates' claim did prevail, it obtained a smaller recovery than would have been obtained under the prior test. The Altai case introduced a new, and still enduring, standard for protecting computer software from the theft of intellectual property it contains.

As mentioned earlier, Yale Law School encouraged pro bono work and Steve has continued to devote time to it throughout his career. Early on, he joined a young lawyers group called the Council of New York Law Associates that was formed by, among others, Carol Bellamy (who went on to become New York City's first female City Council president and the head of UNICEF) and two other Yale Law graduates, named Tim and Nina Zagat. Under Mr. and Mrs. Zagat's influence, the young lawyers shared recommendations about good restaurants when not discussing legal business. The mimeographed lists of restaurants were the first step toward the Zagat publishing empire. Also in the early 1970s, following the first Earth Day, Steve cowrote a report with two other young lawyers, Clifford Case and Myron Kaplan, which argued to the City Bar Association that law firms should help the environment by using recycled paper. Naturally, the paper industry trade association did not like that idea, and it quietly tried to quash the report at the association. Fortunately, a neighbor of Steve's, James MacGregor, then a reporter for the *Wall Street Journal*, heard about the situation and wrote a full-page feature article about the impasse for the newspaper. The City Bar Association reviewed the report, found it accurate, and soon the Bar Association was distributing the report to all law firms in the city whose copy machines then began using (and getting jammed by) recycled paper!

Steve loves the mission and the staff at Save the Children. According to the organization's website, www.savethechildren.org, in 2011 alone the organization reached 185,000 vulnerable, underserved, and often forgotten children in this country through education, health, and resiliency programs, and 92,000 mothers, fathers, grandparents, and caregivers. Around the world, the website states, when disaster strikes Save the Children steps in with food, medical care, and education and remains to help communities rebuild through long-term recovery programs. Not only does it quickly respond to tsunamis and civil conflict, it also works to resolve the ongoing struggles poor children face every day.

However, Steve dislikes the long commute from his home in Brooklyn, New York, to Save the Children's headquarters in Westport, Connecticut. In addition, what was supposed to be a four-day-a-week job actually requires a full-time commitment. Consequently, Steve and the CEO have concluded, in an entirely friendly way, that he would be replaced by a full-time general counsel. "Save the Children was pretty close to a perfect fit for me, so I step down with some regrets."

Steve credits his wife, Betty, with encouraging him five or so years ago to plan ahead so that, when the time came, he would not leave the law firm cold turkey. She advised him to arrange a smooth transition from Weil to whatever he chose to do next. This advice was especially timely because Steve's father had died suddenly, his brother was going through significant life changes including a divorce, and Steve was shouldering extra-heavy personal burdens.

He recalled the way his father had retired from the insurance business. "He walked out the door and never looked back. That was not for me. I hate golf, don't like to fish, and do like work so long as it is stimulating and useful. Betty knows me well enough to realize that I need something to do or I will get antsy. She would like me to turn the knob back a bit toward relaxation so we can visit our children and grandchildren more often and do more traveling. We went hiking with friends in the mountains of Montenegro this year, and we would like to do more of that."

Fortunately, a new opportunity has arisen for Steve to apply his expertise in intellectual property law. He is not willing to discuss this opportunity for publication, but it involves using environmentally clean, renewable sources to provide energy to communities in which live tens of thousands of people. This work would at once be stimulating, exciting in many ways, and useful to many people around the world.

Unemployment is the pits. Unemployed men and women of all ages can identify with the sentiments expressed by a forty-eight-year-old advertising manager who has been out of work for more than six months: "Your whole life your job defines who you are. All of a sudden that's gone, and you don't know what to take pride in anymore."[25] In the words of a discouraged sixty-one-year-old man who was laid off four years ago when the company he worked for closed and is still out of work: unemployment "affects your vision of yourself; it affects your outlook on life; it affects your motivation at times. You start questioning—'Had I done this, had I done that.'"[26] To help maintain a sense of "purposeful engagement" in unemployed older workers and recent retirees, the Tufts Health Care Foundation is funding a nonprofit organization called ReServeInc that matches older adults with part-time jobs in schools, government offices, and community agencies in New York City and Boston and pays them $10 per hour. One ReServist, the former chief economist for New York City, spoke for many when he said, "If there was no compensation, it would mean I'm not worth anything."[27]

Sequestration, the automatic across-the-board federal budget cutting that took effect on March 1, 2013, is targeting federal, state, and local government employees with cascading job losses and furloughs. The companies in the private sector that rely on public spending are expected to follow suit. A month before sequestration, at the end of January 2013, the total unemployment rate—7.9 percent—reported by the BLS was relatively unchanged from the previous year. It dipped to 7.7 percent in February. When it dropped to 7.6 percent in March, economists were quick to attribute the change to more people dropping out of the labor force (they are neither working nor looking for work) rather than more people being hired. Furthermore, hiring is not only proceeding at a sluggish pace, it is also generally paying low wages and offering temporary or part-time work with little or no job security.[28] At 6.0 percent the unemployment rate for older people specifically (i.e., men and women fifty-five and older) was also relatively unchanged from the past year. According to AARP's Sara Rix, unemployment for all age groups is a "much greater problem" than it was at the start of the Great Recession, and for older people, while not quite as dire as for younger people, it is "up sharply": nearly 2 million older people were unemployed in January 2013, an increase of approximately 115,000 from the previous year alone.[29]

AARP's Public Policy Institute has amassed facts about the financial strains besetting many Americans sixty-five and older since the recession as well as longer-term trends, such as the high cost of health care:[30]

- One out of six lives in poverty.
- Half of the age group has annual individual income below $18,500.
- Older females are poorer than their male counterparts. (Among blacks, 24 percent of older women are living in poverty compared to 13.7 percent of older men; older white women have a 9.5 percent poverty rate, compared to 5 percent of older men.)
- Upward of 7 million men and women sixty-five and older are in the labor force, but the unemployment rate for the age group is nearly twice what it was in 2007 and many have been unemployed for a year or longer.

Income losses caused by the recession remain widespread despite signs that recovery is officially under way. US Census data show that median net worth for householders sixty-five and older in 2010 was more than $25,000 less than in 2005: $170,128, down from $195,890.[31] Sentier Research's comparison of median annual incomes among different racial and ethnic groups found a lower starting point and a larger decrease (11.1 percent) for black Americans than any other group.[32]

Once out of a job, older workers tend to remain unemployed longer than younger workers. Rix reports that more than four out of ten older jobseekers were categorized as "long-term unemployed" in January 2013 (defined as being out of work for twenty-seven weeks or more). There is a danger that long-term unemployment could become *structural*: jobless workers lose skills, contacts, and information; they get stigmatized as unemployable; and they become more discouraged and isolated than ever.[33] "TIME IS NOT ON THEIR SIDE" blares a front-page headline in the *Boston Globe*.[34] Long-term joblessness—lasting more than one year—is hitting older workers harder than any other age group. "Older" in this article refers to people *forty-five and older*, who constitute nearly half of the 3.5 million Americans unemployed long term. The Department of Labor says the majority are college-educated white men in (what should be) their prime earning years. Not only are their employment prospects dimming, says reporter Megan Woolhouse, their self-esteem is also plummeting. In the words of laid-off men Woolhouse interviewed for the article, "you feel empty," "you dread the silence" that follows job applications.[35]

In response to the "unprecedented" increase in protracted unemployment across all age groups, the BLS issued an unusual announcement with its monthly rundown of the employment situation: the Current Population Survey has for the first time in years allowed survey respondents to report unemployment of *up to five years* in duration instead of up to only two years. It is not surprising that the number of "discouraged" older workers (the official designation for men and women who want a job but have stopped looking) is higher today than at the start of the recession. And, as a result, many hard-pressed Americans who have exhausted their unemployment benefits and their personal savings, if any, are opting for early retirement or in some cases applying to the disability program.

Another group whose numbers are higher than at the start of the recession is made up of older involuntary part-time workers, involuntary because the only work available to them in an uncertain labor market is part time, owing to hours being cut back or an inability to find full-time employment. Typically, along with the shift to part-time status come wage and salary cuts and loss of eligibility for benefits. A sixty-one-year-old man in this situation has been working for forty-five years but is now a substitute teacher who calls in to work daily and gets hired for one to two days of work per week. He has a second job as an outdoor instructor to supplement his modest income from teaching. He also volunteers at a food pantry.

Still another solution to job loss for people who want to keep working is self-employment. However, becoming a successful "silver entrepreneur" in the same field or a different one requires financial resources, connections, drive, and determination that can be hard to come by. For the period since 2007, the proportion of self-employed workers within the older workforce has been about ten percent.[36] Entrepreneurial boomers in the fifty-five to sixty-four age group are starting new businesses at a faster rate than younger workers.[37]

Against the dichotomous backdrop of a labor market that is said to be ever bigger, older, and more diverse while remaining unfavorable to the employment and reemployment of older workers, the many and varied success stories of professionals still on the job stand out. Let's explore further who they are, what they are doing, and why they are opting for work over retirement.

5

Over Sixty and on the Job

Age is nothing. . . . Attitude is everything. —Marie Therese von Rohr-Truong in Luxembourg, NoAgeSite.com

Previous chapters have introduced individual men still on the job after years of experience in fields as disparate as law, higher education, international development, sports management, film distribution, medicine, social services, and social risk management. While the profiles put a face to the statistics by telling each man's story in some detail, readers also need basic, summative information about all the 156 professionals who completed my survey and the ways in which they are similar to or different from one another and consistent with or deviating from national trends. To that end, this chapter presents the men's average age, where they live, marital and family status, educational achievement, earnings, length of time in the workforce, and so on.

Respondents range in age from sixty to ninety-three. Their average age is seventy (the median is seventy-one), making these working men four years older on the whole than the women I studied. Fifty-seven percent of the men are seventy and older; 43 percent are sixty to sixty-nine.

Respondents hail from twenty-two states, the District of Columbia, Belgium, and Canada. New England is home to eighty-four of the men: Connecticut, Massachusetts, Maine, Vermont; twenty-five are from the mid-Atlantic region: Maryland, New Jersey, New York, Virginia, Washington, DC; eleven are from the South: Arkansas, Florida, Georgia, Kentucky, Mississippi, North Carolina, Texas; eight are from the Midwest: Illinois, Michigan, Missouri; and twenty-six are from the West, Southwest, and Northwest: Arizona, California, New Mexico, Washington. Heavily represented are Massachusetts residents (50 percent of the total) and Californians (14 percent).

A very high percentage of the men are married (88 percent). Nine are currently divorced (6 percent). There are five widowers, four single men, and one partnered man. We might expect more older men to be married than older women since women in the higher age brackets generally tend to live longer than men and are more likely to be widowed. Indeed, the percentage of older married men exceeds the percentage of older married women by twenty points (68 percent of the women I surveyed are married and the rest are divorced, widowed, or single).

US Census statistics on the marital status of older Americans confirm that older men are much more likely than older women to be married. In 2010, more than three-quarters of American men ages sixty-five to seventy-four (78 percent) were married, compared with over one-half (56 percent) of women in the same age group. The proportion married was lower at older ages: 38 percent of women age seventy-five to eighty-four and 18 percent of women age eighty-five and over were married. For men, the proportion married also was lower at older ages, but not as low as for older women. Even among the oldest old in 2010, the majority (58 percent) of men were married. Widowhood was more common among older women than among older men in 2010. Women age sixty-five and over were three times as likely as men of the same age to be widowed, 40 percent compared with 13 percent. Nearly three-quarters (73 percent) of women age eighty-five and over were widowed, compared with 35 percent of men.

Relatively small proportions of older men (9 percent) and women (11 percent) were divorced in 2010. A small proportion (4 percent) of the older population had never married.[1]

All but fourteen of the men in my study have children or stepchildren. Among the 93 percent with children, the number of offspring ranges from one to ten. Most common is a family with two children, which was somewhat lower than the average number of children born to married couples nationally in the 1950s, 1960s, and 1970s when my respondents were starting families. (The national average exceeded three children in the 1950s through the mid-1960s, after which it began to drop. From a low point in 1976 when it was 1.7, the average began to climb steadily, reaching 2.06 children in 2012.) More men have children than the women (88 percent of the women do), possibly due to acquiring stepchildren or forming a blended family, or starting a new family when marrying for the second or third time. Although I did not ask the men to tell me how many grandchildren they have, I received this delightful comment from an eighty-two-year-old professor: "Having twenty grandchildren is an assignment as bewilderin' as it is utterly entrancing!"

One respondent who has devoted himself to family—biological, adopted, and foster—as well as helping other men to be good fathers is Neil Tift. Neil, sixty-five, and his wife, Denise, have two grown children and an adopted teenaged daughter who has special needs. They have been foster parents to many children and adults. Two disabled foster adults currently live with the Tift family. As Father Involvement Program Director at the Child Crisis Center in Mesa, Arizona, Neil strives to teach fathers on and off the reservation about positive parenting and healthy life choices. By including motivated dads in the parenting picture, child abuse and domestic violence can be reduced. Neil appreciates the opportunity "to make the world a better place" at home, at work, and in the community.

PROFILE: JOHN NEIL TIFT

Neil Tift is the Father Involvement Program Director at the Child Crisis Center in Mesa, Arizona (the state's third largest city, located twenty miles east of Phoenix). As a specialist in working with men, his job balances working directly with fathers and developing resources for fathers, such as father-child activities, parenting skills classes, family law clinics, couples workshops, and "boot camp" for new dads. Many of the fathers Neil sees are seeking ways to enhance their skills with and access to their children. Neil and his family moved from Minnesota in 2007 to Mesa because the Native American Fatherhood and Families Association (NAFFA) recruited him to work in the fatherhood program, working with fathers on and off reservations across the state. "There is so much to be done here. Compared to Minnesota, Arizona is terribly underresourced with respect to child and maternal well-being." And, Neil adds, Arizona doesn't have the Vikings, his favorite football team.

He also provides training in Arizona and around the United States for professional staff in social service and government agencies, such as Head Start; family service programs; teen parent programs; Offices of Child Support Enforcement; and Healthy Mothers, Healthy Babies. He urges them to make their programs more inclusive, more father-friendly, and shares father involvement recruitment and retention strategies, such as how to engage fathers in home visits and strategies to making them feel welcome. He also illustrates the rich nuances of maternal and paternal parenting styles. For example, when a child is crying over something, perhaps losing a ballgame, mom typically will try to soothe the child while the dad's approach will be to redirect him. Moms encourage expression of emotion. Dads focus on the regulation of emotion. Mom worries about building self-esteem. Dad wants his son to learn sportsmanship and how to handle loss. "Their approaches are merely different; one is not better or worse than the other," says Neil. Since typical agency staff providing resources for at-risk women and children are predominantly female (often 85 to 100 percent), Neil's challenge is to get those providers to see *men* and fathers as part of the solution.

Neil made a point of differentiating the purpose of father involvement programs from the goals of fathers' rights organizations. "The former do not intend to take anything away from moms; rather they try to *include* dads in the parenting picture. The latter, often representing angry white men, try to take certain legal rights and resources away from moms and give them to dads." He also differentiates anger management programs for men who batter or intimidate women and can't be trusted with their kids from anger management needed by his clients. "They are dads who are nonviolent though they may drive too fast or yell at the kids or their female partner. They have no legal rights, yet they *do* want to be there for their kids. They prove it by being the ones who show up for a fathers' program."

When I asked Neil to cite other evidence that father involvement programs are effective, he mentioned outcome measures such as: self-assessment reports from participants, a reduction in the number of emergency 911 calls to the home, reports from kids about the amount of positive time dad spends with them, and feedback from mom saying she is more comfortable around dad. And, at the agency level, he gets thanked by staff for showing them how they were, inadvertently, keeping men *away and precluding fathers from their service delivery.*

Now age sixty-five, Neil is married to Denise, a marriage and family therapist. They have three children—a grown son and daughter from Neil's first marriage and an adopted teenaged daughter with special needs. They have eleven grandchildren. Neil and Denise have also been foster parents to many children and adults over the past twenty-one years. Two disabled foster adults are part of the Tift family at present.

What drew him into the father involvement field years ago was becoming a single custodial dad after his first marriage ended and discovering firsthand the dearth of resources for fathers who need housing, child care, legal assistance, employment, and other resources. "I would go to agencies whose brochures *said* that they offered assistance to single parents and the staff would tell me that they only provided assistance to single *mothers* and children. Having nowhere to turn, I started a Fathers' Resource Center in Minneapolis. Denise supported me for almost three years until I got fatherhood programming established there. What started almost as a quirk of fate developed into a trend and now has become a movement."

With a master's degree in counseling psychology, Neil has spent his entire professional life working for nonprofits. For twenty-two of those years he has worked in various capacities with fathers. His many career choices include: special education teacher, live-in house parent in a group home for mentally handicapped adults, therapist for men who batter, community organizer, founder and director of a transitional housing program for homeless adults, grant writer, founder of the first Fathers' Resource Center in the United States, and director of training for three national fatherhood organizations in Washington, DC, and Arizona.

In addition to his current work for the Child Crisis Center, Neil teaches psychology and ethics courses at nearby Chandler-Gilbert Community College and previously at Ottawa University. He travels a fair amount with Denise and their teenaged daughter, Hannah, and they volunteer at a local food pantry on Thursday afternoons. He is an ordained deacon and serves at masses at his Catholic parish where he can preside over baptisms, weddings, and funerals. Another of Neil's interests is politics. Recently, he got involved in the Obama campaign because, in his opinion, "Democrats and progressives are an endangered species in Arizona!"

Although his position at the Child Crisis Center is far from lucrative, finances are not the reason Neil intends to keep working. He wants to stay busy, and above all, he is motivated to give back. Giving back is one of three life lessons imparted by his hard-working father during Neil's childhood in Charles City, Iowa: (1) remember that the world doesn't owe you; you must contribute to make it a better place; (2) always respect women; and (3) yell only at the dog. Neil recalls the selflessness of the Presentation sisters who taught him and his three siblings in parochial school. And he recalls how he considered entering the priesthood when he was in college until he realized that what he really wanted was "to be a *dad*, not a father."

"I can make a difference in a small field that has too few service providers and very limited status or visibility." Even so, his contributions have not gone unnoticed: Neil has won the "Spirit of Fatherhood" and "Father of the Year" awards for his work in Minnesota, Maryland, and Arizona. He wants to encourage men with passion for the work to go into fields such as early childhood education, where they can contribute to the healthy development of boys and girls. "It is not enough to *talk* about ending child abuse and domestic violence. Men have to *live* it and share it," he insists. It gives Neil great satisfaction to know that his own son, Zack, is working with young fathers at Catholic Charities in St. Paul, Minnesota.

Neil expects to keep working until his health won't permit it. For now, he enjoys getting up and going out for a run five days a week. "Part of that is an inability to sleep in the morning, and part is looking forward to doing work I really care about. I feel very lucky."

The recession took a toll on the Tifts. They had a hard time selling their home in Minnesota in 2007 and had to sell it at a significant loss. Then the owner of the house they first rented in Mesa cheated them out of the money they put down toward the purchase of her house, and they lost their home. This was on top of a series of serious setbacks for the family from which they seem to have emerged stronger and more resilient. Perhaps this was an echo of Neil's childhood experience of small-town prejudice against his family's devout Catholicism, about which he simply says, "Our faith made us stronger."

Neil's advice for men considering working beyond conventional retirement age derives from his parenting philosophy and personal experience. "The messages too many guys learn about masculinity at an early age fosters a selfish 'I win–you lose' approach to problem solving. Young men, particularly gang members and boys who grow up without fathers in their lives, need messages that move them away from 'win-lose' and help them to make healthy life choices. Older men serving as role models for younger men can make a real difference. By mentoring and teaching younger men about healthy behaviors, they can leave the kind of legacy a granddad wants to leave for his grandkids. You're never too old to affect the way you will be remembered!"

Professional men need to be well educated, and the survey respondents certainly prove that point. Nearly every one (94 percent) has at least a bachelor's degree. Three-quarters of the men have a master's, doctorate, or other advanced professional degree, such as an MD or JD. This is also true of the women I surveyed. While both genders are highly credentialed, I did detect an interesting difference in the type of advanced degree attained. Nearly one-half of the women have a master's, two master's, or credits beyond the master's compared to 22 percent of the men, whereas more than half of the men have a doctorate or other advanced professional degree compared to one-third of the women. That men earned far more doctorates and advanced professional degrees than women does not mean they are brainier. It is no doubt associated with the time women gave to bearing and raising children, the lower-paying occupations open to them when they finished college, and the challenges they faced when attempting to break into fields (and graduate programs) where men once predominated.

Times have changed and the gender gap in educational attainment discussed earlier has been reversing in recent years. According to the US Department of Education's National Center for Educational Statistics, female attainment has been surpassing male attainment at each educational level since 1980.[2] In addition, on average, younger adults in the United States are completing more bachelor's degrees today, whereas older adults have earned more advanced degrees:

Adults sixty-five and older with a bachelor's degree or higher: 22.1 percent

Adults sixty-five and older with a graduate or professional degree: 9.8 percent

Adults twenty-five to twenty-nine with a bachelor's degree or higher: 32 percent

Adults twenty-five to twenty-nine with a graduate or professional degree: 7 percent

Then again, times have not completely changed in some respects. When it comes to taking time out from work or schooling to provide family care, the current US Census tells us that women in the twenty-five to sixty-two age bracket still do most of it: 93.1 percent of women versus 6.9 percent of men. They interrupt work to care for children most often (94.7 percent), or an elder relative (3.8 percent), or a disabled relative (1.5 percent).[3] So when I saw that merely three of the 156 older men I surveyed had taken some time out for childrearing, I was not surprised that they completed more advanced degrees than their female counterparts, who, in contrast, had taken time out for childrearing (58 percent). As to adult caregiving, the percentage of respondents who had provided or were still providing it was low for both the men and women I studied (3 percent and 4 percent, respectively) and did not necessarily entail a career interruption if other family members pitched in or paid help was available.

Educational attainment usually is an important consideration but not the sole factor in salary decisions. A professional's income can depend on many factors besides education, notably part-time versus full-time job status, career field, rank or title, experience level, length of service, job performance (skills and ability), and more. Although several of the main indicators of economic expansion have started to trend upward—for example, increases in construction, manufacturing, and consumer confidence—companies are keeping wages and salaries in check and remain cautious about hiring. A pervasive feeling of anxiety about the economy lingers. One sixty-three-year-old businessman shared a long list of his concerns with me: rising health-care costs, the cost of implementing "Obamacare,"[4] potential changes in the tax rates, the worldwide economic climate and its effect on the United States, the US debt structure and its effect on the economy and retirees, and the solvency of Social Security and Medicare.

To find out how well older men are faring salary-wise in the workforce, my survey asked respondents to indicate current personal income in one of three categories: "modest" (under $30,000), "middle" ($30,000 to $79,000), or "higher" (more than $80,000).[5] All but four of the full-time and part-time workers were willing to share information about their salary range. Regardless of age or field, nearly three-quarters of the senior men (71 percent) have incomes in the higher category, 13 percent have modest incomes, and 16 percent have incomes in the middle range. Since the average annual earned income for American men ages sixty to seventy-four is approximately $50,000,[6] most of my respondents appear to be well above average. Across all the older age groups, the majority—just shy of two-thirds—are working full time. Nearly half of the men who are working part time appear to be doing very well in terms of personal income, despite working fewer hours.[7]

This is true of Steve Schoenbaum, who made a smooth transition to foundation work from medicine and health-care management and is now working part time. After distinguishing himself as a clinical epidemiologist and then a health-care administrator with a focus on health policy and high performance delivery of care, Steve moved to a different arena—national grant-making. He spent a decade overseeing programs for the Commonwealth Fund before accepting a part-time position in 2010 with the Josiah Macy Jr. Foundation. At the foundation, he works on grant making, organizes meetings, and prepares talks and papers on medical education. Steve loves the intellectual stimulation of new challenges and has no idea how long he will continue working. "I'm seventy-one, semi-retired, and feeling great!" he enthuses.

PROFILE: STEPHEN C. SCHOENBAUM

According to a September 2012 report from an Institute of Medicine expert panel, an estimated $750 billion or approximately thirty cents of every dollar spent on health care is squandered because of unnecessary services, inefficient delivery of care, excess administrative costs, inflated prices, prevention failures, and fraud. The report goes on to compare health-care inefficiencies to several major industries, such as banking: "ATM transactions would take days"; home building: "carpenters, electricians, and plumbers would work from different blueprints and hardly talk to each other"; shopping: "prices would not be posted and could vary widely within the same store, depending on who was paying"; and airline travel: "individual pilots would be free to design their own preflight safety checks—or not perform one at all." And the panel concludes that "American health care is falling short on basic dimensions of quality, outcomes, costs and equity."[8]

These are the very issues that have preoccupied Dr. Stephen Schoenbaum for most of his forty-six-year career. With a master's degree in public health and a medical degree from Harvard, in 1967–68 Steve trained in communicable diseases at the Centers for Disease Control (CDC) in Atlanta under the tutelage of noted epidemiologist Dr. Alex Langmuir, founder of the CDC's Epidemic Intelligence Service. "Alex took me under his wing, trained me, and became my professional father figure and a friend." Steve's specialization in infectious diseases first landed him a clinical position at the Brigham and Women's Hospital in Boston. He went on to help establish the Department of Population Medicine at Harvard Medical School, then served as deputy medical director at Harvard Community Health Plan from 1981 to 1993.

During this period, Steve worked closely with his colleague Dr. Donald Berwick to increase the value and quality of health care. Berwick was the plan's vice president of quality-of-care management and an advocate of practices that improve care and reduce cost. He drew attention to waste in health care, for example, overtreatment, failure to coordinate care, and fraud. (Berwick later served as administrator of the Centers for Medicare and Medicaid Services from 2010 to 2011 through a highly contentious Obama administration recess appointment.) The two colleagues wanted hard evidence to show how the vast amounts of money spent on health care could produce better outcomes. "Health care professionals always *thought* they were delivering the very best care, but there was no measurement of it until we, along with others, created the tools collectively called HEDIS, the Healthcare Effectiveness Data and Information Set." Now further expanded and maintained by the National Committee for Quality Assurance, HEDIS is used by more than 90 percent of America's health plans and other providers to measure and compare performance on important dimensions of care and service.

Steve went on to become the medical director and then president of Harvard Pilgrim Health Care of New England from 1993 to 1999. As it turned out, he was the *final* president of that organization. Harvard Community Health Plan of New England had started as Rhode Island Group Health and later was taken over by Boston-based Harvard Community Health Plan. Although the Rhode Island component ran an efficient operation, it was bleeding red ink. Even though expenses were relatively lean, revenue did not match those expenses. Steve was "up to his eyeballs in alligators." He "saw the end coming" but chose not to jump ship. In late 1999, Harvard Pilgrim Health Care jettisoned the Rhode Island entity, which went into receivership and was liquidated. A few months later, the attorney general of Massachusetts put Harvard Pilgrim Health Care itself into receivership but helped to save it.

By late 1999, it was necessary to move on. Steve considered returning to clinical medicine, but chose instead a job that tapped not only his management skills and experience but also his interest in health policy and delivery of care. From 2000 to 2010 he was executive vice president for programs at the Commonwealth Fund, as well as executive director of the Fund's Commission on a High Performance Health System. The Commonwealth Fund is a national grant-making foundation based in New York City that supports independent research on health-care issues and makes grants to improve health care practice and policy.

At the end of 2010 Steve left the Commonwealth Fund and full-time employment, accepting a new position as special advisor to the president of the Josiah Macy Jr. Foundation, where he works two days a week. Macy is a national foundation dedicated solely to improving the health of the public by advancing the education and training of health professionals. At Macy he works on grant making, organizes meetings, and prepares talks and papers on medical education.

Like most private foundations, Macy saw the recession take a bite out of its endowment but continued to support existing commitments and make new grants. Instead of the just passively responding to grant-seeking appeals from organizations, Macy's staff is increasingly proactive, reaching out to potential grantees and advising on the development and functioning of projects.

When I asked Steve how long he plans to continue working, he confessed that he has no idea. "I'm seventy-one, semi-retired, and feeling great! Living and working in New York City, I have to walk a lot. My schedule is flexible and I can work from practically anywhere." Most of Steve's friends in medicine and in academe are still working. "Frankly," he says, "I don't know many people who think in terms of conventional retirement age." At the same time, he points out, there are so many new developments in medicine, it is hard for older professionals to keep up. Their clinical skills may be pretty good, but not cutting edge. Still, there are other ways to stay involved, and they need not retire. "Personally speaking, I need something new to learn every five years or so." He loves the intellectual stimulation of a new challenge, even if he's simply changing positions within the same organization. "I tend to burrow into the work and make changes until I've solved the problem," he notes.

Thanks to the flexibility of his work schedule, Steve can devote time to his family—his wife, Sylvia, their two children, and grandchildren—and to music, which has always been paramount for him. His forté is piano. The day after we spoke Steve was leaving for Hartford, Connecticut, to rehearse a Brahms piano quartet with three string players—a violinist, a violist, and a cellist. The rehearsal was in preparation for an upcoming weekend of intensive coaching. "We have to rehearse in order to get the most out of the coaching opportunity. This way we take care of the basics ourselves, and, during the coaching, we can work on the subtleties."

The author or coauthor of more than 150 professional publications, Steve would like to write a book on ways to make the health-care system more patient-centered. In his view, "For all the talk about *patient*-centeredness, the health system remains *provider*-centered." He is planning a talk for hospital CFOs that will address the question: "How can your organization be more efficient *and* focus on the populations you serve?" Or: "Does the patient benefit enough from the ways your organization functions now?" Among other things, he will tell them about an enterprising Johns Hopkins doctor who introduced a "daily goals" clipboard sheet for individual patients being treated in the intensive care unit. At first, only 5 percent of Hopkins' ICU doctors and nurses could honestly say they knew exactly what the next twenty-four-hour goals were for an individual patient. After using the clipboard sheet for some time, 95 percent knew the goals and, owing to closer attention to individual patient needs, the average length of stay in the ICU dropped by 50 percent. This not only also meant better outcomes for patients who were able to leave the ICU sooner, it also represented huge cost savings for the hospital and for insurers.

Steve remains intensely interested in what has come to be called "accountability" in health-care circles. The previously mentioned Institute of Medicine report on waste in health care today reinforces what he has been arguing for years. Not surprisingly, he says he is ecstatic about the Affordable Care Act, and he hopes it will be implemented fully by 2014 as intended. "Universal coverage is a baseline step. Every other developed country has it. Why not the United States? We're the richest country. It's obvious that you have a stronger society when your people enjoy good health. You need a good health-care *system* to meet the needs. It starts with everyone having coverage and access to health care. It seems obvious. I can't understand the objections!"

It is hardly news that women's earnings lag behind men's: the personal incomes of senior women are fairly evenly spread across the three survey categories. Just 36 percent of the women enjoy higher incomes, compared to nearly twice that percentage of the men. Men are earning in the higher category regardless of age; women's earnings often tail off as they age (women between sixty and sixty-nine tend to earn in the middle and higher ranges, women seventy and older tend to earn in the modest and middle ranges). Nearly two-thirds of the men I studied (63 percent of the total) are working full time compared to 53 percent of the women. Yet, even the men working part time seem to prosper financially more than the women. These differences can be partially explained by women taking time out for raising a family, men choosing higher-paying occupational fields, men working more hours (on average), and pay practices blatantly unfair to women that persist in spite of pay equity legislation.[9] According to the American Association of University Women (AAUW), inequity persists from the first paycheck through to retirement: "college-educated women working full time are paid more than a half million dollars less than male peers over the course of a lifetime . . . women continue to be paid less than men, *even when they make the same educational choices, earn the same grades, and work in the same jobs.*"[10]

A controversial book by Facebook COO Sheryl Sandberg, *Lean In: Women, Work, and the Will to Lead,* focuses on the disparity between the number of men and women in leadership positions in major businesses (just twenty-one of Fortune 500 CEOs are female) and what women can do about it. If they want to get ahead and build a satisfying work life, Sandberg advises them not to shrink from challenges and to be more confident and ambitious. Reviewing *Lean In* for the *New York Times,* Princeton professor Anne-Marie Slaughter explains:

> Her [Sandberg's] point, in a nutshell, is that notwithstanding the many gender biases that still operate all over the workplace, excuses and justifications won't get women anywhere. Instead, believe in yourself, give it your all, "lean in" and "don't leave before you leave"—which is to say, don't doubt your ability to combine work and family and thus edge yourself out of plum assignments before you even have a baby. Leaning in can promote a virtuous circle:

you assume you can juggle work and family, you step forward, you succeed professionally, and then you're in a better position to ask for what you need and to make changes that could benefit others.[11]

Slaughter, apparently more realistic than Sandberg about what is needed for getting ahead, then asks, "Is the dearth of women in top jobs due to a lack of ambition or a lack of support?" Adding to the debate, *Harvard Business Review* blogger James Allworth asks whether advising women to behave more like men to get ahead in the workplace and in their careers is the right approach. Perhaps, he suggests, men have been leaning in *too much*, spending too much time on the treadmill. Put another way, men who *build a life in the context of a career* rather than the reverse often pay a serious price. And, Allworth concludes, men might be better served by emulating women, thereby making workplaces, families, and society better in the process.[12] Implausible? Improbable? It seems to me that this analysis, while appealing at first glance, raises a thorny question: who would keep the treadmill going if men should decide to step off and women do not opt to step on?

On the whole, professional men (like those I surveyed) evidently *do* lean in, snagging the majority of leadership positions in various fields and garnering the rewards that correspond with success. Their economic status is far above the American norm. Whether they are continuing in a career job or working at something else, my survey respondents have been working for a very long time. On average, they have been working for forty-eight years. The number of years worked overall ranges from thirty-three to seventy-three. The men who are eighty or older have worked for an average of sixty years. By comparison, the professional women I studied have been working for fewer years, ranging from a low of ten to a high of sixty-three. The average number of working years for the women is forty.

Of course, as most everyone discovers sooner or later, money and seniority cannot guarantee happiness. As mentioned in chapter 2, psychiatrist George Vaillant thinks he knows what is essential. In his *Aging Well*, the seven major factors that predict healthy aging (from retirement to past eighty) are based on physical and psychological evidence collected over many years for the Harvard Study of Adult Development. He uses numerous statistics to compare the Harvard men, the Gluek inner-city men, and the Terman women, for example,

- Race (Caucasian: 100 percent, 99 percent, and 99 percent, respectively)
- IQ (130–135, 95, and 151, respectively)
- Social class of most parents (upper class/upper middle class/middle class for the Harvard men; middle class/skilled labor/unskilled labor/welfare for the inner-city men; and upper middle class/middle class/skilled labor for the Terman women)
- Graduate school degree attainment (76 percent, 2 percent, and 23 percent, respectively)
- Mean income at age fifty in current dollars[13] ($105,000 as of 1999, $35,000 as of 2000, and $35,000 as of 1988, respectively)[14]

The gender pay gap was even more exaggerated twenty-five years ago: the average income of Harvard men, three-quarters of whom held graduate school degrees, was *triple* the average income of the Terman women, and the Terman women's income was on a par with the Gluek inner-city men's income, regardless of a woman's graduate school degree attainment.

Like the Harvard men in *Aging Well* who were still working at seventy-five (and some of my respondents *are* Harvard men), the men in my study are not only still working, they also possess in some combination the protective factors or "guideposts to a happier life" (listed in chapter 2) that help men respond to difficulties and hardships in their lives, as well as beneficial personal qualities, such as having a future orientation (an ability to anticipate, to plan, and to hope); a capacity for gratitude and forgiveness; empathy; cultivating a social network; and doing things *with* people, not *to* them.[15] Although Vaillant does not rank the guideposts in order of importance, he clearly sees marriage as a significant organizing principle when he says, "For marriage is not only important to healthy aging, it is often the cornerstone of adult resilience."[16] To age successfully, Vaillant concludes, men should enjoy their loved ones, work, and learn something they didn't know yesterday.

By those lights, I think it is safe to say the professional men I studied are aging quite well. Of course, there is a great deal more to know about them, since their average age, residence, marital and family status, educational achievement, earnings, and length of time in the workforce are only part of the picture. We will turn next to their career choices and job status.

6

Where Older Men Work

It's important to do something that pushes your buttons. When I wake up in the morning, I can't wait to get to work. — Bart Guerreri, founder, chairman, and CEO of DSD Laboratories, Inc.

While the older men in my study are working in a great variety of career fields, business is far and away the preferred field for nearly one-third of the men. Their specialties include the following: accounting, affordable housing, automotive, banking, communications, customer satisfaction, dairy processing and distribution, dry cleaning, entrepreneurship, film distribution, finance, fire protection, health care, high tech, historic preservation, house painting, insurance, long-term care, management, marketing, musical instruments, process control, real estate, sales, sports, sports camps, training, travel, waste management, and wine retailing.

Business is the second most popular career field for the older women I studied, but they do not often sit at the helm. One businessman who does is John Kaneb, the seventy-seven-year-old chairman and CEO of HP Hood LLC and part owner of the Boston Red Sox. John previously owned a controlling interest in Gulf Oil. Retirement holds no interest for him.

PROFILE: JOHN A. KANEB

Milk, ice cream, baseball, and family. These top John Kaneb's list of favorites. He is the seventy-seven-year-old chairman and CEO of HP Hood LLC, the iconic New England dairy processing and distribution company. He is a part owner of the Boston Red Sox. And he and his wife, Virginia, have six children and eighteen grandchildren.

First, *the Hood story.* You may or may not have seen the colorful Hood blimp flying over sports and cultural events or visited the outdoor ice cream stand inside a giant Hood milk bottle at Boston Children's Museum, but you likely have encountered the Hood brand name in a supermarket, independent retail operation, convenience store, or other food-service channel. With headquarters in Lynnfield, Massachusetts, research and development operations, and fourteen plants throughout the country, Hood employs some three thousand men and women. The company makes and distributes a variety of branded, private label, licensed, and franchise products, including milk, cultured foods, extended-shelf-life dairy, frozen desserts, and nondairy, specialty, and high-protein drinks. It has seen tremendous growth and change since Harvey Perley Hood founded the dairy business in 1846 in Charlestown, Massachusetts.

Second, *John's career.* John's father was his hero and role model. One distinctive aspect of his management style that John remembers and tries to practice to this day is the respectful way his father treated every employee no matter his status. In 1959, Mike Kaneb had just expanded his petroleum business when he died tragically and suddenly. Son John was then a twenty-four-year-old naval officer and recently married. He was needed in the business. The Navy was sympathetic to his plight and released him. "I had to step into my father's shoes, convince our creditors that I was capable of running the business, and then prove it."

It helped that John had developed essential skills during his undergraduate years at Harvard College that stood him in good stead. "I learned to read or listen and then analyze fairly quickly what was most important. I brought this kind of thinking to bear on business opportunities and problems, asking, for example, Who are the key players? What do we want to be or do? What steps do we need to take?"

The experience of taking over his father's petroleum company showed John that he was good at growing businesses and turning businesses around. In 1994, he and his son Gary purchased a controlling interest in Gulf Oil for the family. Its annual sales tripled before its sale in 2005. Meanwhile, the Kaneb family purchased HP Hood in 1995. "Although the public was unaware of it, the company was in serious financial straits," John explains. "The challenges at Hood were interesting, and we enjoyed the process of making the business successful. We knew we had to protect the trusted brand. There were actually some similarities to the petroleum distribution business in that the solution wasn't high-tech. It was simply about a healthy infusion of money and a lot of common sense." Even the recent recession and the slowed economy did not affect the business, which has remained "pretty steady." Annual Hood sales now surpass $2 billion.

At the corporate level, Hood takes social responsibility seriously, supporting organizations that assist children and their families to achieve better health and nutrition. The company also awards $5,000 Hood Sportsmanship Scholarships each year to eighteen high school athletes attending two- or four-year accredited colleges or universities. On the personal level, John makes time to be active in the nonprofit world. He serves as an Emeritus Fellow of Harvard Medical School, former Chairman of Partners Healthcare Finance Committee, Chairman Emeritus of McLean Hospital Board of Trustees, Trustee Emeritus of Massachusetts General Hospital, and Emeritus Trustee of the University of Notre Dame.

John is particularly proud of the work he did as vice chairman of the National Prison Rape Elimination Commission, which was established in 2003 by President George W. Bush. "I have a hatred of bullying," he explains. "Intimidation is rife in prisons, and I simply felt something should be done about it." In 1999 John learned about a very small group of abuse survivors calling their organization Stop Prisoner Rape. To advance their cause, he came to realize that federal legislation would be needed. For this, he turned to his college friend, Senator Ted Kennedy. "Kennedy, although a liberal Democrat, was able to work well with Republicans. He persuaded Senator Jeff Sessions (R-Alabama) and House Speaker Dennis Hastert (R-Illinois) to work with him. Together they got legislation passed establishing a commission to evaluate the problem of prisoner abuse and draw up a set of standards for its control. Although the prison industry and the Department of Justice were resistant initially, today the federal prison system is operating under the new standards and state and local systems have been incented to follow suit."

Currently, John's major pro bono contribution is chairing the board of the Archdiocese of Boston's Clergy Fund. The fund provides the financial resources for priests' health-care coverage and retirement benefits. Unfortunately, some years ago, sound fiscal management practices eluded the archdiocesan staff; payouts far exceeded income. When John became chair of the Clergy Fund board, he worked with the new CEO and together he and the board achieved a surplus in just four years. It was another successful turnaround.

Third, *baseball*. Ah, the Red Sox, another Boston icon. When they have a tough year, fans, talk show hosts, and sportswriters buzz with speculation, commentary, and criticism. When they are in first place, fans, talk show hosts, and sportswriters buzz just as much. All John would say about his team's ups and downs is, "Amazing!"

Last, but not least, *family*. Among John's considerable achievements, the highest for him is being a successful father and husband. Two of John's sons are in the dairy business with him, one is Hood's CFO and the other is executive vice president. When I asked John whether he mentors his sons, he summed up his approach this way: "I don't mentor them or tell them what to do. I hope to teach by example."

John says he has no problem telling people he's seventy-seven and "an old guy" by some measures. For example, he depends on his assistant, Camille DiCocco, for most things high-tech. His wife, Virginia, is concerned about his workload, but she knows he loves the business and wouldn't dream of retiring. Retirement, or what John describes as "crossing to the other side," is "a desert" that holds no interest for him. Only what he refers to as "a sudden major event" could force a decision to retire. But his health is good—he jogs a mile almost every day and does some weight work to keep in shape. He readily admits that the real reason he continues working, aside from the satisfaction he gets, is that he's not just afraid of retiring, he is "absolutely petrified!" If he stepped down, the decision would be irrevocable; he could not change his mind and come back. He offers cautionary advice to other men in similar circumstances: "Have a healthy respect for the consequences of retiring. Don't go there casually or unprepared, or you may regret it."

Another high-powered businessman is Bart Guerreri, founder, chairman, and CEO of DSD Laboratories, Inc. (DSD Labs), an industry leader in information technology. Bart is an entrepreneur, inventor, design engineer, and business troubleshooter. Work is a passion for this sixty-nine-year-old.

PROFILE: BART G. GUERRERI

"We're back!" says the upbeat greeting on the Guerreris' answering machine, and I don't know whether that means Bart and Andrea are back in Massachusetts from Florida or they are back in good shape after Bart successfully recovered from three bouts with cancer. When I went to interview Bart in his office, I changed out of my usual outfit of running shoes and jeans. As it turned out, he was wearing running shoes and sporting an RIT baseball cap.

Bart, now age sixty-nine, is an entrepreneur, inventor (he holds thirty patents), design engineer, and business troubleshooter. He is the founder, chairman, and CEO of DSD Labs, a registered, privately owned small business whose focus is to provide high-end engineering, Lean Six Sigma, and related technical services to federal, state, and commercial customers. DSD Labs is headquartered in Miami Beach, Florida, with multiple offices located throughout the United States. The company is an industry leader in information technology, including cyber security (in conjunction with its affiliate company, Backbone Security), programmatic support, system engineering, system operations, maintenance, and service-oriented architecture.

A few years ago, his alma mater, Rochester Institute of Technology (RIT), honored Bart with the Distinguished Alumni Award and invited him to give the commencement address. Bart won over the audience by declaring, "I am not qualified to give you advice. What I can tell you is a bit about my history."

He was raised by Italian immigrant parents in a farm town in upstate Ulster County, New York, called Tillson. The hamlet had a population of 835. It took him five years to graduate from high school because he couldn't spell (and says that he still can't). RIT accepted him as a freshman on probation. He made it through with a bachelor's degree in mechanical engineering in 1967.

In a self-deprecating manner that endears him to the graduating students, Bart says that he knows many CEOs, some are RIT graduates, who are all "well-groomed thoroughbreds. I am a plow horse. We talk about business and about the Red Sox." Next he shares two common denominators of success: *passion* and *persistence*.

Work is a passion for Bart. "It's *fun*! It's important to do something that pushes your buttons. When I wake up in the morning, I can't wait to get to work." His other passion is his family, wife Andrea and their three grown children. When Bart announces, "I make all the big decisions, Andrea makes all the little decisions," I wince, until he adds the punch line, "*She* decides what is big and what is little!"

Bart is fond of a Henry Ford adage about lessons learned from a temporary defeat, something along the lines of "opportunity often comes in the form of misfortune." Encouraging the graduates to trust their instincts and not be afraid of making mistakes, he goes on with his story. He founded DSD Labs in 1978, initially for the purpose of designing interface display systems, and for three years was the sole employee. In 1983 he put DSD Labs on hold and founded Linc Telecommunications. Although that company went bankrupt, Bart eventually repaid all his debts to creditors. After the bankruptcy setback, he restarted DSD Labs.

His persistence paid off. DSD Labs grew to encompass hundreds of employees in more than a dozen locations. Today, Department of Defense contracts account for fully half of DSD Labs' work in the high-end engineering market. Clearly, passion and persistence spell success for Bart.

After business comes a cross-section of other occupations. Nineteen percent of the men are educators, the vast majority having positions in higher education. Fourteen percent are doctors, dentists, and scientists. Eleven percent are lawyers. Six percent are engineers of some type. Other fields represented are government, the arts, social services, journalism/writing, philanthropy, and architecture. A look at the titles describing their jobs suggests a wide span of income levels. For every doctor, lawyer, scientist, architect, accountant, owner, partner, president, vice president, director, treasurer, and chairman, there is a painter, musician, writer, librarian, translator, teacher, inclusion coach, paralegal, state representative, and crossing guard.

Applied sociologist and octogenarian Chuck Willie held the Charles William Eliot Professor of Education chair at Harvard University. Even after receiving emeritus status, he has remained active—teaching his signature course on grassroots social action, writing books and articles, serving on boards, giving talks (often at gatherings to celebrate the birthday of his More-house classmate, Martin Luther King Jr.), and consulting, for example, on social problems and school assignment plans. Among several reasons Chuck gives for staying active in his field is keeping in touch with former students. He was my doctoral advisor and remains my mentor and friend.

PROFILE: CHARLES V. WILLIE

Charles V. Willie (also known as Chuck) was born in 1927 as the third child in an African American family of two parents and five siblings. They lived in Dallas, Texas. He remembers short visits to the homes of an aunt in a rural area of Louisiana and an uncle in a rural area of Oklahoma. He had never traveled outside of Texas alone until he enrolled in Morehouse College in Atlanta, Georgia.

This college was established for black male students many years ago and would have closed during World War II if the president, Dr. Benjamin E. Mays, had not inaugurated a new policy of enrolling fifteen- and sixteen-year-old black students even if they had not graduated from high school. Although Chuck Willie was sixteen years old and had finished high school, one of his freshman classmates—Martin Luther King Jr.—was only fifteen years old and was one year short of receiving a high school diploma.

Dr. Mays knew that these young people needed help in developing their own philosophy of life and how to implement it. As part of daily chapel services, each Tuesday Dr. Mays talked to the student body, exhorting Chuck and Martin and their classmates to deal with racial segregation in ways that were legal in Georgia during the first half of the twentieth century. "When you get on the trolley," he would instruct his students, "put your dime in the fare box, go to the back of the trolley, but *leave your mind up front.*" This advice taught them not only how to deal with segregation laws, but also how to maintain a sense of their significance.

Dr. Mays also modeled resourcefulness, and he counseled students how to be open to opportunities. Chuck listened closely and adopted a credo that has served him well all his life. "I worked hard, my timing was good, and opportunities found me." His parents stressed the importance of education, and all five Willie children went to college. Their father, who had an eighth-grade education, was a Pullman porter whose job put him in contact with all sorts of people. Their mother had graduated from Wiley College in Marshall, Texas, taking one semester of coursework per year for eight years. "During the Depression, my mother couldn't get a job, so she stayed at home with us in Dallas, helping with homework and providing nurturing, stimulation, and structure in our own 'Willie Head Start Program' long before there was a national Head Start Program."

Chuck excelled academically at Lincoln High School, played trumpet in the marching band and in the jazz orchestra. He was chief officer of the marching band, sang in the school's chorus, and was elected senior class president. Teachers as well as students steered him toward leadership roles and singled him out for opportunities. He was selected to be "Principal for a Day" in his high school. The head of the Negro Branch of the YMCA Boys Division in Dallas invited Chuck to be his summer assistant. This led to a paying summer job every year while he was in college. One summer he was acting director of the Boys Division of the black YMCA. "I experienced a professional role when I was put in charge. I also realized that my job was more than helping others; it was helping people to negotiate *with* each other. People trusted in me. And, of course I didn't want to let the people down." Chuck also said, "These experiences helped me to understand how to become 'a person for others' and how to 'make an enemy become a friend.'"

Another mentor, his high school music teacher, had encouraged him to apply to *his* alma mater, Morehouse College. Salutatorian of his high school class and Lincoln's highest-ranking male student, Chuck won a Morehouse scholarship for the freshman year. He knows that he owes much of his success to "the people who believed in me and pushed me forward."

Leadership opportunities continued to come his way when he was elected president of his class at Morehouse in the sophomore, junior, and senior years. With the end of World War II, veterans had returned to the Morehouse campus, older and more experienced than Chuck and his peers, but he held his own. "I would bring people together to solve problems among themselves and to do what was fair."

Chuck went on to earn a master's degree from Atlanta University in 1949, followed by a PhD from Syracuse University in 1957, both degrees in sociol-

ogy. He became an *applied* sociologist, concerned with solving social problems in communities and in society as a whole. Soon, he was chairman of
the Department of Sociology and vice president of student affairs at Syracuse
University. In 1974 the Harvard Graduate School of Education (HGSE) appointed him professor of education and urban studies.

His areas of research include education planning and school desegregation, the structure and process of family life, community organization, race
and ethnic relations, and public health. At age seventy, Chuck was appointed
to the Charles William Eliot Professor of Education chair. After receiving
emeritus status, he continued to teach one course on grassroots social action
at Harvard until age eighty.

Chuck is the author, coauthor, or editor of dozens of books and approximately one hundred articles on issues of race, gender, socioeconomic
status, religion, education, urban communities, and family relations. These
include: *A New Look at Black Families*, 6th ed.; *Grassroots Social Action:
Lessons in People Power Movements*; and *Student Diversity, Choice and
School Improvement*.

The *Student Diversity* volume updated an earlier book, coauthored with
Michael Alves, *Controlled Choice: A New Approach to Desegregated Education and School Improvement*. In the belief that *diversity* is integral to school
improvement, Willie and Alves had developed a new school assignment plan
for Boston in the mid-1980s. Chuck explains, "School improvement is a very
broad term, encompassing school *context* along with curricula. Students
learn not only from teachers, books, and other resources but also from their
relationships with classmates. Therefore, diversity in the student body, as well
as in the faculty and staff, must be ensured." Under the "Controlled Choice"
plan, Boston's school system was divided into three zones and parents could
choose five schools for their child, including a neighborhood school, within
their zone. Chuck is proud that 85 percent of parents got their first or second
choice of schools, and only 40 percent chose a neighborhood school. "Most
parents chose and were assigned the best school for their child, whether
or not it was located close to home. Choice also was intended to stimulate
change—parents would avoid poorly performing schools; those schools
could potentially learn from more successful schools and get turned around."
Controlled Choice lasted in Boston for a decade until a new school superin-
tendent took over. With budgets tightening, transportation costs associated

with choice proved prohibitive. To this day, the Boston Public Schools are still experimenting with school assignment schemes, none of which has been as effective as Controlled Choice.

Chuck has served as a consultant, expert witness, and court-appointed master in major school desegregation cases in larger cities such as Boston, Hartford, Dallas, Denver, Houston, Kansas City, Little Rock, Milwaukee, San Jose, Seattle, and St. Louis; and in other municipalities such as St. Lucie County and Lee County, Florida, and Somerville, Cambridge, and Brockton, Massachusetts. Although he has reached eighty-five years of age, he continues to accept invitations to speak in colleges and universities, at professional conferences, and at gatherings to celebrate the birthday of Martin Luther King Jr.

Decade by decade over his long career, more leadership roles came Chuck's way. He was appointed by President Jimmy Carter to the President's Commission on Mental Health and was a member of the Board of Directors of the Social Science Research Council in the 1970s. He served as president of the Eastern Sociological Society (ESS) in the mid-1970s and as vice president of the American Sociological Association (ASA) in the mid-1990s.

Many awards have also come Chuck's way, recognizing him as a distinguished alumnus of Syracuse University; lauding his standing as a scholar, author, and lecturer; and citing his contributions to public service. He also has twelve honorary degrees. The ASA bestowed its Career of Distinguished Scholarship Award in 2005 and the William Foote Whyte Award, Applied Sociology Section in 2004.

In 2006, the ESS bestowed on him its Merit Award, the ESS's highest honor. It recognizes members for outstanding contributions to the discipline, profession, and organization. Despite all the honors, Chuck observes, "There are still some things I haven't learned about my discipline and my discipline hasn't learned about me."

One of Chuck's reasons for remaining active in his field is staying in contact with former HGSE students. I am one among many fortunate enough to call him mentor and friend. While working on my doctorate in administration, planning, and social policy at HGSE in the mid-1980s, I would check in with Chuck, who was my doctoral advisor. He invariably greeted me with, "How's my Favorite Scholar?" I believed that I *was* his Favorite Scholar, and I certainly did not want to let him down—just as he didn't want to let down the people who believed in him along the way. Only some dozen years later at Chuck's Harvard retirement party did it emerge that each of the former students who came to pay tribute to him had believed that he or she was his Favorite Scholar!

Chuck has continued to work into his eighties for other reasons. He wants to be in a position financially to help his three grown children or his three grandchildren with the cost of education, housing, or health care. He wants to stay active as long as he can. "Not just to stay busy—I'm a little too busy—but to be helpful, to meet a need. I try to bring along people of color who have been passed over for years and recruit them for institutional boards that want to be diversified. That's what keeps me involved as Overseer Emeritus at the Boston Museum of Science."

Yet another reason is using and sharing his experience in community organization. After attaining emeritus status at Harvard in 1999, Chuck continued teaching "Community Power, Decision Making and Education" for the next ten years. The course helped HGSE students understand the role of grassroots populations in community organization and development. It involved them directly in effective social action to solve community problems, especially those related to public education. When I asked him why he selected that particular course out of all the courses he could teach, he said, "There were not many courses at Harvard dealing with it. I felt it was imperative to help students understand grassroots social action." From Chuck, students can learn the difference between an ideologue haranguing society for its failings and oversights and a problem solver who seeks solutions that are equitable to everyone.

Today, in addition to writing, giving talks, and consulting, Chuck sings bass in the choir at St. Elizabeth's Episcopal Church in Sudbury, Massachusetts, where his wife, Mary Sue, is the music director. (They met more than fifty years ago at a church in Syracuse, New York, where Mary Sue was playing the organ—she had studied sacred music at Union Theological Seminary—and Chuck was singing in the choir.) They participate in the co-ed book group they helped to organize thirty years ago in their hometown of Concord, Massachusetts. Chuck is blessed by the opportunities that have "found" him, yet he continues to work hard and be as resourceful and independent as Dr. Mays expected a Morehouse man to be.

Septuagenarian Bob Schecter is a part-time, self-employed writer-for-hire whose business is called Bartleby Scriveners. While he enjoys the work and wants the income, he makes sure to leave time for volunteering, charitable projects, tennis, and Scottish dancing. He plans to keep working indefinitely.

PROFILE: ROBERT E. SCHECTER

Bob Schecter's business is called Bartleby Scriveners, a reference to the title character in a short story by Herman Melville. He is by choice a part-time, self-employed writer-for-hire because (a) he enjoys it and (b) he wants the income. Bob writes books, articles, blogs, and newsletters for clients, some of whom are businesses and some are nonprofit organizations. One of his clients is the International Cultic Studies Association (ICSA), a research and educational organization that studies groups—often called "cults"—that practice harmful social and psychological manipulation and control. ICSA, originally named the American Family Foundation (AFF), was founded in 1979 in response to parents' concerns that they were losing their children to organizations like the Unification Church. Bob helped establish and grow the foundation together with a Harvard psychiatrist, a personal friend, who had earlier published a report on the phenomenon in the *Journal of the American Medical Association*. Bob became AFF/ICSA's director of publications. By 1990, however, the nonprofit was unable to raise enough money to support its small staff—even though the psychiatrist was always unpaid. That's when Bob, who continues to abstract world press reports on "high demand" groups for ICSA, started Bartleby Scriveners.

It was not his first career change, however. Bob had spent several years (1967–72) at the University of Zambia Institute for Social and Economic Research in Lusaka studying the oral traditions of a small kingdom in Zambia. He earned a doctorate in African history from the University of Wisconsin–Madison in 1976 and went on to teach African history for a few years at two different universities. He left teaching because he did not really enjoy it, yet he remained keenly interested in Zambia and the friends he had made there.

Now seventy-one, Bob aims to write a book a year. With three books about business topics under his belt, he is now working on one about Massachusetts and the Civil War for the Massachusetts chapter of the Military Order of the Loyal Legion of the United States, an organization formed by Union Army officers in the wake of President Lincoln's assassination. "I am doing profiles of the ancestors of the present members who served as officers in the Union forces, as well as of noted general officers from Massachusetts. I will also include people and industries from Maine, Massachusetts, and New Hampshire that contributed to the war effort."

Fully half of each week is taken up by volunteering in the Framingham, Massachusetts, area where Bob and his wife, Mary Louise, reside. Bob is very active in the local Rotary Club, one of more than 34,000 Rotary Clubs worldwide whose members—1.2 million strong—are business and professional people committed to volunteer service at home and abroad. Bob has built support for a middle school computer literacy project in Zambia that became one of Framingham Rotary's projects. Under his leadership, the club raised money at both the district level and internationally to provide computer education to poor middle school students in Zambia. "I enjoy the fellowship, the weekly luncheons, and the charitable work at Rotary. Oh, and I almost forgot, the mentoring. I mentor a fifty-year-old Nigerian man who runs a successful home health-care agency and is studying for a doctorate in music therapy at Regis College."

Somehow Bob finds time to help the Framingham Public Library. Bartleby Scriveners gives time and talent pro bono, designing and laying out the brochure publicizing the library's "one book, one community" initiative, Framingham Reads Together.

Bob plays tennis three days a week with a rotating group of eighty players. He describes them fondly as "old timers who feel lucky to be alive." They are professional men and women, both retired and employed. "One thing that I am pleased about is that I have been consciously trying to improve my game, and it *is* getting better. None of the other players seem to be doing that! Unfortunately, I am not as fast as I used to be in the writing department, not as good at connecting the dots. Even though I have all the new technologies at my command, I have to hire someone when I run into a problem."

During the years Bob spent at the University of Zambia, he met a Scotswoman who introduced him to Scottish country dancing, which he and Mary

Louise enjoy to this day in Boston. I was interested to learn that Scottish country dancing is a social form of dance performed by three, four, or five couples in simple or complex sets. As such, it differs from the Highland dancing that is performed competitively or solo. I was also interested to learn that it was through Scottish dancing that Bob had met the Harvard psychiatrist with whom he worked at the AFF/ICSA.

Bob and Mary Louise make their decisions independently with respect to working, when and how much. Mary Louise retired six years ago after a long career teaching music in the Weston, Massachusetts, public schools. She juggles several part-time jobs now: accompanist to the school choruses in Weston; lifeguard at a wellness center's therapy pool; director of a German-speaking chorus in Walpole, Massachusetts; and director of the children's chorus at the MetroWest Performing Arts Center in Framingham. With a mixture of pride and bemusement, Bob says that Mary Louise is "compulsively employed." As for himself, he plans to continue working "indefinitely."

Bob has traveled to Zambia four times in the past seven years and plans to go there again next year with Mary Louise to check on the computer literacy project, visit close friends, visit the people whose history he compiled forty years ago, and see some new places in southern Africa. Unlike Melville's Bartleby the Scrivener, who preferred not to do *anything*, Bob knows what he wants to do and gets it done.

Michael Avsharian, age eighty-two, is a classically trained violinist who prefers teaching young people to performing. He is also part of the three-generation executive team that runs Shar Music Company's showroom, workshop, and warehouses in Ann Arbor, Michigan. Shar is the go-to place for strings, instruments, bows, cases, bags, and other essentials for musicians. Michael vows to continue working "as long as I'm alive and can do it."

PROFILE: MICHAEL AVSHARIAN JR.

At age eighty-two, Michael Avsharian Jr. works full time at Shar Music Company in Ann Arbor, Michigan, where, as executive vice president, he oversees purchasing and does "general troubleshooting." When I called to interview him, he was busy in the warehouse.

Today, Shar's showroom, office, workshop, and warehouses are family run by three Avsharians—Michael Jr.; his younger brother, Charles; and Charles's son, Haig. However, it was Michael Avsharian Sr., an émigré from Armenia by way of Turkey in the 1930s, who started Shar Music Products in 1962 as a small discount mail-order company selling strings to string players. He got the idea from Michael Jr., who had discovered that buying violin strings overseas cost less than buying them at local music stores. Charles took the idea one step further by proving to his father that symphony orchestra players were eager customers; professional musicians had little or no access to the variety of strings they needed in those days, except for those living in a few major cities. Michael Sr. set up shop in his house, offering low prices and quick turnaround service (trademarks of Shar Music to this day) and soon was calling on Michael Jr. for help. Ever self-effacing, Michael says, "I only gave technical advice. My father was the entrepreneur with the native talent. He was fond of saying that none of his earlier business ventures could compare to Shar, that he had his greatest success *once he retired*."

Here's where the technical expertise came from. Although Michael's parents were not musically trained, they loved music and raised two sons and two daughters who all were accomplished musically. Michael studied violin in his youth under pioneering music educator, violinist, and conductor Elizabeth Green, who had fortunately relocated to Ann Arbor. And, at the Meadowmount School of Music summer camp in New York State, he studied with renowned violin teacher Ivan Galamian, considered the greatest violin teacher in the world in the second half of the twentieth century. Elizabeth Green ultimately incorporated Galamian's teaching and playing strategies into an instructional textbook that became a best seller. In it, virtually all of the illustrations feature the hands of prize pupils Michael Jr. and Charles.

Michael went on to earn his bachelor's degree in violin performance from Juilliard and a master's in violin performance from the University of Michigan. He then embarked on what he thought would be a long and satisfying career teaching classical violin at the University of Oklahoma and at the University of North Texas. Eight years into his university career, when his father unexpectedly needed help with the start-up company, Michael responded by resigning his faculty position in Texas and returning home to Ann Arbor for good.

In those early days, Shar struggled to get a foothold in the business, Michael recalls. "String players obviously had a vital need for strings. One man who had connections to distributors in Germany controlled virtually all sales, and he was like a dictator. He blocked any competition by telling his distributors not to sell to Shar. My father went to Europe and found a distributor who was willing to ship to us, but the dictator put a stop to that, too, by threatening to cut the fellow off. This went on and on. Shar would have gone out of business had not my father appealed to our senator from Michigan, who happened to chair the Senate's antitrust committee. The committee's intervention, allowing us to buy imported strings, 'opened the floodgates' for Shar. The dictator stopped blocking our way, the word got around, and our little mail-order business began to grow."

Even with Shar's head start in the mail-order business, competition intensified. It wasn't long before Michael's younger sibling, Charles (who also studied under Elizabeth Green and Ivan Galamian and went on to the Curtis Institute), left *his* position teaching violin at the University of Michigan to join his father and brother as Shar's chief executive officer. Modest as ever, Michael says it was all thanks to Charles's brilliant mind for business and his bold nature that the business expanded. "My Dad and I were more conservative. Charles recommended doing things that seemed risky at the time but proved to be the right moves. Shar Music thrived and became a powerhouse." Today, the company's extensive inventory offers individual and institutional customers a far greater variety and more gauges of string than typical music stores can possibly carry. In addition to strings sold at a discount, Shar also sells (and rents) bowed string instruments, bows, cases and bags, electronic accessories, and more. The company is a big purveyor of Suzuki-method materials for teaching and learning a variety of instruments, such as violin, guitar, harp, viola, cello, flute, and piano.

Another member of the close-knit Avsharian family is Michael's nephew and Charles's son, Haig, who represents the third generation of Shar partners. Now president of the company, Haig is an exceptionally good manager who knows how to recruit and hire talented people. The three partners excel in different ways and have formed a well-balanced team.

Michael admits that he is old-fashioned and hasn't kept up with the new technologies, such as Web-based sales. He relies on an IT manager, one of many specialists on staff. "I can get away with it at my age, and I'm an owner, so I can't be fired," he chuckles. "I may not be a tough enough businessman—

Charles and Haig are tougher, and I'm probably *too* agreeable—but customers and employees do come to me with their questions. I'm the answer man who knows the business from its origins fifty years ago."

In the course of the interview, Michael revealed his true passion—giving private violin instruction. For nearly sixty years he has been giving lessons to young violinists. "I'm energized by the kids I teach, and it's exciting to see their skills develop. Most are pre-college age, some are university students." Michael says he never really liked to perform; he always loved to teach. He neglects to mention how some of his former students have gone on to illustrious violin teaching and performance careers. Catherine Cho, a faculty member at Juilliard, is but one example.

Shar has been like a second home to Michael since he became a widower many years ago. He raised two children, then aged eleven and fourteen, after his wife passed away. Characteristically, Michael credits his wife for how well the children turned out by insisting that *she* was the major influence on them. These days, one of his greatest delights when he does have leisure time is visiting his grandchildren in Colorado. Another pleasure, a close second to music, is reading. "If I had more free time I would go to the library and browse."

As should be apparent from reading this profile, Michael is an exceptionally modest man who says that it has always been his nature to avoid drawing attention to himself. He also believes in accepting what he cannot control and adjusting to his environment rather than endeavoring to change it. He cites an example: whenever he got water in the basement of his house, he would simply mop it up. It was only when his son's drum set was set up in the basement that Michael took steps to remediate the water problem. More recently, with his vision, hearing, and stamina declining ever so gradually, he has adjusted by slowing down a bit.

Michael expects to continue working "as long as I'm alive and can do it. I particularly enjoy the stimulation of solving problems and getting the job done, and I'm not going to give it up. Shar provides a living, but more than that it's a *way of life*, and one that keeps me perfectly happy. I'll keep doing what I'm doing forever."

The vast majority of men (more than four-fifths, or 81 percent) are working in the private sector, the remainder (19 percent) work in the public sector.

Steve Grossman spent four decades managing and growing the family business, Grossman Marketing Group, before leaving the private sector to become Massachusetts State Treasurer and Receiver General in 2011 when he was almost sixty-five. He follows Oliver Wendell Holmes's advice to be a vital, engaged person who makes a useful contribution every day. He is "leaning strongly" toward a run for governor in 2014.

PROFILE: STEVEN GROSSMAN

Steve Grossman is Massachusetts State Treasurer and Receiver General. Public service is a Grossman family heritage. In 1910 Maxwell Grossman, Steve's grandfather, helped John F. (Honey Fitz) Fitzgerald get reelected as mayor of Boston. When Steve was a senior in high school, a conversation with his grandfather turned out to be a defining moment for Steve, for his grandfather spelled out the three most important things in life—get a good education so you can support a family, succeed in your career, and give back to the community. And Steve proceeded to do just that, getting his bachelor's degree at Princeton University and an MBA at Harvard Business School; raising a family with his wife, Barbara; managing and growing the family business for the next four decades; then merging a new career *with* public service in his position as state treasurer. "I have always gravitated toward leadership opportunities. I was chair of the Massachusetts Democratic Party in 1991 and 1992 and the Democratic National Committee from 1997 until 1999. I ran for governor in 2002 but did not win the nomination. When the state treasurer's job opened up at the tail end of the 2007–9 recession, I decided to go for it. I was elected in 2010 with 1.2 million votes and took office in January 2011 when I was almost sixty-five." Naturally, I asked Steve whether he aspires to higher office. He replied that he is leaning strongly toward running for governor again and intends to be in the best possible position for the race in 2014.

A commitment to public service is not the only trait that runs in the Grossman family; longevity does as well. His uncle Jerome is ninety-five and receives round-the-clock care, yet still gives monthly talks about politics. Steve's mother, Shirley, is ninety-one, takes courses and is active socially. Steve's father, Edgar, was his business partner for many years. "We were best pals who never had a real argument over business or other matters. He used to remind his kids that the seven most important words are 'Thank you, I love you, I'm sorry.' My dad was also a big believer in working throughout one's lifetime, and he did work until just a few weeks before his death at age eighty. When it came time to etch something special on his gravestone, I recalled how he loved Baltimore's third baseman and Hall of Famer, Brooks Robinson, who was known for advising Red Sox fans to 'make optimism a way of life.' The fact that we put 'He made optimism a way of life' on his gravestone tells you something about my dad—and, probably, about me."

A little more than one hundred years ago, Maxwell Grossman founded the Massachusetts Envelope Company. His sons Edgar and Jerome joined him in the business. Grandson Steve came on board in 1969 and became CEO in 1975. Steve's sisters also work for the company—Amy, who is marketing director, and Meg, who serves as treasurer. Their mother still works there, assisting Meg two days a week. In 1995 the company expanded its offerings and changed its name to MassEnvelopePlus. A fourth generation of Grossmans came aboard in the mid-2000s and the name was changed to Grossman Marketing Group to reflect further expansion with respect to products, services, and territory. It is now a full-service provider of marketing communications materials and promotional products to customers in fields as varied as biotechnology, law, financial services, major league sports, and the arts. Two of Steve's sons took over leadership of Grossman Marketing when Steve stepped down to become state treasurer, and he no longer has an active role in the company.

When I asked Steve about his accomplishments during the two years he has been in office, I expected him to mention several, such as establishing the Small Business Banking Partnership to help grow small businesses and promote job creation; improved operations and efficiencies at Treasury to protect the public's money, including better debt management and putting Treasury contracts out to competitive bid (thus saving taxpayers in reduced service fees and administrative costs); pension reform and benefit modernization; and increased state lottery and unclaimed property revenues. However, he singled out something else entirely as his proudest achievement: building relationships.

"A person in business or political life needs to be meticulous about nurturing, building, and maintaining relationships if he is to be well regarded in the community at large. My parents stressed the importance of treating each person as if they were of infinite worth because they are. It follows from that there is a big difference between wanting to be respected and being treated deferentially. When I meet someone I would rather be called 'Steve' than 'Mr. Treasurer.' And I consider the team I have built at Treasury as trusted and talented colleagues with whom I work on commonsense problem solving, not as people who work for me."

A typical week's schedule for the trim and energetic treasurer includes giving a breakfast talk at Temple Beth Am in the town of Randolph; meeting with small business owners, bankers, and industry leaders in the western Massachusetts city of Springfield to discuss economic development, Treasury issues, and the Small Business Banking Partnership; addressing the MetroSouth Chamber of Commerce in Easton; addressing the Needham Business Association's annual dinner; attending the governor's annual State of the Commonwealth speech; and cochairing the Financial Literacy Advisory Committee of the Massachusetts Department of Elementary and Secondary Education.

A person who makes as many speeches as Steve does has a collection of apt stories and quotes for almost any occasion. He summons, for instance, a line from the 1884 Memorial Day speech by Oliver Wendell Holmes Jr. in Keene, New Hampshire. On that occasion, Holmes asked his listeners to remember the noble sacrifices men and women made during the Civil War, owing to firm convictions regarding the justness of their cause, whether they were Union or Confederacy sympathizers. "As life is action and passion, it is required of a man that he should share the passion and action of his time at peril of being judged not to have lived," Holmes declaimed. For Steve, Holmes's message serves as encouragement to be a vital, engaged person who makes a useful contribution every day.

Steve describes himself as a happy person who loves to work. When I ask about the remote prospect of retirement, he admits to worrying about one thing—finding other ways to keep his mind sharp. "And, like everyone else, I need to make a living as a result of the difficult economic circumstances we have all been experiencing." Family life is a major source of Steve's contentment. He is married to Dr. Barbara Wallace Grossman, a professor in the Department of Drama and Dance at Tufts University and vice chair of the Massachusetts Cultural Council. Barbara is also active in professional associations, such as the American Society for Theatre Research. They have three sons and four grandchildren. After forty-four years of marriage, this two-career couple has what Steve calls "a symbiotic relationship." Barbara prods him to exercise more, work less, and make more time for the grandchildren. She works as hard as he does, however. Neither spouse wants to retire and sit around waiting for the other.

Steve has three heroes beyond his family members—the prophet Isaiah, Pope John XXIII, and Leonard Fein. Fein, a former professor at Brandeis University, is the founder of Mazon ("sustenance")—A Jewish Response to Hunger. He started Mazon in 1985 to help Jews share a portion of the cost of significant "life-cycle events" such as weddings, bar mitzvahs, and other celebrations, with organizations working to reduce world hunger. Mazon fulfills the commandment in Isaiah 58:10: "If you offer compassion to the hungry and relieve the oppressed, then your light will rise in the darkness and your night will become like the noonday." In addition to supporting Mazon, Steve serves on the advisory boards of the Women's Lunch Place and of Cambridge College. (A lot of other philanthropic work had to be put on hold when he became state treasurer, as Steve cannot do fundraising.) He sums up his sociopolitical philosophy with watchwords derived from his grandfather Maxwell's family, career, service-to-community mantra. "It is not what we earn that's important but what we *do* to create a just and humane society."

The next profile describes a man who also works in state government, Jack Buckley. Jack is the deputy director of the Massachusetts Division of Fisheries and Wildlife. At MassWildlife he oversees administrative functions, the land acquisition program, fisheries management, and the endangered species program. Now sixty-four, he is one of the highly experienced "old-timers" on staff who know how to function effectively within the bureaucracy. He enjoys his job, especially preservation of open space; but he does not plan to work forever—he would like to have the time to pursue his many strong interests outside of work.

PROFILE: JACK BUCKLEY

Jack Buckley is the deputy director of the Massachusetts Division of Fisheries and Wildlife, an agency of the Massachusetts Department of Fish and Game, within the Executive Office of Energy and Environmental Affairs. Mass-Wildlife manages more than one hundred Wildlife Management Areas and thirteen wildlife sanctuaries with responsibility for more than 195,000 acres of lands and waters.

Now at the peak of his career, some forty-three years ago Jack discovered a program at the University of Massachusetts at Amherst that combined a second bachelor's degree with a master's degree in Fisheries Biology. (He already had a bachelor's degree in history.) He focused his graduate work on shortnose sturgeon. After graduate school he worked at the University of Massachusetts for three years on shortnose sturgeon research projects. In 1982 he was hired as fisheries chief for the District of Columbia government, responsible for overseeing the District's fisheries resources.

For the past twenty-five years he has worked as a senior manager in the Commonwealth's fisheries and wildlife agency, juggling a variety of responsibilities. First, he oversees administrative functions, such as budgeting, personnel, and issuing regulations and permits for hunting, fishing, trapping, and recreational land use.

Second, he manages the land acquisitions program whose primary goal is protecting biological diversity, what he deems a legacy issue. The state spends 6 to 10 million dollars a year on locating land parcels, negotiating, and purchasing open space. Typically, the state acts in partnership with conservation organizations, such as the Nature Conservancy, the Massachusetts Audubon Society, the Trust for Public Land, Sudbury Valley Trustees, and other nonprofits.

His third area of responsibility is fisheries management. This includes inland streams, rivers, ponds, lakes, and five fish hatcheries containing 2 million rainbow, brown, brook, and tiger trout for stocking various state waters. Also involved is safeguarding the relationship between land and aquatic resources, for example, between a river and its riverbank.

Fourth, he oversees the endangered species program. The state list contains 429 endangered species at present. The division issues regulations for the permitting process (a controversial program because people don't like the government telling them what they can and cannot do with their land when endangered species are involved).

Jack, now sixty-four, plans to retire in a few years. The long commute into Boston from his home in Hopkinton is wearing on him. He would like to travel more often and for longer periods with his wife, Jeanne Kelley, who happens to be the recently retired director of my local library. One aspect of Jack's job that he particularly enjoys is the international work associated with the United Nations environmental protection program. "It is interesting, rewarding, and a good change of pace. The program, based in Geneva, moves even more slowly than operations here in the US." Jack points out that wherever he travels—Thailand, the Middle East—he is always connected to his job via his iPad and iPhone.

"I really like what I do and I enjoy my colleagues. The division is going through a transition. Most of the staff has been with the agency for a very long time, as I have; fifty years on the job is not unusual (even though most state employees have retired at sixty-five and taken their pension). Gradually, we will be replaced by younger scientists, who represent the future."

Like many older men who have years of work experience, Jack knows what he excels at. One of the highlights of his career is the preservation of open space. "Land protection represents a lasting legacy and is the most significant action we can take to preserve the Commonwealth's biological diversity," he explains. Jack functions well within the state government bureaucracy and knows how to get funding for the division's programs. He thinks he has been effective where he is because he knew how to make good choices. When he works with other agencies, he usually spots what is likely to be productive and avoids what threatens to be a wasted effort. "I have a reputation as a skilled bureaucratic infighter. I tell people what I honestly think because I believe I am being paid for my honesty."

Jack gets up at 5 a.m. every day to get in a run before leaving for work. He takes concertina lessons and plays the fiddle or practices the concertina for two hours a night and tries to do some reading before bed. One night a week he plays in a session with a pick-up band at a local bar. "They usually play from 8 p.m. to 11 p.m., while I'm ready to go home at 10:00 p.m. because I need to get up early to run."

When I ask Jack what he thinks about older men continuing in the workforce, he replies that it is a personal decision. Some people can't wait to retire because they dislike their jobs, but that definitely does not apply to him. Much as he has enjoyed his career, he does not plan to work forever because he believes that a job is a *part* of your life, it is not your life. He has many strong interests outside of work that he would like to have more time to pursue. He is reminded of the Tom Wilkinson character in the film *The Best Exotic Marigold Hotel*, who peremptorily declares, "Today's the day," quits the halls of Parliament, and heads off for India. In Jack's view, "You do the best you can and when you're done, you're done."

Well over three-quarters of the men (78 percent) hold jobs in metropolitan areas. Thirteen percent are working in nonmetropolitan locales and eight percent work in both metropolitan and nonmetropolitan areas. On the whole, professional work has always been more available in major metropolitan areas, and salaries tend to be higher for urban workers than for workers in nonmetropolitan areas in the same occupation. According to the BLS, approximately 86 percent of US nonfarm wage and salary jobs are located in urban settings. Significantly, compared to nonmetropolitan areas, metropolitan areas have higher employment concentrations in nearly all of the higher-paying occupational groups.[1] For example, as a share of total employment, metropolitan areas have about twice as many legal and business and financial operations jobs, and more than three times as many computer and mathematical science jobs. Metropolitan areas also have higher employment shares of management; architecture and engineering; life, physical, and social science; and arts, design, entertainment, sports, and media occupations. Among the occupations with above-average wages, only education, training, and library occupations have a higher employment share in nonmetropolitan areas than in metropolitan areas. Workers with especially high wages because of their location in metropolitan areas (referred to as a "wage premium") include: lawyers, financial managers, advertising and promotional managers, economists, art directors, administrative law judges, producers and directors, editors, writers, and authors.[2]

Economic status has a close association with residence. Recall that many of the older men I surveyed live in New England, the mid-Atlantic states, and western states. Massachusetts and California residents predominate. The majority of the women I surveyed for *Women Still at Work* live in the New England and mid-Atlantic states, where the highest rates of professional and managerial women and the highest annual earnings for full-time, year-round employed women can be found. Many of the women are doing very well for themselves in financial terms, yet they are not on the whole as prosperous as the men.

The older men I surveyed are more likely than older women to work in the private sector and in a metropolitan area where higher-paying jobs are to be found. Two-thirds of the professional women have jobs in the private sector (compared to 81 percent of the men) and more than two-thirds work in a metropolitan area (compared to 78 percent of the men). Like the men, professional and managerial women also work in a wide variety of career fields, but the greatest number are found in the so-called helping professions whose doors were open to women in the 1960s and 1970s—namely, education, health care, social work, or social services—as well as in business and the arts. Although nowadays women can land good jobs in banking, publishing, medicine, and law, choice jobs in those domains used to go almost exclusively to men. Years ago (and to this day), far more men than women in the United States have pursued lucrative careers in the STEM fields—shorthand for science, technology, engineering, and mathematics. These differences suggest that career choice, sector, and location explain at least partially the financial advantage men have over women.

Don McEachern's doctorate in chemical engineering in 1963 was only the first opportunity to study subjects that would be interesting and useful for a career designing advanced nuclear reactors. At seventy-seven he is manager of Nuclear Fuels at General Atomics in California. The work is obviously challenging; the technology has to be both effective and safe. After nearly five decades in the business, Don still has lots of energy (that was immediately apparent when I met him) and is most content when he has a stimulating project to work on. He relishes opportunities to learn with his colleagues and enjoys teaching younger staff. He has outside interests but none as compelling as his work. He admits to fearing retirement.

PROFILE: DONALD MCEACHERN

Don McEachern defies the stereotype about older workers not being willing or able to learn new things. "I am interested in learning and understanding—every day. In fact, throughout my working life I have taken classes in special subjects that I thought would be useful—management, finance, marketing, engineering, statistics, physics, languages." And useful they have been.

At seventy-seven, Don works full time at General Atomics in California designing advanced nuclear reactors. This requires knowledge of nuclear technology and materials, performing analyses, and conducting experiments. Funding mainly comes from the US Department of Energy.

After nearly fifty years working on nuclear reactors at the Los Alamos Laboratory in New Mexico and at General Atomics in La Jolla, California, Don has given up managing organizations and large projects in favor of developing new business, planning, consulting, and teaching younger staff based on his many years of experience with nuclear technology. His current title is Manager of Nuclear Fuels.

"The work is extremely challenging," he says. "The nuclear business is plagued by many problems, as is well known. We try to solve those problems in ways that make the technology both useful and safe. We deal with costs, safety, environmental risks, efficient utilization of resources, and more." Don was in Japan recently to attend an international meeting on nuclear technology and not, as I had assumed, to study the Fukushima Daiichi nuclear power plant disaster. (In March 2011, a 9.0 magnitude earthquake triggered a massive tsunami that killed thousands and severely damaged the power supply and reactor cooling systems of the coastal Fukushima nuclear plant.) Nonetheless, Don could give me a very simple explanation of the difference between Fukushima's technology and General Atomics' high-temperature gas-cooled nuclear reactor technology:

> Our technology is much safer than the type of reactor at Fukushima. At places like Fukushima, the uranium that generates the energy is contained in long, skinny metal tubes; the energy is extracted using water; the water is converted to steam that powers turbines for generating electricity. When Fukushima lost the ability to circulate water in its cooling system, the metal containers melted and the operators lost temperature control of radioactive fuel and materials. The H_2O separated and the hydrogen exploded. In contrast, our concept uses ceramic material, not metal, to contain the nuclear fuel at high temperatures (higher than Fukushima's reactors could), and we use helium, not water, to cool the nuclear fuel. If something happens, we *can* conduct the heat out of the system. There is no hydrogen to cause explosions and no problem with release of greenhouse gases.

There has been considerable interest in General Atomics' technology, but it has not been widely implemented owing to a hiatus in building nuclear power plants in this country since 1975. Presently, four southern US states, as well as approximately twenty foreign countries, are planning to build electrical generation nuclear plants or thinking of building new plants to use in the so-called process industries. For example, the petrochemical industry needs a high-temperature reactor to generate hydrogen efficiently. The hydrogen is useful in many ways, such as making lower-grade petroleum that can be turned into lubricants, oils, gases, and greases.

Don plans to continue working at least one more year. Is he afraid of retiring? Yes, he thinks he is. "I am not happy unless I am busy and the work environment here provides stimulation not easily duplicated elsewhere. I have made work the center of my life and find working as an engineer more interesting than other activities. To be successful in the nuclear technology workplace, one has to focus on important issues and deal with them in the most rational and objective manner. I like that. One has to deal with facts, with real issues. There is no room for posturing or illogical conclusions. Working in that kind of environment is fulfilling. It is not like politics, which I find appalling. Also, there are certain social rewards associated with the workplace where thoughtful people concentrate together on a mission. There are opportunities to meet new people and share experiences. I know this can be done outside the workplace, but I am hesitant to take on the challenge."

"I still have a lot of energy," Don continues, "and I am not comfortable unless I have some projects to work on. The workplace is structured to provide interesting things to do. I am not sure that I would be successful in finding equally interesting and significant projects outside the workplace. Since I have not developed a great many competing interests outside of my work, no doubt I do not appreciate the possibilities of alternative activities."

Although Don and his wife, Dixie, enjoy socializing and attending music and theater performances, most of Don's close friends are coworkers. He finds younger coworkers—bright, energetic men and women—a pleasure to work with. The ones who have graduated recently know newer computer methods and other productivity-enhancing tools that he doesn't know, although he assures me that he has a good working grasp of them. He considers mentoring General Atomics' younger employees to be one of his major contributions.

When Don was studying for his PhD in chemical engineering in the early 1960s at the University of Wisconsin, there were no female students in his program. "It's puzzling. In elementary school *girls* were the smart ones, and they were good at math. What kept them from going on to STEM careers (science, technology, engineering, mathematics)?" Today, engineering classes are about 30 percent female. Don sees no differences in the abilities of male and female students. He would like to see STEM education pushed even harder in our schools. "We are not growing enough STEM people in our country. We are importing many of them from abroad, and that is a real failing."

When I asked Don whether he has noticed any changes in his life since reaching sixty or seventy, he admitted that he is often fatigued at the end of the day. "I look old and I am aware that I am old. That is the reality. Consequently, health and fitness are extremely important to me. I watch my diet carefully and exercise vigorously several times a week." Don loves to go on trips sponsored by the Sierra Club that require strenuous activity. Most recently, he has hiked across the topmost parts of Scotland, canoed the Buffalo River in Arkansas, hiked in the Dolomite Mountains in Italy, and gone rafting in Alaska.

After reading my book *Women Still at Work*, Don told me that he found the women's responses to my interview questions quite different from his. He thought their reasons for continuing to work expressed more affect. And here Don does fall back on a convenient stereotype: "What do you expect?" he seems to shrug. "I am an engineer."

Other factors affecting income from the job are full-time versus part-time status and number of years in the current job. According to the most recent US Census, 44.3 percent of men and women sixty-five and older who participated in the labor force worked full time and year-round in 2011.[3] (The District of Columbia's rate surpassed all states': 62.2 percent.) The men in my study clearly prefer full-time work. Just under two-thirds of the men are working full time and 38 percent are working part time. Seven of the twelve men in their eighties-nineties are working full time. The rest of the full-timers are divided fairly evenly between the sixty- to sixty-nine-year olds and the seventy- to seventy-nine-year-olds. The pattern I see for older women is somewhat different. As is true of the men, there are slightly more full timers (53 percent) than part timers (47 percent) among the women. However, age definitely plays a bigger part in the women's employment decisions. Part-time work is generally favored by women seventy and over, and women sixty to sixty-nine tend to choose full-time work.

Eighty-two-year-old Ed Myers of Austin, Texas, has three part-time jobs. He has been teaching in the water for more than sixty years. Serving in the US Navy before attending college, he taught naval recruits about water safety. Once he enrolled at St. Lawrence University, he established a swim program. Now, at a mature age and in very good shape, Ed is still teaching swimming and lifeguarding at the Town Lake YMCA in Austin, where he is beloved. But the YMCA job is only one of Ed's part-time paid positions. He is a sales manager for a computer services company—an Austin-area staffing agency called Senior Work Solutions found the job for him—and he is a professional model for television commercials and print advertisements. He also volunteers his time instructing a swim and water exercise class for Alzheimer's patients in the YMCA's Senior Retreat program. All told, Ed puts in thirty-five hours a week or more and he expects to continue because he really enjoys it, plus the income comes in handy when he and his wife want to travel.

Another teacher (of the dry-land variety), North Carolinian Dr. Ed Neal, has been consulting in higher education on a part-time basis for the past five years. He was a recognized leader in POD (Professional and Organizational Development in Higher Education) when I was a rookie faculty developer in the late 1980s to early 1990s. Ed provided an honest snapshot of his career in faculty development, curriculum design, and higher education pedagogy:

> Although I started my academic career as a history professor (in 1968), I became more interested in the dynamics of the classroom than in the exotic charms of my chosen field, so I switched to faculty development. I established the Office of Faculty Development at University of North Carolina (UNC) at Chapel Hill in 1974 and served as the director for thirty-four years, retiring in 2008. I started part-time consulting outside the university in the early 1990s, so when I retired it was easy to continue the work (and, of course, there is no heavy lifting). Consulting is still very much a part-time occupation. For example, I've been working with the Biostatistics Department at Duke University for about twenty hours a month for two years, helping the faculty design and implement a new master's degree program (which includes trying to train the faculty in

effective teaching techniques). Every fall I teach a ten-class post-doctoral seminar, "College Teaching," at UNC and I repeat the course in the spring for postdocs at the National Institute for Environmental Health Sciences. I also usually present four or five pedagogical workshops a year at colleges and universities in the area, although that kind of work has tapered off because of the recession. I became editor of the *Journal of Faculty Development* in 2000, and I'm doing a better job than ever before because now I have the time to do it properly.

I really love teaching (not only for the ego boost it provides), and I think I still have something important to contribute, especially since the field has been hijacked by a fascination with technology. I've talked with many people who work in distance education or who serve as technology consultants to faculty members, and I fear that at least 75 percent of them know nothing about principles of cognitive psychology and have only a passing acquaintance with the relevant educational literature. Even now, faculty members from UNC still contact me with questions and problems, since the teaching center has ceased providing individual consultations and is now focusing on "the technological enhancement of teaching."

The number of years men have spent in the current job ranges from 0.5 to 73. The average is twenty-two years in the current job and the median is eighteen. What keeps the average and median low for these older men is their propensity for starting a new job in the same field or changing fields altogether (29 percent and 20 percent, respectively) after working for many years in an initial career. Examples of career changes include the following: hairdressing to film distribution, airline supervisor to crossing guard, practicing law to university teaching, owning a travel agency to K–12 teaching, health-care administration to historic preservation, practicing law to financial advising, journalism to political advising, engineering to university teaching, typography sales to house painting, costume jewelry sales to fundraising, and architecture to state government service. A sixty-eight-year-old who describes himself as an entrepreneurship and business plan consultant in this country and abroad has deftly moved from one business venture to another. He asserts, "I never had a 'career' of any sort. Instead I changed work as I got bored or discovered something new." He lists his noncareers as mechanic and racing car team manager, securities salesman, insurance salesman, marketing director, sports car designer and manufacturer, lawyer, auto industry consultant, author, and publisher. This is a self-appraising fellow who wishes he had "patience, equanimity, and a less judgmental nature" instead of "quick reactions and knee-jerk jerkiness." Perhaps he doth protest too much, for his impatience seems to have served him well.

Jim Fannin had been working for fifty-four years overall when I interviewed him. He had moved from the highest ranks of hospital administration to working in historic preservation with *and* for his wife, and from being a "suit" to doing an artisanal craft which also involves some heavy physical labor. This change from full-time work in one career field to full-time work in another was one of the most radical and successful I learned about through my research. Jim and his wife have so much cemetery conservation and historic preservation work they can't possibly retire.

PROFILE: JAMES C. FANNIN JR.

In the 1960s, after Jim served three years in Army intelligence and completed a master's degree in hospital administration at Columbia University, he landed his first job at a community hospital in Long Island, New York. Those were the "halcyon days" when Medicare was new and reimbursements to hospitals were generous. For the next twenty-seven years he served as COO or CEO of various other hospitals until mergers and acquisitions became the order of the day. As COO at what was then called Framingham Union Hospital in Massachusetts, he had a wonderful working relationship with the CEO that was interrupted by the unplanned early retirement of the CEO. A new CEO came on board, but he and Jim did not see eye to eye. "We were oil and water at best," says Jim. "I decided I didn't need the stress of hospital administration any longer, although I didn't know what the alternative would be. And I was in my early fifties. Luckily, I escaped at the right moment."

It was the right moment because Jim's wife, Minxie Jensvold Fannin, and her friend, Monique Lehner, both trained architectural historians, had established Fannin-Lehner Preservation Consultants in 1984. Minxie had developed the idea of cemetery conservation after going to a Boston conference on the work being done in its old burying grounds. Jim agreed to take on the cemetery preservation work. There were incidents of vandalism and the ordinary ravages of time and weather taking their toll. Fannin-Lehner specializes in the field of historic burial ground conservation and historic preservation consulting. The firm works with architects, landscape architects and historians, structural engineers, and metal conservators and a historic masonry contractor on the different aspects of gravestone and monument condition assessment and conservation in New England, the Midwest, and Mid-Atlantic regions of the country. Consulting services include preparing documentation for individual and district listings on the National Register of Historic Places and National Landmark nominations. Minxie serves on the boards of the Society of Architectural Historians/New England chapter and the Boston Preservation Alliance; is a member of the Collections Committee of the Bostonian Society; and is the former chair of the Massachusetts Senate Art Committee.

In the late 1980s when he became senior associate in the firm (Minxie is managing principal), there was no program available to teach Jim all he needed to know about burial ground gravestone and monument conservation and tomb and mausoleum rebuilding and restoration—all the methodical processes of cleaning, resetting, adhesive repair, drilling and pinning, and infills. His only training was a cartography course taken as part of his economic geography major at Dartmouth College years before. He could do the hand drawing and measuring required of cartographers before computers were available, but that wasn't enough. Jim was fortunate to attend a two-week course on the conservation of outdoor sculpture put on by the National Park Service, which included a good deal about stone as well as metals, and he attended numerous other conferences and workshops on all types of natural stone. In addition, Jim found a fellow from Vermont doing gravestone restoration who would allow Jim to "shadow" him and, eventually, to help him to learn on the job.

One of Jim's early challenges was restoring Eleazar Wheelock's gravestone at his alma mater. Wheelock, the founder of Dartmouth College, had died in 1779, and his and wife Mary's gravemarker badly needed attention. Other notable clients Jim regularly tends to include two cemeteries in historic Salem, Massachusetts, where Jim has been working for many years and a cemetery in the middle of town in Granville, Ohio. "I have been working on stones there for twenty-two years. Our firm did an assessment of all 1,200 stones and found that nine hundred were in bad shape. So far, we have done all the 'easy' ones and many of the hard ones, but the remainder are a huge challenge."

Jim stays current with changes in stone processing and adhesives and with strategies for preserving the built environment by attending annual meetings of the Association of Preservation Technology as well as any conference, meeting, or workshop concerning stone and collaboration with colleagues. The Internet is a plus, making the search for historic documents less arduous. Needless to say, one thing has not changed over time: stone is still very heavy. Jim, age seventy-seven, has to be able to lift stone fragments as well as eighty-pound bags of concrete mix. The weather can be problematic, too hot or too cold or rainy. Therefore, most of the physical labor gets done in the summertime; the recording of photographs, proposals, and other paperwork is done the rest of the year. Jim does have a crew to help him in the cemeteries, mostly academic types who are available to work in the summer. "It is quite a challenge to reassemble three or four pieces of stone. The people who work for us have to understand and respect *antiquity*. There is no protocol—you often figure it out as you go along—which makes for very little routine in this line of work. I find it very rewarding to take inanimate objects that are in terrible shape and get them to look good."

In addition to scores of newspaper and magazine articles written about the firm, Fannin-Lehner Preservation Consultants have won two major awards for their work: in 2009 the Oakley Certification of Merit from the Association for Gravestone Studies and in 2010 the Paul Tsongas Profiles in Preservation Award from Preservation Massachusetts. The firm is also known for leading workshops on historic preservation.

The decision about when to retire will be made jointly, but Jim already knows how Minxie feels: "Retirement is a no-no." To keep in shape for their physically demanding work, the Fannins cycle 1,100 miles every year outdoors, and take spinning classes at a health club. They get up at 4:30 a.m. most mornings to go to a 5:45 a.m. spinning class. Cycling not only increases fitness, it also reduces the stress associated with having too many jobs to do at once and needing to keep clients satisfied. "It is a juggling act. I thought the recession would hurt us, but demand never slackened, especially in Massachusetts. When the Community Preservation Act passed here in 2000, adopting communities had to assign a 1.5 to 3 percent surcharge on property tax bills for open space preservation, preservation of historic resources, development of affordable housing, and the acquisition and development of outdoor recreational facilities. There are very few corners of Massachusetts where we haven't done work."

The couple seems to make friends everywhere. They maintain friendships from their university days, from the health-care world, from the historic preservation world (including longtime clients), and at the health club. Most of the older friends are retired. When Jim and Minxie attend college reunions, all their friends seem to talk about are their ailments, which makes the Fannins even more determined to remain active.

They are visiting their son and his family in Hong Kong for a midwinter vacation, then, as Jim puts it, they will "get back in the traces" when they return. "The jobs flood in. We are booked into next year. We can't retire. It wouldn't make sense. And, in reality, even if we wanted to step away, there is no one to take over the business."

A modest portion of the women I studied had, like the men, decided to start anew one or more times, sometimes because the grass appeared greener elsewhere, sometimes because job cutbacks or other fiscal exigencies forced them to start over. Consequently, even after many years in the workforce less than one-third of the men (25 percent) and the women (30 percent) described themselves as "at the peak" of their career. Aside from these similarities, however, there are differences with respect to time spent in the current job. The average time in the current job for women (16.3 years) is even lower than the men's average. The median for women (fifteen years) is three years *less* than the median for men. The range for women—three months to fifty years—is wide, but it is less wide than the range for men. There are at least three possible explanations for the differences in years in the current job: a higher upper age for the men responding to my survey; women getting a "late start" due to breaks for childrearing in the past; and the greater number of full-timers among the men.

Whether by personal choice or, more likely, because of financial pressures, twenty-eight of my respondents (18 percent) also have a *second* job. Most of the men with second jobs are in their sixties and their jobs include: on-call firefighting/EMT, teaching/tutoring, music instruction and performance, writing/editing, medical review, event security, and outdoor instruction. The other ten men with second jobs are in their seventies and eighties and their jobs are mostly in teaching, writing, lifeguarding, acting, retail sales, and disability claim review. For psychiatrist Dick Winslow, whose profile you will read in chapter 8, reviewing disability claims for the Social Security Administration is a part-time second job. He is more interested in the intellectual challenge of the work than the income it provides. Allan Shedlin took a second job as a Trader Joe's "crew member" to supplement the modest income from his primary job and obtain health insurance coverage (his profile is in chapter 3).

As older men and women have discovered, self-employment, consulting, and business ownership make it far easier to continue working and to maintain earning power. Entrepreneurs can parlay their considerable know-how, skills, experience, and all-important networking contacts into a new venture. It requires having the desire and confidence, as well as enough capital to get started and a product or service that meets clients' or customers' needs. The Small Business Association saw the number of self-employed people fifty-five to sixty-four soar 52 percent from 2000 to 2007, and that was *prior to* the Great Recession.[4] Seventy of my respondents (45 percent) describe themselves as self-employed or consulting, and the other 55 percent work for an employer. (The percentages are reversed for the women: just under half work for an employer and the rest are self-employed or consulting.)

Eighty-five-year-old Donald Brick is a silver entrepreneur par excellence. Until the demands of worldwide travel became too much for him two years ago, Don was president of the US branch of Hi-Tech Solutions (HTS), an Israeli firm. He relinquished the position to a younger man, whom he mentors, became special consultant to HTS, and formed his own company, Donald B. Brick and Associates, to build upon the systems he designed using license plate recognition (LPR) technology. He recently agreed with his wife that it was time to downsize and move to a condo, but he is not about to lessen his commitment to the business.

PROFILE: DONALD B. BRICK

It is very easy for eighty-five-year-old Donald B. Brick to keep up with new technologies—it is all part of his dual responsibilities as president of Donald

B. Brick and Associates, Inc., in Burlington, Massachusetts, and special consultant to HTS, an Israeli firm. With a doctorate in engineering and applied physics from Harvard University and some sixty-five years of experience in artificial intelligence, pattern recognition, and command-and-control research, design, and marketing, he knows all the fundamentals as well as the very latest applications. He intends to continue working as long as he can, as long as he is physically and mentally able. "I have a lot to contribute," he says, "and I enjoy my work. I see how retired friends spend their time, and that's not for me. I *have* things to do, so I don't have to *look for* things to do. The business gives me a big reason for living. It keeps me out of trouble and makes me feel younger. And I like being with younger people."

Don was part of a cluster of Harvard postdocs who were hired by Sylvania in the mid-1950s to do research and development for the defense industry.[5] Information processing was Don's specialty. Sylvania was so impressed with the group's work that it built a new building to house their R&D lab. An outgrowth of the ten years Don spent at Sylvania is the LPR software systems in use today on highways all across the country—think E-ZPass, QuickPass, FasTrak, TollTag, or I-Pass. Similar systems, in use in parking lots, parking garages, gated communities, and shipping ports, also hearken back to the pattern recognition work he pioneered at Sylvania. Image processing software for video security and parking and traffic monitoring and recording identifies vehicle owners to be allowed through a gate, charged a toll or fee, or detected if they try to avoid paying. An interagency group of thirty states shares the same type of violation enforcement and toll collection system.

Access and surveillance systems like these raise questions about potential invasion of privacy (questions I asked). Don's answer is matter of fact: "It is being done anyway because of overriding safety, security, logistics, and law enforcement considerations." And then he launches into a story about the time he was wandering through the parking lot at the mall while his wife shopped, and he was carrying a handheld LPR device. A woman observed his unusual behavior and told him to stop or she would call the police. He calmly replied that it was not illegal, but she called anyway. Soon, two policemen arrived and asked him to explain what he was doing. He did, and they became completely fascinated with the device.

Don is the proverbial cat with nine lives. Not counting his first jobs—at age thirteen filling orders in a wholesale drug company near home in Paterson,

New Jersey, and at age fifteen selling shoes—he has made at least five major career moves, buying and selling companies, generally within the information processing systems field. One of his more short-lived ventures involved a computerized maintenance system for highway departments. However, maintenance workers strenuously objected to the tracking function, and it was "deep-sixed." Between business ventures, he worked for eight-plus years as technical director at Hanscom Field in Massachusetts on radar systems and the command-and-control-infrastructure of the US Air Force.

He next consulted for a number of companies, one of them being Alphatech, a company owned and run by a number of present and ex-MIT professors who knew the business of government-sponsored R&D but did not understand the marketing of commercial products like the LPR system, a byproduct of the government R&D. Don took over that function. Soon, he and a few colleagues split off and formed their own company, which morphed into the US operations of HTS. Until the demands of worldwide travel became too much for him two years ago, Don was president of the US branch of HTS. He relinquished the position to a younger man, whom he mentors, and became special consultant to HTS and formed his own company, Donald B. Brick and Associates, to build upon the systems he designed using LPR technology. Nonetheless, there has been no letup in new ideas and challenges. For example, to expand into new markets and see those ideas flourish, he has had to learn both the shipping business (to implement container recognition in shipyards on the West Coast and in Europe and Asia) and the parking business. For all these accomplishments, the achievement closest to Don's heart remains the scientific paper he contributed to the invitation-only Festschrift (or celebratory publication) honoring legendary Professor Norbert Wiener on his seventieth birthday in 1964.[6] In this paper, Don applied Wiener's nonlinear signal processing concepts to the detection and classification of noise-like signals.

Don's wife, Phyllis, thinks he works far too much. She has retired from her job as associate director of the American Technion Society in New England (an organization that supports the Technion-Israel Institute of Technology, a.k.a. the "MIT of Israel") but keeps busy with fundraising activities. They do see their three children and seven grandchildren fairly often and enjoy attending their grandchildren's special occasions and events, such as their youngest grandson's high school basketball games. Don can no longer play tennis or ski since having both knees replaced, but he does try to go to the health club regularly. As he nears eighty-six, he is saddened by friends' passing. He admits to slowing down a bit and says names tend to escape him at times. He really doesn't feel old, even though people who look at him might see an elderly person. He and his wife recently decided to downsize, selling their home in Lexington, Massachusetts, and moving to a condo in nearby Burlington. "We looked at several attractive retirement complexes but decided against them because we couldn't see ourselves surrounded by older people!"

Self-employment is a popular option for older men and women who have been laid off and for those who have retired but changed their minds. *New York Times* reporter Steven Greenhouse detects "myriad forms" of retirement behavior across the country. He highlights an elastic "in and out, off and on" pattern by which people *un*retire after retirement from a career job and start a new business or take a part-time job.[7] Some may have "gotten the message" too late that having enough money to retire comfortably (i.e., maintain one's preretirement standard of living) means saving more, so they are working longer than expected. Many people got the message when the recession put a big dent in their savings. As discussed in chapter 4 and documented by the Employee Benefit Research Institute, an increasing number of Americans (not just seniors) do not plan to retire until age seventy or later (26 percent, compared to 12 percent in 2002), and fewer intend to retire before age sixty-five (24 percent, compared to 50 percent two decades earlier).[8]

Although the Greenhouse article astutely captures the "in and out, off and on" behavior of retirees and *un*retirees, his examples skew to the *financial* pressures driving their decisions. Financial pressures indisputably are keeping many men on the job, but as we shall see in the next profile and in chapter 7, money worries are neither the top reason nor the only reason men give for delaying retirement.

Ted Grenham has retired and *un*retired a few times. His longtime marketing career at Digital Equipment Corporation (DEC) ended when he accepted a generous early retirement package. An encore career in real estate fizzled when the recession took its toll on the economy. Golf was really enjoyable for a while, but he missed work and the structure it provided to his life.

Fortunately, his next encore career—selling outdoor equipment and garden supplies part time at Home Depot—has proved to be just right. Although he does not earn a lot, that is not why he is working at seventy-four.

PROFILE: TED GRENHAM

After college at Boston University, Ted worked for a hotel chain for a few years. With the computer industry heating up, he went into sales at UNIVAC (Universal Automatic Computer I) for thirteen years. For the next twenty-three years, Ted was marketing director for various new software applications and hardware products at DEC. He marketed DEC products to businesses, colleges and universities, and medical centers, not directly to consumers. He loved it. "It was the best place to work!"

DEC was taken over by Compaq Computer Corporation in 1996–97, which in turn was taken over by Hewlett-Packard in 2002. After the second merger, Hewlett-Packard offered a very lucrative early retirement package to anyone over age fifty-five who had worked at the company for ten years or longer. Early retirees would keep all their benefits and any stock options they had. Ted was sixty-three and planning to work there for another three years, but the offer was simply too good to ignore.

"As soon as the early retirement program was announced, I knew I had to choose an encore career. I decided to obtain my real estate license before leaving Hewlett-Packard and was all set when the time came to leave." Like his wife, Cynthia, Ted sold real estate for Coldwell Banker Residential Brokerage. He enjoyed working directly with clients, "people spending their own money." After a few years, he joined a division of Coldwell Banker that was marketing new housing projects. "What really appealed to me about that was the fixed schedule; you don't ordinarily have fixed hours in residential real estate. However, within two years the project was entirely sold out. There were no new or interesting projects available—it was 2007, the recession was upon us, the housing industry tanked—so I decided to retire."

Retirement did not last long. In just two or three months, Ted admitted that he missed working a lot, even though it was the summer and he could have played golf every day. "Work is ingrained in me. I think not working is unhealthy. It is not about the money, it is more about having structure in your

life." A friend from DEC who had taken a job at Home Depot in Marlbor-
ough, Massachusetts, encouraged Ted to apply for a job there. He was hired to
sell outdoor power equipment, grilling products, and garden supplies and has
been doing that part time ever since. "My friend said it would be fun, and he
was right. What I enjoy the most is dealing directly with customers, answering questions and helping people who are first-time homeowners. Having
owned a home for over forty years, I have expertise to share. Even the occasional cranks don't bother me. I just let the irritability roll off or get one of the
new sales associates to deal with it." Ted also is pleased when former customers return to the store to thank him and tell him how his advice worked out.

What Ted likes least is negotiating his time off. He and Cynthia take
long trips to visit their children and grandchildren in Oregon and Australia
every year, and the families gather in Cape Cod for a vacation every summer. Tuesdays and Thursdays are sacrosanct—they are his golf days in the
good weather and his days for taking architectural walking tours through
Cambridge and Boston. So Ted works at Home Depot on weekends and one
day during the week. Conveniently, Cynthia usually works on weekends, too.
Their grown children say, "Wow! This is what retirement looks like?"

Ted is pleased to tell me how Home Depot gave him and another older
fellow a chance to prove themselves. It has turned out so well—they are still
employed four years later while many of the younger workers have been let
go—that the company is now willing to take a chance on other mature workers. Every new employee goes through a ninety-day trial period, especially
during the summer. The company then keeps people on who are good workers. Ted's pay is higher than minimum wage, but is certainly not enough
to support a family. "That is not an issue for me, but there are many folks
working at the store who are struggling to hold things together." He is aware
that many of his fellow employees are men and women who *have* to work,
whereas he has a choice. "It is socially defining. A number of the employees
are struggling with addictions of various kinds; some have no family or support system. I know I am much better off than they are. We get along very
well, but that is a conversation we stay away from."

I wondered how Ted feels about not having a managerial position. He
assured me that he does not feel the need to be a manager. "I have a whole
new perspective on working now. At seventy-four, I can relax and not worry
about climbing the career ladder." He does enjoy being one of a select group

of employees who are invited to attend the "road show" of new products held at the company's regional headquarters in Canton, Massachusetts, every year. Ted has also been recognized in another way. Twice in a row he has been nominated by every manager in the store to receive Home Depot's executive award for outstanding customer service. In 2009, the very first time the award was given, the CEO presented it to Ted. In 2010, the senior vice president of Home Depot did the honors.

"Few salespeople select Home Depot as a career—they cannot afford to. But if you are not supporting a family and you have another purpose for working there, the job can be very meaningful. I do get a lot of respect." That reminds Ted of something he learned years ago from a vice president at DEC who was his manager: the importance of listening to and learning from others. Even if an idea was the manager's, they would think it was theirs, so the fellow had the respect of everyone who worked for him. This work ethic has stood Ted in good stead over the years.

The profiles in this chapter not only illustrate a wide variety of career paths taken by older men—business, higher education, writing, music, government service, science, technology, historic preservation, and sales—they also portray career changers, full-timers, and part-timers. Moreover, the profiles reflect attitudes about retirement articulated by men who are confident about working longer. For example, Don Brick *has* things to do, so he doesn't have to *look for* things to do. Ted Grenham says it's not about the money, it's about having *structure* in his life. Michael Avsharian agrees: his work does more than provide a living, it's a *way of life*. Steve Grossman, too, says it's not what we earn that's important, it's what we *do* to create a just and humane society. For Bart Guerreri, work is simply fun, a passion. Jack Buckley also loves his work, but sees it as *a part of* his life, not all-absorbing; so he looks forward to retiring in a few years. In contrast, the prospect of retirement "absolutely petrifies" John Kaneb. An even closer examination of men's reasons for working past conventional retirement age follows in the next chapter.

7

Why Older Men Work

As life is action and passion, it is required of a man that he should share the passion and action of his time at peril of being judged not to have lived.—Oliver Wendell Holmes Jr., 1884 Memorial Day Speech

Chapter 1 highlighted two things that piqued my curiosity the most when I undertook the current book project and the preceding one—the reasons men and women give for opting to work well past conventional retirement age, and how men's work life stories might differ from the stories told by the women I studied. Does contributing experience, know-how, and institutional knowledge give them satisfaction and keep them on the job? How important to them is making money? Men responding to my survey could check multiple reasons for continuing to work and add others. Table 7.1 displays in priority order their reasons for deferring leisure and retirement in favor of persisting in the labor force.

Topping the list of reasons by a full seventeen percentage points is the *satisfaction* older working men are getting, the *meaning* nearly all of them find in work. Using their professional *abilities, skills,* and *training* falls in second place, followed by their *enjoyment of clients, patients, students,* or *customers;* the sense that they are *helping others, contributing to society,* and *making a difference; having good health and high energy;* and *enjoyment of their colleagues and coworkers.*

Table 7.1. Reasons for Older Men Staying in the Paid Workforce (by percentage)

Satisfaction; find meaning in work	91
Use abilities/skills/training	74
Enjoy clients, patients, students, or customers	69
Help others/contribute/make a difference	67
Enjoy good health, high energy	63
Enjoy colleagues, coworkers	62
Need the income	48
Keep busy, get out of the house	47
New job in same field	29
Save in 401(k) plan, other retirement plan	27
At peak of career (high earning power, authority)	25
Boost Social Security benefits	22
Changed career field	20
Rising health insurance costs	15
Accrue pension benefits	14
Other financial pressures	11
Opportunities for training, retraining, updating skills	8
Seniority status (e.g., per union contract)	6
Started career late	3

When the Society for Human Resource Management asked US employees about their job satisfaction and engagement in the organization's 2012 annual survey on those topics, the "opportunity to use skills and abilities" was found to be the most important aspect of job satisfaction for 63 percent of SHRM respondents, especially to employees with college and postgraduate degrees.[1] It is important to note, however, that only 3 percent of SHRM's respondents were "Veterans" (born before 1945), the age cohort that is generally comparable to my respondents. The vast majority of SHRM's respondents who deem use of skills and abilities as most important for job satisfaction are younger men and women: Baby Boomers, born 1945–1964 (43 percent); Gen X-ers, born 1965–1980 (32 percent); and Millennials, born after 1980 (21 percent). SHRM respondents also rate "job security" and "compensation (pay)" among the top three contributors to job satisfaction.

Jon Kapstein's reasons for working track closely with SHRM respondents' opinions on job satisfaction and engagement. When my survey snowballed to Brussels, Belgium, I heard from expat Jon Kapstein, freelance journalist, political advisor, and part-time consultant on European Union government affairs. Jon, seventy-three, gives me three reasons for continuing to work: (1) the satisfaction he gets from "making order out of the chaos of daily events,"

(2) his enjoyment of challenging work, and (3) being able to afford living internationally despite the highly uncertain economy. Then he tags on a fourth: being paid and respected at his age for his useful knowledge and abilities.

PROFILE: JONATHAN KAPSTEIN

Jonathan Kapstein has deftly parlayed his considerable abilities and experience into career-extending work as a political advisor and part-time consultant on European Union government affairs in Brussels, Belgium. After earning a master's degree from the Columbia School of Journalism in 1962 and for a considerable portion of Jon's long working life, he was a journalist with *Business Week* magazine on foreign assignment in Rio, Toronto, Milan, Johannesburg, and, finally, in Brussels, where he still resides with his wife, Nancy. Over the years, he gradually reinvented himself by developing expertise in government matters. Four years ago, he completely changed gears by moving to freelance journalism and becoming a business consultant on European Union affairs.

> Twice I had to learn entire new industry sectors when changing careers after a quarter century as a staff journalist on foreign assignment. The first complete sector change was at age fifty from journalist to chemical company executive. The second was at age sixty-seven/sixty-eight when I went to the aviation sector. I mastered both on my own because what I brought to the new employers was expertise in monitoring European Union legislative and regulatory affairs.

When he turned sixty-five, Jon had already spent fifteen years as director of government affairs in Europe and Africa for a major American chemical corporation. The firm asked him to stay on in a corporate position for another two years to age sixty-seven/sixty-eight as director of international public affairs based in Europe. He agreed because the work was both enjoyable and interesting. Then he was hired as a full-time contractor for the same position in Europe with a major American airline for two more years to age sixty-nine/seventy. This was challenging work, requiring mastery of an altogether new sector. Jon describes the position as "beset and bedeviled by internal head-office politics."

At seventy, he joined an international aviation consulting group based in Switzerland as the person responsible for monitoring developments in the institutions of the European Union. Now seventy-three, and still consulting for this group, Jon says he is fairly well paid for part-time work and could easily be full time if developments warrant.

However, the recession and continuing slump have made it more difficult for the consulting group with which he is affiliated to attract new clients. As Jon sees it, "Continued work on a regular basis is clearly more age-dependent and economy-dependent than I'd like. If this consulting contract disappeared tomorrow, I'd have to sit back and consider what might or might not be available. I don't think I'd hunt aggressively for another consulting contract. Perhaps, considering my major life career as a journalist, I'd do more freelance writing." He also had another job in 2012 that provided what he calls "casual income" for teaching journalism online to third-world, midcareer journalists on behalf of the German government's international development agency.

Jon continues: "I suppose the weak economy has prevented my earned annual income from growing over the past four years. Certainly the economic downturn has also made Nancy and me prudent in watching our retirement income, but then a lifetime of overseas work has always generated a sense of fiscal care."

One thing's for sure. The Kapsteins enjoy their international lifestyle so much, they have every intention of remaining overseas. They do miss their children and grandchildren who live stateside, however. "The only problem with working internationally is not enough time spent with family; yet, on balance, it is always exciting to use work as a means of increasing our exposure to new experiences."

Another major attraction for remaining in Brussels is European medical coverage. Jon supplied me with a primer on the subject.

> The European medical coverage systems are far superior to what exists in the United States. Contrary to the myth in US politics of the evils of so-called socialized medicine, only one country has that system: the UK. Again, contrary to American mythology, it works well. Meanwhile the other countries in Europe have different but mandatory insurance plans. The consumer gets to pick the insurance company, the minimum (which is similar to what the US calls the deductible), the hospital plan, one's own physician, and specialist, and so on

through a range of choices and preferences. One positive result of the Law of Unintended Consequences is that European hospital emergency rooms are just that. They are trauma centers, not crowded by the general public using them as primary care providers as is common in the US.

Statistics show that Europe is far better on preventive care than the US, although both are more or less equal on the treatment front. Statistics also show that the US consumer ends up paying more for medical care than Europeans who do pay higher taxes. Since everyone is covered, the average cost to the payer is pushed down by being spread out. Finally, statistics show that the US ranks shockingly far down the international comparative tables in life expectancy, infant mortality, long-term chronic-disease care, and other broad measures.

The end result is that many Americans, especially those with international experience, are choosing to retire in Europe. Just anecdotally, I even know several US Army colonels who have done that, although they are eligible for the military system's TriCare, which is a health plan for career military and retired military families far superior to Medicare and the Veterans Administration system.

Meanwhile, Jon observes, there are fewer and fewer Americans overseas representing American company foreign operations.

We have lost the international cadre of business expertise, which has been taken over by Dutch, English, French, German, and other nationalities who run American companies overseas. In parallel, American clubs overseas have seen their membership collapse within the past fifteen years. The reason is the US tax system. We are the only country that taxes citizens worldwide rather than on the basis of residence. Although there is an exclusion for foreign earned income up to a certain amount and although there is, in theory, a tax-offset system, neither works. American companies find it just too expensive to maintain expats, unlike other countries. Many companies will not move an American with a family to a foreign post because of the added internal corporate cost. With companies that pay an equalization amount, that sum is taxed as income with the year-on-year multiplier effect of a tax on a tax.

Sooner or later, the lack of American international business expertise will come back to bite the American economy on the butt. The only saving grace is a personal one. It provides me as a retired American living in Europe with the opportunity to work as a freelance journalist or provide consultative services that often mean explaining the US to Europeans and Europe to Americans. It's like falling off a log, but I fear for my country's future.

When I asked Jon to give me his top reasons for continuing to work, he ticked off three: (1) the satisfaction he gets from "making order out of the chaos of daily events"; (2) his enjoyment of challenging work ("If it's not challenging, I'm not interested"), such as having a positive impact on current affairs; and (3) being able to afford the experience of living internationally. Parenthetically, he adds, "You might expect that I'd cite as a top reason being paid and respected at my age for my useful knowledge and activity, but that only occurred to me afterward. I don't think of myself as old even though my hair is more white than gray. From time to time I do wonder whether I have the same drive to succeed that I had in my mature, midcareer working years, but this thought doesn't keep me awake at night."

Furthermore, he is not troubled by retirement or aging stereotypes: both consulting and freelance writing are generally independent of age issues. "I may be reminded when some pretty young woman offers me her seat on the bus or metro. Though this kind of courtesy is common in Europe, not just for me."

Jon expects to continue working "As long as it is enjoyable and paid—provided, of course, that I remain in good health. My father, my uncles and aunts, and my older sister were or are all vigorous, creative, and fit right through long lives, as I hope to be." To combat the ordinary stress and fatigue of working, Jon enjoys reading, writing, travel, and the theater. Keeping fit is important to him: he swims for one hour four or five days a week.

He also volunteers for American and international groups overseas. "It's important to stay in contact with others who often are of different ages and in different circles than those encountered during my daily routine. This adds to a lifestyle of remaining intellectually challenged, active, vigorous, and in good shape and good health while having a great deal of fun." Nancy Kapstein is also an active volunteer with various groups that support the activities of Americans overseas, and she writes an online tourist newsletter. One of her publications, *The Hints Book: Living and Working in Belgium*, was credited as a resource for *Inside Brussels*, a guide for journalists covering Belgium and the European Union.

Jon does admit to a problem that has arisen since he shifted to working part time from a home office. "It's the old saw that one's spouse marries a life partner for better or worse, for richer or poorer, in sickness and health—and now for lunch as well." In nearly forty years of working as a journalist full time overseas on four continents, he always had a one- or two-person office with wide regional responsibility. But he always made sure his office was not at home. It was important for him and for the family to separate the two. "The major change in lifestyle in the last three years has been my working from home, which has required some mental adjustment on my part—and, I am sure, a considerable amount on my spouse's part."

Jon told me that at first he wondered if the experience of an American working and living overseas was relevant to my study. But he soon realized that the interview questions apply equally, domestically and internationally. "The difference is that Americans often continue to work far into older years, whereas Europeans tend to retire much earlier. The cynical European comment is that Americans live to work and Europeans work to live, but that is not necessarily true. What is true is that Americans derive great satisfaction from work and are easier with the concept of working later in life. This does not apply, of course, to those forced to eke out a living due to corporate corruption-and-collapse à la Enron or by the long-running economic downturn or, indeed, by huge and uncovered medical bills. The latter is not a problem in Europe or the rest of the developed world."

Partial as the Kapsteins are to Europe in general and to Brussels in particular, Jon hastens to add the following pronouncement: "To be sure, we are both still proud Americans from New York and New England. Even at my age I also stand tall on indefinite status as a US Navy reservist."

While using their *abilities*, *skills*, and *training* is just as important to my respondents as to SHRM's, I think the men I am studying mean something somewhat different by *satisfaction*, for three of the next top-ranked reasons in table 7.1 (*enjoying clients, patients, students, customers; helping others, contributing to society, making a difference; enjoying colleagues and coworkers*) are more about giving of oneself than receiving. Generally speaking, my respondents seem to be at an age where *finding meaning in work* becomes more important than financial gain. Supporting this notion are the relatively low ratings of the seven financial items in my survey: *needing the*

income; saving in 401(k) plan or other retirement plan; reaching the peak of career (high earning power, authority); boosting Social Security benefits; meeting rising health insurance costs; accruing pension benefits; and *having other financial pressures.* To call finding meaning in work more important than financial gain "altruism" may be too much of a stretch—after all, 48 percent of the men say that they depend on the income from work—but a glance at their comments bears out the point.

For every man who said "A good salary will make things easier in later life," "I need the money," "Adding extra income to my Social Security benefits," "Uncertain about the adequacy of my retirement savings," or "It's an opportunity to make substantial income from expertise gained in the last twenty years," there are men whose work has become almost a cause. Three of them happen to be sixty-nine years of age. "My work is truly a calling," a child psychiatrist confides. "There is tremendous need for child psychiatry," and, he goes on, "I have been trying to help as many children and families as possible." A long-term-care advisor enthuses, "It's a great joy to help people at a difficult time in their lives." And an anesthesiologist says, "The income is nice but not an absolute need." What he really enjoys is "the challenge of new anesthesiology agents and being part of a paradigm shift" in his field. There's a sixty-five-year-old businessman who enjoys giving back to others and a sixty-seven-year-old social service provider who feels that he is making a difference for his clients. And there are older men, like Norman Bridwell and Henry Schniewind, who say they are working so they can help their adult children and their grandchildren financially.

Norman Bridwell, the creator of *Clifford, the Big Red Dog* and other stories, is beloved by children (and their parents) all over the country and the world. Norman, eighty-four, helped Clifford, his publisher, and his fans to celebrate Clifford's Big Five-O in September 2012. Children and their teachers won't let Norman stop working.

PROFILE: NORMAN R. BRIDWELL

Norman Bridwell has been working for more than six decades. He feels *obligated* to keep working because he gets letters every week from children and teachers asking for another story. Were it not for Norman, Clifford the

Big Red Dog would never have been born let alone celebrating his fiftieth birthday (in human years). Norman is the author and illustrator of the beloved literary classic as well as other children's books about witches and funny-not-scary monsters. His Clifford series has more than 126 million books in print in thirteen languages. Clifford's animated television series, in its twelfth season on PBS Kids, is seen in dozens of countries. In honor of the Big Birthday, Clifford's publisher, Scholastic, presented a live Clifford musical in theaters and performing arts centers nationwide from October 2012 through March 2013. Scholastic also ran a Be Big Campaign, a contest promoting community action that demonstrates Clifford's BIG ideas for making the world a better place.

Clifford's September 24, 2012, birthday celebration in New York City was webcast to more than five thousand classrooms around the country and Scholastic made it available as an app. For the event, Broadway was closed off temporarily when Scholastic unfurled a nine-story banner down the front of its building. Norman answered questions from kids and from TV host Diane Sawyer. In the evening, Norman was reunited with four of his ex-editors (the ones still alive, he was quick to inform me). One of them was the Harper & Row acquisitions editor who had looked at his unique drawings of a red horse-sized bloodhound fifty years ago and told him he was not a very good artist—if he added a story to the pictures, that might help. It certainly did.

For eighty-four-year-old Norman, the celebration was exhilarating but overwhelming and exhausting. Nevertheless, he was glad that his wife, Norma, had insisted that they make the trip from their home on Martha's Vineyard to attend. Their daughter—the *real* Emily Elizabeth, who plays a prominent role in the Clifford stories—and a seventeen-year-old granddaughter also attended. Emily, a pre-K teacher and art teacher, told the press that when she and her younger brother, Tim, were small children, they did not realize that their father's drawings and stories about the big-hearted dog were enjoyed by children everywhere; they thought the stories were theirs alone. (That may be one of the stories' many appeals for young readers today.)

Norman has been making up stories and doing funny drawings since his own childhood in Kokomo, Indiana. "I had four dogs and a vivid imagination when I was a boy," he recalls. After attending art school in Indianapolis and at Cooper Union in New York City, he became a commercial artist, working (when he could) as a freelance filmstrip and slide illustrator. In 1962, Clifford was born and that all changed. "I never dreamed Clifford would live fifty years. If I'd known, I would have written him sooner," Norman tells me.

He goes on to explain why he can't stop working. "It's the letters from kids and teachers that pull me back into it. I get the greatest satisfaction from knowing that I have entertained children. Children are always a treat for me. And teachers tell me that Clifford gets their students started as readers." Adults learning English as a second language may also get to know Clifford. Norman takes pleasure in recounting the story of a young Chinese man who told him that he was helped to learn English by reading Clifford books. He liked the illustrations, became an artist himself, and now owns a graphic design studio.

Norman receives some fifty letters per week and answers all of them himself. He used to make school visits, but he doesn't do that anymore because declining health has forced him to curtail his travel. He thinks it is important to encourage kids to be proud of who they are and what they do. Someone may criticize their work—editors, for example, may reject it—but they shouldn't give up. "You never know who the child will become, what he or she is capable of accomplishing some day, perhaps as an artist or a writer. Still, that's a hard way to earn a living. Many want to do it, and few succeed. I was fortunate to have fifty years of success creating books, despite a few flops along the way."

Even though the recession and ongoing economic slump have affected book sales to schools and individuals have less money these days for purchasing books, Clifford and Norman are still hugely popular. "I approve the television scripts about Clifford, but I don't write them. Ironically, the television programs compete with my books," Norman observes.

After undergoing a quadruple bypass, Norman suffered a second heart attack. His cardiologist told him that there wasn't much more he could do for him. The doctor gave him two more years to live, and that was several years ago. "I am going downhill rapidly and probably don't have much time left until the end," Norman says matter-of-factly, "so I am never bored with my leisure time." When he is not answering the mail, Norman enjoys reading a good book, such as a history of the French Revolution or a World War II story. In addition, he and his wife come to Boston regularly for Norma's art classes at the Museum of Fine Arts and the occasional doctor's appointment. Norman tells me how proud he is of his wife for donating her paintings to Vineyard charities.

Although he still enjoys sketching and drawing, since the second heart attack Norman has found it harder to come up with story ideas that he hasn't already implemented. He has always been especially fond of turning things around to get a different viewpoint, thinking about what a real dog would do and imagining what clumsy Clifford would try to do and the trouble he would cause. These days, an editor often suggests story lines to him, and Norman produces the illustrations. Happily, there are at least two or three more Clifford adventures and witch stories in the pipeline.

Henry Schniewind, a psychiatrist, actually has two other chief reasons for working at age seventy-five besides helping his three children and their growing families: supporting humanitarian aid in a variety of forms and donating to a scholarship fund for older students at the Berklee College of Music that he set up a decade ago after he himself studied piano there.

> At this point the travel involved in visiting each of the children once a year (in France, Oregon, and Florida) and the donations and the taxes mean that I continue to work. I consider it an easy obligation to pay back some of what I received all along. No one is self-made. It takes a "village." So I am continuing to pay my "rent" to the "village" that helped me along in the hope that it will make the journey a bit easier for some other people. Altruistic? Yes. But since this feels right and is gratifying, I am not drained by it. I am fortunate to have good health still and to have my "marbles." So why not keep working and supporting?

Henry admits to being unsettled for a while by turning seventy-five, becoming a grandparent, and ascending to the oldest generation in his family.

> It was not easy landing at this stage of life. For the better part of a year I was rather out of sorts over it and not quite sure how to come to terms with it. Freud said the most important things in life are *lieben und arbeiten* (to love and to work). My professional training also taught me that one gets past this kind of denial by acknowledging and accepting what is, giving voice to it,

grieving, and regrouping. That's easier to say than to do, however. Then, one morning on my way to work, a poem came to mind that captured my reality and my feelings exactly and I burst into tears. That was the beginning of moving on into the next stage.

Here is the poem, "Generations," that Henry composed:

> We who confidently
> Rode the crest of the wave
> Are now about to break on the beach
> And come to rest.

Quite a few men say they "love," "like," "enjoy," or "have a passion for" what they do because it is interesting or fun. A seventy-two-year-old doctor says, "I love work. I can't imagine sitting home doing nothing. I will continue to work as long as I am doing useful things." Engineers seem to be especially content with their jobs, based on the frequency with which I heard the "love my work" refrain from them. (It occurred to me as I was reading a *New Yorker* article on the history of culinary revolution that the engineers to whom we are indebted for versatile and efficient kitchen equipment, for example, the microwave oven and the Cuisinart food processor, must have taken great pleasure in knowing how much their inventions were appreciated.[2]) That goes for engineer Don Brick equally well, the eighty-five-year-old self-employed businessman and consultant on LPR software systems (whom you met in chapter 6).

Like the men, the professionals who are the subjects in *Women Still at Work* cite myriad reasons for persisting in the labor force. Most commonly, the women find their work satisfying and meaningful when they feel they are being productive. There is complete agreement between the men and the women on this point: 91 percent of both genders give it as the top reason. They also agree about putting their considerable abilities, skills, and professional training to good use, although more of the women give it as a reason than the men (85 percent and 74 percent, respectively). For both men and women, enjoying their clients, patients, students, or customers is a very appealing part of the job. Sixty-nine percent of the men give it as a reason (taking third place on the list), and 80 percent of the women are in accord.

John Sayour's credo is to find different ways to brighten the lives of others, whether they are his business clients, students, family members, or younger people he is mentoring. He is seventy-one and plans to work another fifteen years.

PROFILE: JOHN A. SAYOUR

John Sayour started out as a street kid from the Bay Ridge section of Brooklyn. The neighborhood called him "Big John," and the nickname stuck. He is still called Big John in the financial and insurance circles in which he works, even nationally. Something else that stayed with him from the early days was Red Skelton's credo. In the mid-1950s when John was a teenager, he loved watching Red Skelton's variety show on television. He would start laughing at Gertrude and Heathcliff, the Two Seagulls, even before the cross-eyed, wing-flapping comic ever said a word. What really affected John, though, was an interview Skelton gave right after his son died of leukemia. When Skelton was asked why he had gone on with his show so soon after losing his son, he replied that he believed he was given the gift of brightening someone's life, and his son would have wanted him to continue doing just that. This made such an impression on John that he decided to adopt Skelton's credo as his own. "It became my driving force, my mission to make someone smile, to make someone's day brighter. I saw that as my job, and, after fifty-plus years in the workforce, I still do."

John owned a ladies lingerie business in the garment industry in New York City for twenty-three years. The business was highly profitable, enabling John to live a country club lifestyle in a Westchester suburb. However, in 1982, when a study reported that the intimate apparel industry as a whole was growing at only 2 percent per year and his business was growing at 15 to 20 percent per year, he decided it was time to close up shop and find another industry. "It was just a matter of time until a larger fish would eat me," he recalls.

John then joined the Northwestern Mutual Life Insurance Company (NML) in a Connecticut satellite office as an exclusive "captive" agent, although he remained his own boss. "I don't like to have to answer to anyone.

My freedom is important to me and important to my clients," he explains. He stayed with NML for twenty-six years, producing at the top 6 percent of the industry levels (becoming a member of the prestigious Million Dollar Round Table), until he retired at age seventy. Retirement proved temporary, however. His strong reputation as a mentor/coach for NML agents landed him a new full-time job in the same field in 2011. The New York Life Insurance Company recruited him to mentor the carrier's new agents in the Southern Connecticut office, and he continues to sell insurance and help individual and business clients manage financial risk.

When I asked John what is most fulfilling about his work, he said his greatest satisfaction comes from imparting good financial sense to his clients, for example, getting a young family to invest in insurance products. "I try to get them to shift money from spending on nonessentials (wants) to investing in savings for the future. We know that the top three necessities are shelter, food, and clothing. Too often for families, consumer gadgets like extra TVs come next. I want them to understand that *savings* should be number four. When it clicks, they buy into the counseling and advice more than any sales pitch per se."

For example, John is a staunch advocate of selling insurance to parents on their children, after they have taken care of their own needs. He is especially happy for clients of his who purchased a policy for their autistic child *before* the disabling medical condition was diagnosed. The value that builds up in the policy belongs to the child. In addition, a benefit on that policy provides the guarantee that the child, as a grownup, can buy up to an additional $1.2 million of life insurance with *no* regard to the medical condition and with *no* rate increases. His future needs can be met. Those particular clients are eternally grateful.

In addition to his primary job, John has been teaching a course on insurance at Westchester Community College and an industry leadership course. However, he would like to teach undergraduates at the university level. When he approached Sacred Heart University about an adjunct position, he was told that he needed an MBA. He went back to their graduate school and in 2012 added MBA to the alphabet soup of professional credentials that follow his name—CFP™, ChFC, CLTC, LUTCF, CLU, RHU, REBC. The initials indicate completion of the many rigorous courses for industry education required of a board Certified Financial Planner, Chartered Financial Consultant, and so on. "This is the first time I'm actually *applying* for a job," he laughs. "If there is a Sacred Heart opening, I hope to share my leadership skills and my business ownership experience with the students, most of whom will end up working in small businesses after they graduate. They will need guidance to manage and survive whatever is coming down the road in the next twenty-five years. You could say that their initial guidance will be my legacy."

Another of John's goals is to continue to grow personally and to continue to be important in people's lives. As he has done for some forty years, John draws inspiration from and recharges his batteries at a retreat in the Weston, Massachusetts, Jesuit Seminary. He loves "people probing," learning about lives. "I find the *hero* in each person I meet. Something extraordinary always emerges when I listen intently to their stories." Big John's four children and six grandchildren are spread out all over the map—Norway, California, Connecticut, and Vancouver. "They, and my working friends, most of whom are all younger than I am, think I'm nuts to keep working at the pace that I do, but they know it's what I love to do and it's the source of my energy and my enthusiasm."

John would be in good shape financially if he retired. Despite having given up most of his clients when he moved from Northwestern Mutual to New York Life, he was having the best year of his career when we spoke. So long as his health holds up, John intends to keep working for another fifteen years. "I'll be sharing the gifts that God gave me. Giving to others gives so much back to me." To this end, he attends the Alfred E. Smith Memorial Foundation dinner annually, a benefit for the Catholic Charities of New York. (At the 2012 event, presidential candidates Mitt Romney and Barack Obama delighted the audience with jokes told at each other's expense and their own.) John liked to tell people, with a gentle smile on his face, that "Romney and Obama were joining him for dinner that evening."

It would be easy to say that John practices what he preaches when he endeavors to impart the knowledge and skills he has accumulated over the years, but I much prefer the imagery he uses to describe his approach to teaching and advising: "If Reason is the rudder, Passion is the sails, and Kindness is the hull, we can sail the seas anywhere. That's a sublime gift to give the world."

Even when professionals are fairly well off, they can be working for financial reasons, such as maintaining health benefits. As a seventy-two-year-old

Table 7.2.   Finance-related Reasons for Working Late in Life (by percentage)

Reason	Men	Women
Need the income	48	57
Save in 401(k) plan, other retirement plan	27	30
At peak of career (high earning power, authority)	25	30
Boost Social Security benefits	22	28
Rising health insurance costs	15	21
Other financial pressures	11	16
Accrue pension benefits	14	15

businessman told me, "If I had a lot of money, I would not work. I would travel and write and keep fit. Now I need income, but I am lucky to be doing something very interesting." Unless one happens to be ultra-rich and belongs to the vaunted "1 percent" of Americans, it is hard to shake the sense of economic malaise besetting our country (and much of the rest of the world). Few are immune to feeling little twinges or sharp pangs of financial insecurity. Let's compare older men's and older women's finance-related reasons for working by viewing their tallied responses side by side, as shown in table 7.2.

The side-by-side comparison tells us that older men and women have very similar priorities about staying in the paid workforce, but women perceive financial pressures to be greater: more than half of the women indicate that they need the income; less than half of the men do. The women rightly believe they are in rougher shape than the men vis-à-vis retirement savings, Social Security benefits, rising health insurance costs, and other financial pressures. Women are somewhat more likely than men to cite as a reason for persisting in the labor force the higher earning power that comes with being at the peak of one's career. Actually, the gender difference regarding peak of career (25 percent of the men versus 30 percent of the women) is marginal. Both men and women said that they got a new job in the same field or changed careers midstream or later, thereby accumulating fewer years in the current job and putting peak of career out of reach, but that accounts for merely 20 percent of the men and 30 percent of the women. It could be surmised that the women got a delayed and possibly shakier start on the career ladder than men and they want to hold onto what they worked hard to accomplish.

More than half (58 percent) of the women told me that they took time out to raise a family (as I myself did). A few more did so to care for an adult family member. Three men had taken time out for childrearing and five had provided adult caregiving. Except for those few, the men were not delayed by family care, so their low response rate to the peak-of-career question is harder to explain. The median years in the current job—eighteen—is one clue to "peak" status being remote, even after working for many, many years overall. Then, too, perhaps they (and many of the women) simply did not view it as salient, compared to other reasons for staying on the job.

There is almost no difference between the men and the women with respect to accruing pension benefits, most likely because pensions are quickly becoming obsolete. The BLS reports that steady retirement income from a pension is no longer assured for many workers, as risk has been transferred from the employer to the eventual retiree. Traditional "pay out" plans are being replaced by defined contribution or "pay in" plans in which the employee pays in and the company contributes a specified amount. Overall, fewer older women receive pension income than men do, and, if women do get pension benefits, the median pension is slightly more than half of what men receive.[3]

In addition to job satisfaction; using abilities, skills, and training; and the financial reasons discussed here, older women are wont to say they fear boredom and an atrophied intellect if they aren't working, and there are echoes of this concern from almost half of the men. For instance, an attorney in his eighties says, "I am staying in good physical and mental health so I'll be able to communicate intelligently," and a sixty-seven-year-old wine retailer says he needs "the mental stimulation that comes from being challenged and from working with other people." A sixty-eight-year-old videographer desires "to learn more each day and to keep my mind as sharp as possible." Many men and women equate working with staving off boredom. "I am not sure what I would do all day if I didn't work. I don't sit still well and get bored easily," confesses that sixty-eight-year-old entrepreneurship consultant whom I quoted in the previous chapter.

Originally in advertising and filmmaking, seventy-year-old Tom Lazarus is a playwright, screenwriter, script consultant, writing teacher, and author of *The Last Word: Definitive Answers to All Your Screenwriting Questions*. He has been teaching in the UCLA writer's program for the past twenty years. His play, *Do unto Others*, was part of Winterfest 2013 in Los Angeles the same month that his play, *Stevie Stern as Kick Ass Mary*, was staged in Santa Monica. Tom is forthright about what compels him to work:

I'm an artist and continue to create as I continue to work. In many ways I'm defined by my work and take great satisfaction in the process of working. The process is more important than the product, as I work all the time and enjoy it all the time. I find that when I'm not working, when I don't have a project rolling around in my head, I have a tendency to start drifting down psychologically. For that reason, ever since I can remember, my way of dealing with that is being productive, impossibly productive. I have to figure out why that's a negative . . . though I have my suspicions.

Mentoring early careerists is another contributor to heightened satisfaction with work because it combines helping others and enjoying colleagues and coworkers with using one's abilities, skills, and training. One sixty-nine-year-old businessman says he spends a great deal of time mentoring and cheerleading because the shrinking workforce is creating tremendous challenges for younger workers, challenges he never had to deal with. For a seventy-year-old city manager who runs his own firm, a prime motivator for staying on the job is mentoring his younger employees. "For me (and others my age with whom I have talked), mentoring is one of the major rewards of working," he says. Like this city manager, many professionals who were fortunate enough to be guided along their career path by older colleagues now enjoy passing along what they know to the next generation and, in the process, giving back to the field. Bruce Chabner, Jim Levinson, Larry Lucchino, Chuck Willie, Steve Grossman, John Kaneb, and John Sayour, whose profiles you have read, exemplify the powerful influence mentors and role models of different generations can exert on career choice, conduct, and duration. The men foresee mentoring early careerists becoming part of their professional legacy.

Benefits could be another reason for working late. Many men and women, regardless of age, hold onto a job because they depend on the benefits as well as the income. In addition to compensation, employee benefits may include the following categories: health and wellness, retirement savings and planning, career development, and workplace flexibility. Health insurance is particularly prized, especially when one's employer pays the lion's share of the cost. Telecommuting, as it is often known, is a family-friendly benefit that allows employees with young children as well as employees responsible for elder care the flexibility to work from home for at least a portion of the week. The SHRM says organizations offering some form of telecommuting has increased.[4] When next year's SHRM survey results are reported, it will be interesting to see whether employers continued to allow workplace flexibility, or, like Yahoo! CEO Marissa Mayer, revoked the privilege of working from home.

Three-quarters of the men I surveyed have a few or many benefits contributed partially or wholly by their current employer (or purchased for themselves, as some self-employed men are able to do). Their benefits include the following (in descending order of frequency): health insurance, retirement savings plan, vacation days, life insurance, sick leave, pension, and disability insurance. Other types of benefits contributed by some employers are: long-term care insurance; dental, vision, or legal coverage; shares in the company; an automobile; and professional development opportunities. With respect to professional development as a benefit, relatively few men say that opportunities for training, retraining, and updating skills help to keep them on the job (8 percent). Women in slightly higher numbers agree that such opportunities are minor reasons for continuing to work into one's senior years (11 percent).

One-quarter of the men currently have no benefits, most likely because they are part-timers, self-employed, or collecting benefits from a previous employer. (Some of the men rely on their wife's benefits.) Thirty percent of the men continue to receive benefits from a previous employer, including some of the men with no benefits from the current employer and some who get benefits both from their current job as well as a previous job. Just as older male professionals are faring better than older female professionals in terms of finances, the men are more apt to receive benefits from their current employer than the women are. The gap is large—75 percent of the men versus 50 percent of the women.

Deriving satisfaction from one's work and receiving benefits are key incentives for staying on the job, provided that one remains healthy. Many people have to stop working temporarily or permanently when their health fails, no matter their age. Fortunately, nearly two-thirds of older men (63 percent) say that their health is good and they have high energy. (A slightly higher percentage of older women [66 percent] are similarly blessed.) Good health is both a *reason* to keep working—in fact it is one of the men's top five reasons (see table 7.1)—and an essential qualification or *prerequisite* for working in the senior years. The small number of men and women who told me that they are troubled by physical ailments or limitations are, nonetheless, all still working. They are unwilling to be defeated by their problems. To take one example, here is how a sixty-seven-year-old business owner gamely summarizes his current situation:

> Life turned out differently than expected, and entrepreneurial pursuits make the most sense for me. An attempt at retirement (sort of) was not fulfilling, even with charity work, family, and sports. In the past ten years I have beaten TB, had a heart attack, survived septicemia, and been hit by a car while on a bike. But I will not abandon a positive approach and an effort to live a full life. I spend time exercising to be able to work and maintain mental and physical health.

In addition to considerations of health and fitness, the next chapter looks at a variety of other significant personal challenges and concerns, such as family responsibilities, competing demands on one's time, finances, and issues in the workplace, that are associated with remaining in the workforce.

8

Personal Challenges and Concerns

Old age is like a minefield; if you see footprints leading to the other side, step in them. —George E. Vaillant, *Aging Well*

Next we consider family responsibilities, competing demands on one's time, financial and health concerns, and issues in the workplace. Working during one's senior years is not all fun and games, of course. When I asked my survey respondents to indicate their personal challenges and concerns (allowing for multiple responses), just over one-third (35 percent) said they have none. "It's not an issue yet, but I am on guard," remarks a sixty-nine-year-old lawyer. The major concerns expressed by some of the men are not specifically job related. A seventy-five-year-old engineer worries and wonders what he will do after retirement. A professor, age sixty-eight, is "watching this country's political leaders' failure to create a more just and equal society." He is not very optimistic about our country's future. And a businessman, age sixty-three, is stressed by "the rising cost of health care, potential changes in the tax rates, the worldwide economic climate and its effect on the United States, and increasing US debt."

Thirty-five percent of the men admit to experiencing a little or a lot of stress or fatigue because of their work. A seventy-five-year-old physician in private practice says he doesn't have the stamina he had in earlier years and he gets "stressed out" more easily at work and in nonwork situations. "Overall, though," he concludes, "it's the best time of my life." An eighty-six-year-old physician is bothered by "the odious burden of paperwork." An eighty-two-year-old professor decries "education becoming ever more prescriptive and proscriptive." A sixty-three-year-old doctor laments "the rapidly changing political landscape in medicine, making good patient care a lesser priority." The women I studied are more prone to suffering stress and fatigue from their work than are the men—44 percent of the women (a 9 percent difference) testify to having a little or a lot of stress and fatigue. It is hard to know whether women are simply more "upfront" about it than the men (who may not want to appear vulnerable), or whether they actually do find their responsibilities more wearing. The fact that fewer older women than older men can say they have no personal challenges or concerns (21 percent of the women, 35 percent of the men) seems to corroborate *both* possibilities. Further evidence of women having work-related stress: more women than men say they are bothered by a pervasively negative organizational climate at work (nineteen women, fourteen men).

Twenty-one percent of the men say they do not have enough time for everything they want or need to do. This can be recreational time or time for volunteering, and it can be time they would like to spend with a spouse, children, and grandchildren. It can, as one fellow grumbles, be finding time to organize and dispose of accumulated possessions that are no longer needed but which have personal memories attached to them. "Working on multiple projects about sixty hours per week, plus taking care of the house, etc., leaves little time for family and friends," frets a sixty-seven-year-old businessman. "It is difficult to balance it all" is a common refrain from these older men (and a frequent regret of older women, as well).

Physical limitations concern 19 percent of the men. Some, like a sixty-five-year-old researcher, are resigned to "the normal physical changes of aging." Others, like a seventy-year-old businessman, acknowledge, "Isn't it all about health? If you have it there is a lot to do, learn, and share." One fellow, a seventy-five-year-old attorney, worries, "By the time I decide to quit, I may be too disabled to enjoy activities with my family." Consistent with national statistics showing that older women on average are healthier and live longer than older men, 5 percent fewer women than men are troubled by physical ailments or limitations of any kind.

Dick Winslow is a psychiatrist in Washington State who works in public sector mental health clinics evaluating and treating low-income patients, many of whom are refugees from war-torn countries. Despite having a bad back and a rare neuro-ophthalmological disorder, Dick, age seventy, has no intentions of retiring. That would mean giving up his identity as a working professional and his role as a contributing person.

PROFILE: RICHARD S. WINSLOW JR.

Depending on where and when you befriended Richard Winslow, you might call him Dixie, his high school nickname; Homer, a college sobriquet referring to Winslow Homer; or Dick, as he is known around Mercer Island, Washington, where he and his wife, Susan, live today. A long conversation with Dick reveals him to be a man who carefully weighs his decisions, a caring individual and a modest one.

Professionally, he is known as "Doctor." For some thirty-three years Dick has practiced psychiatry, evaluating and treating patients in public sector mental health clinics. They are low-income patients and the services are subsidized. He deliberately chose cross-cultural psychiatry over private practice because he gets to work with diverse, often immigrant populations, many of whom were severely traumatized in their countries of origin. "I have learned to help people who escaped with their lives from war-torn places, such as Southeast Asia, Bosnia, East Africa, and the Middle East, as well as American-born people of all ethnicities who are out of the mainstream." He also enjoys being part of a multidisciplinary staff, sharing the patients with social workers and other therapists. "Then too," he adds, "it helps to be an *older* clinician since many patients like to have a psychiatrist who is older than they are."

Dick also holds down a second job reviewing disability claims for the Social Security Administration part time. He insists that it is not for the money—he likes the income, but does not need it—rather it is for the intellectual challenge. "I get to see thousands of medical records for patients whose psychiatric problems are often interwoven with physical problems. I can compare the quality of medical treatment available not only in the Pacific Northwest but also nationwide. That's a real eye-opener."

Until the summer of 2012, Dick had a third part-time job at a different public mental health clinic, an arrangement that suited him because he enjoyed the variety of options it afforded. However, his seventieth birthday that summer was the turning point. With the switch to electronic recordkeeping, the bureaucracy at the clinic had become more focused on documentation than patient care, and staff caseloads had increased. "I was expected to save time by typing in my notes as the patient was speaking, but I refused to be a transcriptionist. A patient deserves eye contact!" His supervisor had been hinting that it was time to go, and the department chair wrote about department priorities and questioned whether Dick would be rehired. Given the negative organizational climate, it seemed a good time to leave. The clinic did in fact promptly replace him with a woman half his age. He knows she will do a fine job, in part because he had supervised her during her training. Dick comments on the contrast between the cultures at the two clinics—the one he left and the one where he still works. "Where I am now, staff respect me; they elected me president of the medical staff, or 'senior dude.' It must be the white hair that makes me look so wise!"

Hearing about Dick's life experiences and career moves, it is not hard to discern patterns. In 1964, his senior year at Harvard, Dick traveled with the Krokodiloes, the college's a cappella singing group, on a trip to India. "I wasn't the group's leader. That was my talented friend, Jim Levinson. I was just the tallest! But, seriously, that trip opened my eyes to the wider world." (Jim's profile is in chapter 3.) Dick spent the next two years in the Peace Corps in the high mountains of Peru. "Among my accomplishments were acquiring proficiency in Spanish (which is useful to this day in my practice) and lending my height to a Peruvian basketball team." Once back in the states, for the next three years he did graduate work in Russian language and literature at the University of Washington. By 1969, events at home and abroad—the civil rights movement and the war in Vietnam—seemed more compelling than laboring over a doctoral dissertation. Dick decided to study Vietnamese intensively for a year so that he could do civilian community development work in Vietnam. "Aside from meeting some wonderful Vietnamese people and having the opportunity to speak the language, that was a disappointing experience—I did not get to do much humanitarian work; instead I was just a cog in the military wheel."

Dick returned to the University of Washington to study for an MD. Late in the program he did a rotation with three family doctors who scheduled their patients in strict seven-minute intervals. A seriously ill patient would get twenty-one minutes, everyone else would get either seven or fourteen minutes. "I could see that a doctor could stay in good shape by running from room to room, patient to patient, but as a 'people' person, that did not fit my personality or my pace. I wanted to take as much time as needed with each patient, which is the reason I selected psychiatry as my area of specialization." After his psychiatric residency, in 1980 Dick moved to Alaska with Susan and their firstborn child. Susan had been a special education teacher, but she retrained in Alaska to become a labor and delivery nurse (her profession today). Dick treated Native Alaskans, some of whom spoke little English, so he often worked through interpreters. "While I was amazed by the differences between their culture and mine, I was comfortable in the environment. That was the start of my interest in community psychiatry and working with people who lacked all sorts of advantages we take for granted."

Dick wants me to be sure to identify him as a loving husband and parent, and now grandparent, in addition to being a psychiatrist. "I have been lucky in many respects. Now that our two children are grown and past the difficult stage, we have become even closer to them. I don't even mind when they tease me about my idiosyncrasies, like my fashion sense and the way I comb my hair. And we adore our toddler granddaughter, who is the happiest, brightest part of our lives right now. My biggest regret is not being able to pick her up because of my bad back."

Another impairment a few years ago was a rare neuro-ophthalmological disorder (blepharospasm) that made his blink reflex go haywire and his eyelids shut tight. He couldn't drive and at work had to reassure his patients that he wasn't falling asleep listening to them and he wasn't on drugs. "Groundbreaking surgery has mostly fixed the problem, but I still get injections—it's Botox of all things!" True to form, Dick sometimes goes to medical conventions to help staff the booth of the blepharospasm disorder foundation. "I try to educate other doctors about the disorder. Lots of doctors come from Latin America and I can converse about blepharospasm in Spanish with them."

In his free time, Dick enjoys watching British television shows with his wife. He takes full advantage of Washington state's policy allowing residents age sixty or older to audit college or university classes for a nominal fee. He has audited courses in history and in astronomy, a subject that has fascinated him since childhood when he became an amateur sky observer. He also participates in a book group composed of a dozen men who enjoy getting together every four to six weeks to discuss a book and talk about sports, politics, and the economy.

Ever modest, Dick asks me not to hold him up as an example for other men. "It is hard to give up one's identity as a working professional. How would I spend my time? I am not trying to achieve anything—not fame, power, or a promotion. I just don't wish to lose my role as a contributing person. That wish doesn't make me anything special." This point I have to refute. Dick (Dixie when I knew him) was voted "The Most Respected" boy in our high school class, and that vote was certainly prophetic.

Nineteen percent of my respondents are troubled by the decreased value of their investments or other financial setbacks experienced since the onset of the recession. For instance, the recession forced Neil Tift (profiled in chapter 5) and his wife to take a big loss on the sale of their home in 2007. Other examples are men who are providing financial support to grown children with families and a teacher who is depressed because he cannot afford to do the things that interest him. On the whole, however, most of the men would seem to be in good shape financially. Here again we find national statistics borne out—more women than men are worried about the declining value of their investments or other financial difficulties (one out of three women in my study compared to 19 percent of the men).

The Great Recession took a toll on Badi Foster's retirement savings when the endowment of the Washington, DC–based philanthropy he worked for was wiped out, taking his retirement account with it. His multifaceted career with international overtones and stints in higher education had culminated in a decade at the helm of the Phelps-Stokes Fund. When he turned seventy, Badi took emeritus status at the fund. He continues there part time because he is committed to the fund's mission—fundamental social change through education and service—and also does consulting.

PROFILE: BADI G. FOSTER

The first thing Badi Foster told me was, "Barack Obama isn't the only person who grew up with a funny name. Mine is pronounced Buh dee.'" He went on to explain, "My parents were Bahá'ís and they named me after a martyr of the faith. Bahá'i was founded in the mid-nineteenth century by Bahá u'lláh to spread a message of peace and unity. Our core belief says that all humanity is one family. In the world's current state of moral collapse and strife, that offers a potent reminder."[1]

Badi's parents, an interracial couple, met through Bahá'i. When they were in college during the Depression, they were pained by the political and social ferment that beset blacks so harshly. A Louis Armstrong song invoking the burdens of skin color, "Oh, Lord! What did I do to be so black and blue?" spoke volumes to the activist couple. They were inspired by construction of a Bahá'i House of Worship north of downtown Chicago in Wilmette, Illinois, open to persons of all races and religions.[2] In the late 1950s they decided to move their family from Chicago to Africa, believing that they could propagate their faith and lead exemplary lives there. Consequently, Badi went to high school in Tangier, Morocco, and learned to speak Moroccan Arabic, Spanish, and French. He returned to the States, earned a bachelor's degree in international relations from the University of Denver, followed by a master's in politics from Princeton. He was awarded a series of fellowships and completed a doctorate in politics, again at Princeton.

Instead of aiming for advancement in the professoriate when he left Princeton—the "false gods" of perks and tenure were not for him—he embarked on a different sort of career in higher education. He led planning for a new college of public service at Rutgers University, and then accomplished the same thing at the University of Massachusetts in Boston. He also lent his expertise to the Ford Foundation on higher education projects in Uganda, Tanzania, Zambia, and Tunisia. One of his mentors, Paul Ylvisaker, recruited Badi to Harvard's Graduate School of Education where he spent several years in various teaching and administrative positions. In the 1980s and 1990s he ventured into the for-profit sector where he developed and implemented corporate education and training programs in the fields of health care and transportation. During this segment of his career, in 1990 he was tapped to chair the board of the National Institute of Literacy, a position requiring Senate confirmation. However, Badi was disillusioned by the many barriers in the business world to creating viable black-owned enterprises; he returned to higher education in 1998 as director of the Lincoln Filene Center for Citizenship and Public Affairs at Tufts University.

Badi has spent the past twelve years of his career as president and CEO of the Phelps-Stokes Fund, a Washington, DC–based philanthropy that fosters equity and unity among diverse ethnic and racial groups while promoting the core value of education for human development as its primary mission. Phelps-Stokes claims to be America's oldest continuously operating foundation serving the needs of African Americans, Native Americans, Africans in Africa, Afro Latinos in the Caribbean and South America, and the rural and urban poor. In his philanthropic work at Phelps-Stokes, Badi has found his true calling. "I work with enlightened people whose mission is educating *my people*. The fund resonates with my most cherished values: they all converge around fundamental social change through education and service performed on behalf of those who have been wronged." To illustrate how he has clarified what this work means to him, Badi shares a metaphor about three paper cups. The first is the man, the second is his job, and the third is the organization. There are three questions to ask about each—What? For whom? Why? The three cups may or may not fit together or may be upside down, depending on the answers. For Badi the fit is perfect. "We tend to focus on the mind and the body, but nurturing the spirit creates energy, a special dimension that allows you to do extraordinary things."

In 2012 when he was turning seventy, Badi took emeritus status at the fund. He continues there part time, consults for the governmental Department of Choco in Colombia part time, and intermittently studies his family's history. "My grandmother's grandmother was a slave. When I got into the dreadful history of slavery here in Loudoun County, Virginia, I developed what I call 'PTSD slave syndrome' that forced me to stop my research for a while."

In addition to enjoying congruence or harmony among the personal, professional, and spiritual aspects of his life, Badi has another compelling reason for continuing to work—when the Great Recession wiped out the Phelps-Stokes Fund's endowment, Badi lost the entire retirement account that he and his wife, Juanita, were counting on. Badi told me this with a remarkable degree of equanimity. I might have attributed his calmness regarding such a calamity to Badi's faith had he not shared a part of his family's history that had taught him a significant life lesson. Badi and Juanita were the proud parents of two sons, Nabil and Qasim, born six years apart in the 1970s. The younger boy, Qasim, had a peanut allergy which he and his family knew how to manage. However, at school Qasim was given something to eat that sent him into anaphylactic shock. School and emergency personnel failed to recognize the severity of the reaction and did not act in time to save the child. After Badi and Juanita buried their nine-year-old son in 1986, nothing that life threw at them in subsequent years could compare in importance. Badi reflects somberly, "Qasim's death put everything in perspective and was a catalyst for many things in our lives." Then he adds on a lighter note, "Some good can come from such a horrible tragedy—we have not had a family argument since 1986!"

With age comes the possibility of losing dear friends and loved ones—painful losses that are hard on everyone. As spiritual leader Ram Dass says in his blog on Conscious Aging, "Although relationships change in all stages of life, it often seems harder to find new connections to replace the ones we lose as we age."[3] Yet, only 12 percent of the men (and even fewer of the women) acknowledge such loss as a personal challenge or concern. The somewhat greater tendency for men to indicate this may merely be attributable to the male respondents being four years older on average than the females I surveyed—average age seventy for the men, average age sixty-six for the women—and thus even more apt to have experienced personal losses. A sixty-nine-year-old translator tells me that he is pained by his parents' deaths. One older man is saddened by "the loss of contact with successfully launched adult children who live far away." Still others (10 percent of the male respondents) are concerned about elderly parents or relatives or an infirm spouse in their care. Whether or not Ram Dass has credibility with men and women old enough to recall his earlier persona (Richard Alpert) and LSD, his recommendations for dealing with feelings of loneliness and isolation in the elder years make good sense. They range from caring for others to connecting in cyberspace and being *in community* in various ways and through various media. That is why "Doing unto Others" is an apt title for the next chapter.

9

Doing unto Others

You don't stop running because you get old. You get old because you
stop running.—Jack Kirk, ninety-six-year-old super-runner, in Christopher
McDougall, *Born to Run*

Caring for others and contributing to one's community bring their own satis-
factions as well as burdens. Participation in the paid workforce, no matter how
enjoyable and rewarding, can leave scant free time for activities with family and
friends, relaxation and recreation, creative and cultural pursuits, travel, board
membership, and church, temple, or community service. This chapter discusses
how older professional men choose to spend the leisure time they do have and
compares their choices with those of older professional women.

According to the Bureau of Labor Statistics, 26.5 percent of Americans
(about 64.5 million people) were unpaid volunteers through or for an organization as of 2012.[1] The greatest number of volunteer hours went to religious,
educational or youth-service-related organizations, and social or community
service organizations. Women volunteer at a higher rate than men (23.2 percent of men, 29.5 percent of women) across all age groups, educational levels,
and other major demographic characteristics. The volunteer rate varies with
education level—the more education, the more engagement in volunteer
activities, including undertaking more than one volunteer job. Employed per-

sons (29.1 percent) volunteer more than unemployed persons (23.8 percent); part-timers are doing more volunteering than persons employed full time.

Aside from the small number of men who told me they have "no free time" or "little time to spare," most of the older men I surveyed somehow manage to find time to volunteer in addition to participating in the paid workforce—69 percent of the men are doing some type of volunteer work, such as community service, fundraising, or political activity. Peter Gossels epitomizes citizen service to the community—as portrayed in chapter 10, he served as moderator of the Wayland, Massachusetts, town meeting for thirty years. However, the role undertaken most frequently is that of trustee, board member, or board chairman. Their board service is for a museum or library, affordable housing agency, hospital, university, or nonprofit organization with a charitable/philanthropic, historical, arts, environmental, or sports orientation.

Stokley Towles's board service illustrates the meaning of his favorite quote from Winston Churchill: "We make a living by what we *get*; we make a life by what we *give*." Since transitioning from full-time to part-time work at Brown Brothers Harriman & Co. (BBH)—he is a partner at the oldest and largest private investment bank and securities firm in the country—Stokley has had more time for philanthropic and cultural pursuits. Among his volunteer positions was chairing the board of trustees of the Museum of Fine Arts in Boston and spearheading the fundraising campaign for the New American Wing of the museum. In addition, he and his wife funded one of the contemporary art galleries. At seventy-six, he sticks to a well-established routine because he is strengthened by the work environment and wants to stay up to speed.

PROFILE: STOKLEY P. TOWLES

Six years ago on the occasion of Stokley Towles's seventieth birthday, his three grown children presented him with a bound copy of "Towles's Familiar Quotations," a compendium of quotations chosen by Stokley's friends and family in his honor. Some of the quotes were from well-known individuals and some were Stokley's own wise or witty sayings. Taken together, they paint a loving portrait of a mature yet impish man.

"Success is getting paid for doing what you love to do." This quote from David Starr Jordan, Stanford University's first president, neatly sums up

Stokley's attitude toward his fifty-two-year career at BBH in Boston's financial district. He made general partner in 1978 and became a limited partner two years ago.

Riding up in the elevator to the nineteenth floor offices of BBH, a passenger can follow minute-by-minute stock market fluctuations registered by the DJIA and the NASDAQ. BBH is North America's oldest and largest partner-owned and managed bank. Founded in 1818 by the four Brown brothers, the company merged with Harriman Brothers & Co. and W. A. Harriman & Co. in 1931. The core functions of the new firm are commercial banking, investment advisory services, corporate finance, and custody, that is, providing a "warehouse" for international trading in which BBH settles the trades, holds securities for clients, and manages processes involving dividends and taxes, among other services. On a daily basis BBH computes the net asset value of mutual funds that are listed in newspapers across the country.

The custody part of BBH's business has grown rapidly since the early 1960s when a freshly minted Princeton Phi Beta Kappa, Harvard MBA-educated banker named Stokley Towles was hired. He was part of a small group responsible for developing custody into a thriving global product: BBH now has $3 trillion in assets in custody for clients in eighty to ninety countries today. "I'm an idea person. Compared to the 1950s when everything was done 'by the book,' the 1960s was a period when new ideas mattered more and more. My bosses were open-minded; they always listened, gave counsel, and supported my efforts. They were my role models and remained good friends, too."

Stokley has friends who have retired, and he meets with them over lunch where they muse about getting close to eighty, taking it one day at a time, and how it takes longer to do things. In his estimation, "If you retire at sixty or even sixty-five, you might have the energy to start another career or venture you're passionate about. You shouldn't wait too long! However, once you retire, people have less interest in what you say. When you're still working, you're assumed to be in touch and clients ask your opinion about business strategy." Thus, retirement's definitely not for him lest he lose *momentum*. His preferred routine is to get up every morning, buy a coffee and muffin, and go to the office. He wants to be *productive* and to be around people who appreciate his being around despite or because of his singularity: there are no others his age at BBH in Boston. "I benefit from structure and I enjoy interacting with people, so I'm strengthened by the work environment." His philosophy of life is to keep going until you can't, either because of poor health or no longer being useful. Two long-favored beliefs follow from this: "To him to whom much is given, much is required" and "You have to prove your value every day."

Having gradually transitioned from full-time to part-time work in his seventies, Stokley has been able to "slack off a bit," travel more, and devote more time to philanthropic and cultural pursuits. Not only does the BBH organization foster a good work-life balance for employees, Stokley personally is serious about the "much is required" admonition. Until three years ago he was chairman of the board of trustees of the Museum of Fine Arts in Boston. During his time at the helm, the Museum of Fine Arts successfully completed the largest fundraising campaign on behalf of a New England arts institution, topping its $500 million goal by $4 million and erecting the museum's dramatic New American Wing. He and his wife funded one of the seven new galleries dedicated to contemporary art collections, the Jeanne and Stokley Towles Gallery. He is also a trustee of Vincent Memorial Hospital, St. Philip's Church, and the Santa Barbara Art Museum in California.

Pictures of three handsome children have pride of place on Stokley's desk, alongside a paperback copy of *Rules of Civility*, the 2011 novel written by his son Amor Towles, whose day job is in the financial services field. Stokley raised his children to be independent, honest, hard-working, and active members of society. The word *persevering* gets special emphasis. He would like to think his eleven grandchildren will share these values.

Stokley told me of another transition that is under way. While he remains very committed to the arts and culture, he would like to become more active in educational and social issues that he cares about. There are a lot of people hurting from the economic downturn today who could use some help. It's a matter of finding the right way to be constructively involved. Two other quotations from his birthday book reflect this different yet equally important side of the man. The first comes from Winston Churchill: "We make a living by what we *get*; we make a life by what we *give*." The second is vintage Stokley: "Well, it's a good thing that we're doing. Don't you think? I always want to leave things a little better than I found them."

Longtime civil rights activist and political leader Leslie Burl McLemore devotes time to several volunteer positions in addition to his social justice and citizenship education work on behalf of the Fannie Lou Hamer National Institute on Citizenship and Democracy in Jackson, Mississippi. These include organizing an effort to restore a local cemetery, participating in a school-based mentoring program, advising the Mississippi Humanities Council, conducting voter registration for the NAACP, spearheading fundraising for scholarships at his alma mater, and serving on three civil rights–related commissions. Now seventy-two, he plans to contribute in one capacity or another for several more years.

PROFILE: LESLIE BURL MCLEMORE

Dr. Leslie Burl McLemore directs the Fannie Lou Hamer National Institute on Citizenship and Democracy in Jackson, Mississippi. Honoring the work of American voting rights activist and civil rights leader Fannie Lou Hamer, the institute's mission is "to promote positive social change by examining the tools and experiences of those who struggle to create, expand, and sustain civil rights, social justice, and citizenship." Its vision is "to nurture a generation of young people engaged in and committed to discourse on these topics." The Hamer Institute offers educational programs, lectures, symposiums, and town hall–style discussions on citizenship, democracy, and civil rights issues past and present. There are summer youth programs and continuing education workshops for public school teachers and community college faculty. Book discussions on such topics as "The Changed and Changing South" and "Medgar Evers" foster a sense of community on the Jackson State University (JSU) campus. A core message of the institute says that history is made in all places and by all kinds of people.

Known as a civil rights activist, authority on the Southern civil rights movement, and local political leader, Leslie Burl McLemore served two and a half terms on the Jackson City Council, was interim mayor of Jackson in 2009, and then interim president of the university in 2010. With a master's degree in political science from Atlanta University and, in 1971, a doctorate in government from the University of Massachusetts in Amherst, he worked for more than forty years as professor of political science at JSU, where he taught courses on black politics and the civil rights movement. "To be candid, I never considered retiring in the traditional sense. I accepted emeritus status when I had had my fill of grading papers. I was nearing seventy years old and wanted to give more of my time to developing the Hamer Institute. I found that it rejuvenated me."

Leslie was born into a sharecropping family in Walls, Mississippi, in 1940. Before he enrolled at Rust College in 1960, he led a boycott of classes at his high school in 1959. During his freshman year at Rust he participated in a boycott of a segregated theater in Holly Springs. "Discrimination really tried the soul in 1960. I was one of the founders and president of the first college chapter of the National Association for the Advancement of Colored People (NAACP) at Rust. I became involved with the Student Non-Violent Coordinating Committee (SNCC) in 1962 when I met Bob Moses. Rust professors encouraged my activism but also cautioned me to be sure to get my coursework done. They taught me to be disciplined and responsible. At such a small college, you couldn't hide in the back of the class. The professors would call on everyone and you had to be prepared and well read," he recalls vividly. "Because I was involved in the early voter registration drives, I was a veteran of the movement by the time I was a senior." It was then 1964, and Leslie became a SNCC delegate to the newly formed Mississippi Freedom Democratic Party. In no time he was elected as a vice-chair of the party and became involved in negotiations and meetings.

Here is where the formidable Fannie Lou Hamer entered the picture. Mrs. Hamer helped to organize the Mississippi Freedom Summer in 1964 for SNCC and its partners, the Congress on Racial Equality (CORE), the Southern Christian Leadership Conference (SCLC), and the NAACP. The foundation for their efforts can be traced back to 1954 when Medgar Evers and his wife Myrlie were working for the NAACP in Mississippi, and to 1960 when Freedom Riders came to McComb, Mississippi, to help Bob Moses organize a voter registration drive. The so-called 1961 McComb Project became "ground zero" for mass demonstrations that quickly spread to other cities and towns. Civil rights leaders in the state—the NAACP's Aaron Henry, SNCC's Bob Moses, SCLC's Arnell Ponder, and CORE's Dave Dennis—formed an umbrella organization called the Council of Federated Organizations, or COFO, that attempted to unify the various black grassroots organizations with their sometimes competing philosophies and tactics. (The Hamer Institute helped to establish the COFO Civil Rights Education Center which is located on John R. Lynch Street, the heart of the Civil Rights Corridor in Jackson.)

In 1962 when Mrs. Hamer was forty-four years old and working as a sharecropper and record keeper on a plantation in Sunflower County, Mississippi, she attended an SNCC voter registration meeting where she learned for the first time that black people actually had a constitutional right to vote. Since she was "sick and tired of being sick and tired," she volunteered to go to the courthouse in Indianola and register to vote. Her temerity led to eviction from the plantation and several attempts on her life which she barely survived, yet Hamer persisted, becoming an SNCC Field Secretary, traveling around the country speaking and registering people to vote.

By 1964, Mrs. Hamer and other activists, including young Leslie Burl McLemore, had cofounded the Mississippi Freedom Democratic Party (MFDP). Convinced of the validity of their cause, they headed for Atlantic City, New Jersey, to challenge the legitimacy of Mississippi's all-white, anti–civil rights delegation to the Democratic National Convention. Although the Democratic leadership was unsympathetic to the MFDP, Mrs. Hamer was allowed to present their case before the Credentials Committee. The proceedings were televised and viewers all over the country heard how discriminatory practices, such as illegal tests and poll taxes, and outright intimidation were preventing blacks from voting in many states. The Credentials Committee's concession was to give two delegates speaking rights; the rest of the delegation was seated as honored guests. The Voting Rights Act passed in 1965. At the 1968 Democratic National Convention, Mrs. Hamer was seated as a member of Mississippi's official delegation.

After running unsuccessfully for Congress in 1964 and in 1965, Mrs. Hamer worked on behalf of Head Start, a Freedom Farm Cooperative in Sunflower County, and Martin Luther King Jr.'s Poor People's Campaign. She continued to fight for civil rights until her death in 1977 at the age of fifty-nine. She is remembered for her courage and leadership, as well as for singing Christian hymns and freedom songs to fortify herself and her followers when threatened by hostile crowds.

The Hamer Institute originated in 1997 as an action plan hatched among a group of five fellows participating in a National Endowment for the Humanities (NEH) Summer Seminar for College Teachers, held at Harvard's W. E. B. Du Bois Institute. Leslie was one of those founding faculty members.

"Our group of five was interested in social change, so instead of spending time updating a bibliography on civil rights along with the rest of our colleagues, we decided to replicate the NEH model itself, targeting K–12 teachers and students instead of college teachers and making Jackson State University our base. The NEH was an early funder and has continued to support our work for fifteen years. We have also received grants and donations from institutions of higher education, corporations, small businesses, and individuals."

One thing Leslie regrets is not having time to write articles about the civil rights movement when he was a full-time faculty member. He was pulled in many directions—getting involved in community affairs, building up JSU's political science department, and writing proposals. "I wrote lots of proposals for purchasing computers and for helping junior faculty complete advanced degrees and further their careers," he explains. "You could say that helping all those junior faculty members get established is a significant part of my legacy. Another piece, now that I am working part time, will be a book about the 1964 Freedom Summer I plan to write with a colleague. Time is too precious to waste. "

Leslie Burl McLemore is hardly a time waster. In fact, he readily admits that he is "driven to volunteer." He is leading an effort to restore the Mt. Zion Cemetery in his hometown of Walls, Mississippi. He participates in a school-based mentoring program for youngsters attending the Walls Elementary School (which was his high school in the 1960s). He is still involved in an advisory capacity with the Mississippi Humanities Council. He is a member of the Civil Rights Education Commission, the Mississippi National Museum Commission, and the Mississippi Freedom Trail Commission. He conducts voter registration for the DeSoto County chapter of the NAACP. And he is spearheading the class of 1964's fundraising drive for Rust College scholarships. "In 2014 it will be fifty years since our graduation. The first year we raised $25,000, this year it was $100,000, and we hope to reach $150,000 by 2014. Our goals are modest. Most of the classmates are folks of modest incomes and many are retired, so we have to be realistic."

Leslie and his wife Betty Mallet make the two-hundred-mile commute between Jackson and their home in Walls on different schedules, so family time has to be protected. "Betty has a busy law practice in Jackson. She is much younger than I am and hopes I will keep working for a long time. Actually, she's thrilled that I am still working!" Their son Leslie II finished law school, got an LLM at American University, and stayed in Washington to seek a job in the second Obama administration.

Recognition for Leslie's contributions to social justice has come in the form of several awards: the W. E. B. Du Bois Award from the Association of Social and Behavioral Scientists in 2010 and the Fannie Lou Hamer Award from the National Conference of Black Political Scientists in 1995–96. However, when I asked Leslie what he is proudest of, he replied, "Without question it is my role in helping to create the Hamer Institute and being able to continue working with my colleagues there. I plan to contribute in one capacity or another for several more years. The ongoing challenge is to get young people to appreciate their right to vote, a right that we had to fight hard for." When the time does come for him to step down, Leslie would like COFO's current director, Dr. Daphne Chamberlain, to succeed him as director of the Hamer Institute. The fact that she earned her doctorate in history from Ole Miss, previously off limits to blacks, speaks volumes about the success of the civil rights movement which Leslie Burl McLemore helped to bring about.

Additional popular roles for older men who volunteer include: serving as a member of a church or temple committee, town committee, or community agency; assisting in house-building for the poor via Habitat for Humanity; acting as a writing coach/editor; and donating various forms of professional service pro bono, such as reviewing charts for a home nursing service, providing legal assistance, mediating court disputes, chairing a hospital's finance and audit committee, and deploying to natural disasters as a Red Cross mental health manager.

One man's volunteer job is "home helper." Another man drives carpool and supervises homework for his grandkids. The rest are performing unpaid work in a variety of capacities on behalf of many organizations:

- job coaching for working-poor breadwinners
- mentoring youngsters at a Boys and Girls Club
- assisting with university outreach
- mentoring business school students
- helping children with cancer

- judging at a high school science fair
- coordinating a foundation's auction
- working on an organic farm
- serving as general counsel to a major ballet company
- participating in Rotary projects in the United States and overseas
- facilitating synagogue attendance by handicapped adults
- organizing art for a hospital's intensive care unit
- befriending the local library and historical society
- trying to find employment for struggling musician friends

My findings about volunteering deviate from the national data in two areas. The first difference is fairly small. The BLS says part-timers are more available for volunteering than persons employed full time. That seems perfectly logical, yet somewhat more of the full-timers in my study (64 percent) are volunteering than the part-timers (61 percent). The second difference is startling. The BLS says women volunteer at a higher rate than men. My findings contradict the national data on this point: among the women, 52 percent are volunteering, and while that is more than double the national average and quite respectable, it is 17 percentage points less than the rate for men (69 percent). This difference may well derive from men's greater tendency to work for an employer—more than half of the men do, while the majority of the women are self-employed or consulting—and from their companies encouraging (and sometimes requiring) their employees to perform community service or donate professional services pro bono. The difference might also be related to women putting more time in on housework than men do, which could be a valid reason! Let's just agree that both men and women who volunteer demonstrate generosity and a strong sense of engagement, be it civic, social, cultural, or religious in nature.

Leisure time activities are as important to older men as they are to older women. True, one seventy-three-year-old lawyer hastened to remind me that *work* comes first: "My job/work gives focus to the day. Leisure fits around it." But most subscribe to the old saying (apparently a proverb that has been around for more than 350 years) that all work and no play makes Jack a dull boy. As a library trustee and member of two book groups, I was pleased to find that reading—print and electronic materials—is the favorite pastime of both men and women. Nearly three-quarters (72 percent) of the men and more than four-fifths of the women (85 percent) enjoy reading in their spare time. At least two of the men profiled in these pages are active members of book groups—Chuck Willie and Dick Winslow. Chuck belongs to a coed book club in Concord, Massachusetts, that he cofounded with his wife thirty years ago. Dick is the linchpin of a men's book group in Mercer Island, Washington, that gets together every four to six weeks to talk about books, sports, politics, and the economy.

Reading, sports and fitness, travel, and computer use are the top four leisure-time activities for *both* men and women. However, after reading, the preferences of older men and older women diverge slightly. Sports and fitness are in second place for the men: 62 percent are participants in or spectators of a variety of activities, including tennis, skiing, hiking, kayaking, cycling, boating/sailing, golf, and working out at the gym. Examples drawn from among the men I interviewed include: Jim Fannin, who cycles regularly to keep in shape for the heavy lifting required by cemetery preservation work; Paul Fideler, who does weightlifting, stretching, and biking to keep fit and to stave off hip and possibly knee replacement surgeries; Jack Buckley and Neil Tift, who get up early every morning to run before leaving for work; Bob Schecter, who plays tennis three times a week; Ted Grenham, Bruce Chabner, and Andrew Fogelson, all of whom are avid golfers; John Kaneb, who jogs and lifts weights; Jon Kapstein, who swims; Don Brick, who gave up tennis and skiing after having both knees replaced but goes to the health club regularly; and George Doubleday, who does yoga and Pilates, bikes, walks, skis, and swims.

George Doubleday's calendar is chock-full of commitments. In addition to working at Geographic Expeditions (he is the seventy-two-year-old chairman of the San Francisco–based tour operator and outfitter), he tackles outdoor chores on his Sonoma County property, takes piano lessons, is a member of two boards, hosts family visits, and keeps fit. The long-range planning he is doing for GeoEx includes finding someone to replace him—eventually.

PROFILE: GEORGE DOUBLEDAY

Dividing his time between busy San Francisco and a retreat in Healdsburg, California, seventy-two-year-old George Doubleday is chairman of Geographic Expeditions, a tour operator and outfitter that offers 150 journeys to all seven continents. Groups, families, and couples can choose from what the GeoEx website (www.geoex.com) describes as "a varied portfolio of overland tours, treks, walks, and expeditionary voyages to the world's most astonishing places." GeoEx travelers pay a premium for customized, handcrafted trips that are carefully planned for sustainability, that is, leaving a minimum amount of "footprint" or impact on natural resources. It is no wonder that the company has won top honors from *Outside* magazine, *Travel and Leisure*, *Condé Nast*, and *National Geographic*.

In Healdsburg, George and Cynthia Doubleday have eleven acres on a hillside overlooking a peaceful valley in Sonoma County wine country. Cynthia is an architect who is working on houses for three different clients at present. The Doubledays each have three children from previous marriages and ten grandchildren between them. Like many far-flung families today, their offspring reside in Seattle, Dallas, New York City, Genoa, Italy, Portland, Oregon, and Santa Barbara, California. George gardens and does other outdoor chores, such as splitting wood and trimming bushes, on the three tillable acres. He is supervising the building of a tractor shed and taking piano lessons. He does yoga and Pilates, bikes, walks, skis, and swims. He serves on the boards of the San Francisco Aeronautical Society and the Pan Am Historical Foundation. Until he mentioned working out in a cardio rehab gym program twice a week, I would have never guessed that such an active man suffered a heart arrhythmia in 2011 that sidelined him for a while. He is back at GeoEx doing long-range planning on a part-time basis (supposedly), by which he meant all five days during the week when we spoke. "I like it. I get huge energy and great satisfaction from being here."

George told me that his career developed by happenstance when he finished college. In 1961 he started out as a fighter pilot in the US Marine Corps, then joined Pan Am Airways as a management trainee. He mastered crew scheduling, operations analysis, flight operations, and interviewing new pilots. "It quickly occurred to me that pilots were having all the fun, so I asked to be trained as a copilot. I flew for seven years until I became staff vice president for worldwide operations control, a twenty-four/seven job that made it hard to maintain proficiency." George's next assignment for Pan Am was serving as regional managing director for Southeast Asia. From 1978 to 1981, Hong Kong became home base for George and his family. "China was just opening up, and it was a very exciting time. I was able to visit nooks and crannies no one had ever heard of in places like Malaysia and Borneo." On trips with his three children, George had a great time snorkeling off the Great Barrier Reef, skiing in New Zealand, and visiting with tribesmen in Papua New Guinea—all on the same trip.

He also enjoyed trekking in Nepal with friends who owned a remote jungle lodge. Those friends told him they were looking for a company in North America to send clients to them in Nepal. When the Doubledays moved to San Francisco in 1981, George teamed up with his friends in Nepal and with a daring mountaineer, a woman named Jo Sanders, in a new joint venture. Sanders was already running a company called InnerAsia and, just as importantly, she held a permit to operate trips with the Chinese Mountaineering Association. The new partners decided to keep the name InnerAsia. Shortly thereafter, in 1982, Jo Sanders was stricken by a cerebral hemorrhage and, tragically, had to withdraw from the business. George took over full management responsibilities. "At the time it was still a small business and one fraught with difficulties. For example, clients no longer wanted to travel to China after the Tiananmen Square student protests precipitated a massacre in 1989. That situation forced us to add destinations *outside* of Asia. As a result, we concluded that the company name should reflect our growing diversification. It became Geographic Expeditions, which was eventually shortened officially to GeoEx."

George also has had what he refers to as three "corollary" businesses that are "fun but not terribly successful." One is a rug company in Tibet that buys highland sheep wool from farmers and employs one hundred Tibetans as dyers, washers, and weavers. "Given China's heavy hand in Tibet, it is very satisfying to be helping to preserve an endangered livelihood and lifestyle. That gives me a good feeling even though there is no profit in it." The two other businesses are no longer operating. A consulting business advised American firms about technology transfer from the United States and Canada to India. "We were ahead of the curve on that one." A cross-linked polyethylene pipe manufacturing company in Shanghai provided an alternative to copper piping, but local manufacturers undercut the company's price, and George's partners didn't have enough local influence to compete.

GeoEx, however, has thrived and employs more than forty staff members today. George is extremely proud of the team he and his partners have built. "GeoEx has expertise in each area of the world. We can advise clients and set up itineraries tailored to their particular interests— wildlife, art, history, culture, scenery, safari drives, river trips, climbing, or a certain location. Our employees are hugely talented and many of them have been with us a very long time. I would like to offer them better retirement benefits."

George no longer is responsible for day-to-day management of the company. He told me that he would like to find a way to "step away gracefully," but that all depends on whether he can find the right person to replace him. It seems like that will take quite a bit of time.

Health club membership is a booming industry for adults fifty-five and older. They are clearly heeding the messages about the benefits of regular exercise—mental as well as physical—for quality of life. According to the *Houston Chronicle* online, 25 percent of some 41 million health club members in the United States are over fifty-five years old, making this the fastest-growing segment of health club memberships.[2] One explanation for the surge is fitness-conscious baby boomers moving into the senior ranks. Another explanation is health insurance providers offering cash incentives for joining a gym.

Yet a third explanation is scientific evidence that regular physical activity helps protect against cancer, osteoporosis and fragility, cardiovascular disease, diabetes, and dementia. Neuroscience research is discovering that loss of memory as we age is not inevitable. Although genes play a role, studies show that regular exercise spurs biochemical changes leading to new brain cells (neurons) being produced in a process called neurogenesis, as well as more effective connections between neurons, thus aiding learning and memory even in old age. Along with intellectual stimulation, socializing, and being active— for example, aerobics and resistance training or merely walking for thirty to sixty minutes a day three days per week—have been shown to increase cognitive performance in older adults. Researchers at Northwestern University's Cognitive Neurology and Alzheimer's Disease Center are studying men and women over age eighty whom they call "SuperAgers" because their memories are exceptional, that is, as good or better than fifty- and sixty-year-olds.[3] The cortex within our brains may gradually shrink, but loss of memory as we age can be lessened.

More than half of the women I studied (54 percent) are "into" sports and fitness, but for the women, travel holds second place (68 percent). Men also enjoy travel; at 60 percent it is their third favorite leisure activity. Like many older folks who travel to visit family, Ted Grenham and his wife rack up frequent flier mileage on annual trips to see their children and grandchildren in Oregon and Australia.

More than one-third of the men say that they spend leisure time on the computer, and one-third say that they enjoy making music or listening to music. Steve Schoenbaum stands out because he is a serious pianist. Jack Buckley stands out because he plays the fiddle or practices the concertina for two hours a night. Bob Schecter is a Scottish country dancing enthusiast. Somewhat less than one-third of the men devote free time to gardening and yard work. George Doubleday splits wood and gardens. Writing, solving crossword puzzles, creating various art forms, participating in religious programs, and taking adult education classes are strong interests for some of the men. One lifelong learner is Dick Winslow, who audits classes at the University of Washington. Social media, all the rage with younger people, appears to have minimal appeal for senior men, however.

Pastimes mentioned by men multiple times are, in order of frequency: family time, home improvement projects, movies, film club, theater, boating, sailing, woodworking, church choir, fishing, friends, motorcycles, photography, and technology (building and repairing computers). Other leisure-time activities that received just one mention include: caring for an antique car, assisting relatives, participating in a bereavement support group, watching British television shows, camping, cooking, supporting environmental efforts, genealogy, doing investment research, studying a foreign language, meditating, collecting model trains, people-probing (learning about lives), performing living history, studying history, and solving Sudoku puzzles.

Clearly, these mature age professionals are active and engaged in work as well as nonwork activities. Dare we borrow a term from neuroscience and call them SuperAgers?

Men Still at Work

If you have your health, you can earn a living and be active and involved with people and issues, and you can help change things for the better.
—Peter Gossels, Attorney

It is clear that professionals are remaining in their career jobs longer than in the past. Indeed, the BLS expects the overall trend in favor of higher labor force participation rates for all older men and women alike to continue in the near future.[1] By 2016, the two oldest groups of workers (sixty-five to seventy-four and seventy-five and up) are each expected to grow by more than 80 percent, far outstripping the rate for younger groups (under fifty-five) and more than twice the rate for fifty-five to sixty-four-year-old workers. Even when retirement from a career job does occur, it does not necessarily mean a permanent exit from the workforce if a suitable part-time position, consulting job, or business ownership is obtainable.

Like many human career changers, "job hopping" worker ants graduate from one function to another as they age. Swiss researchers who tagged worker ants to study their behavior discovered that younger ants are primarily nurses, a middle group cleans the colony, and older ants go outside to forage.[2] While foraging is the most dangerous job, it may or may not mean that older ants are less valuable to the colony and thus expendable. Moreover, the career changing process is not clear cut: some foragers are in fact young and some nurses are old. One interpretation says that those are rogue ants taking jobs not suitable for their age.[3] Another interpretation from a University of York researcher is that age per se is not the criterion—what matters is the amount of fat stored in their bodies. Leaner ants go out to forage and older ants tend to be leaner. It is tempting, isn't it, to perceive this segment of the natural world as a metaphor for the behavior of mature human workers who are lean in the sense of being fit for work and whose contributions are considered valuable. Continuing in the workforce in the senior years may be relatively uncommon—even as the *rate* of participation is accelerating, in terms of *numbers* more older men and women are retired—but uncommon, or exceptional, is hardly equivalent to rogue.

Given the recent financial crisis and its after-effects, it would be easy to assume that money woes underlie the decision to postpone retirement and keep working. And it is true that insufficient savings, depleted investments, and fears concerning rising health-care costs are enough to keep many workers on the job. Whether they are seniors or members of the younger generations following us, if they are struggling to keep afloat, they may not have a choice. Economic uncertainties are real enough, but they do not tell the whole story, at least for those fortunate older men and women who *do* have a choice. Recall that it was curiosity about the reasons they give for remaining in or returning to the workforce well past conventional retirement age, as well a suspicion that men's work life stories might differ from the stories women tell, that led to the two separate-but-linked investigations I undertook. Admittedly, I was relieved and also amused to find the men as willing as the women to tell me their work life stories, for I had mistakenly anticipated that it would be more difficult to get busy men to talk about themselves.

Men (and women) in their sixties, seventies, and eighties readily shared their reasons with me for working late. Under the umbrella of *job satisfaction*, they give many examples: "Staying active (by working) keeps me in good health and good spirits." "I enjoy the work, it's my passion . . . it's fun!" "By working I give back to others." "I stay engaged." Using their abilities, skills, and training is also very important to them, as is enjoying colleagues and co-workers, as well as their clients, students, patients, or customers. In addition to relishing strong and enduring family bonds (most are married with children and grandchildren), they cite higher education as one of the keys to their success. Many earned advanced degrees, put them to good use in professional capacities, and now have the income to show for it. Many benefited from mentoring and in turn are mentoring early careerists. Most are making time for volunteer work and most enjoy one or more leisure pursuits as well. All recognize that good health and stamina are essential. They want to stay alert, keep their minds sharp and their bodies fit. They want to stay in the game, as sports fans would say. Still, their busy lives are not without costs, particularly the stress and fatigue associated with the workplace and the demands of business travel, and, even if they are self-employed, not having enough time for all that needs to be done.

In addition to the many attributes older working men and women in this demographic share, there are also differences. On the whole, the men started their careers earlier than the women, more than half of whom had taken time out for childrearing. The men are staying in the workforce longer and are more apt to be working full time. Mainly because of choice of career field (business is number one for men, education is number one for women) and partially because of entrenched pay inequities, the men earn higher salaries and receive considerably more Social Security income than the women. The men are more likely than the women to hold jobs in the private sector and in a metropolitan area (where higher-paying professional jobs are usually to be found). Even when educational attainment is on a par, career choice, sector, and location are important determinants of income level. These are some of the factors, in addition to life's vicissitudes, that help to put older women under greater financial pressure than older men.

Women more than men report a growing awareness of being out of step, particularly with younger folks' fashions and lifestyles. Older women, but not older men, speak of being invisible and feeling they no longer "count" in the wider world. Professionals of both genders seem to know themselves well by the time they reach the senior years: the men tending to define themselves, as their fathers did, primarily by what they do for a living and the goals they have reached; the women tending to see themselves reflected in home, family, and collegial relationships and responsibilities first, and as career women second. Although they are unlikely to be thought of as Martians and Venusians today,[4] given the era in which my respondents grew up, avoiding those stereotypical definitions of masculinity and femininity was difficult if not impossible.

To be sure, many older working women take great pride in the strides they made as professionals under the influence of a burgeoning feminist consciousness. Consequently, it is to be hoped that their daughters and granddaughters do not have to fight quite as hard for equal treatment in the workplace. However, recent controversies over flex-time scheduling and working from home, and debates about whether women can "have it all," suggest that work/life balance and glass ceiling issues are still very much with us. What's more, despite federal law prohibiting age discrimination, stereotypes about aging also remain. Employers may say they do not give credence to "lower productivity as the career clock winds down," but a reluctance to hire older workers, especially older workers who have been out of work for a while, indicates otherwise.

In the concluding chapter of *Women Still at Work* I presented a highly accomplished and exceptional older woman as the pièce de résistance. For the same purpose I have selected one participant from this study, octogenarian Peter Gossels, who embodies many of the impressive qualities associated with older men still at work. Peter had been practicing law for fifty-six years when I interviewed him. His is an inspiring story of escape from war-torn Europe as a young child, building a professional and family life in the country that took him in, and dedicating his time, talents, and treasure to the improvement of public education, religious practice, and civil society. He doesn't think of law merely as his career: "It shapes my life, and *it is who I am*." Some lines from Sartre's 1945 lecture, *Existentialism*, seem to convey Peter's philosophy:

> And when we say that a man is responsible for himself, we do not mean that he is responsible for his own individuality, but that he is responsible for all men . . . a man is nothing else than a series of undertakings . . . the sum, the organization, the ensemble of the relationships which make up these undertakings. . . . Consequently we are dealing here with an ethics of action and involvement.[5]

PROFILE: C. PETER R. GOSSELS

A refugee from war-torn Europe, eighty-two-year-old attorney Peter Gossels is deeply rooted in his community and still immersed in his work. In 1939, when he was eight and his little brother, Werner, was five, their mother, Charlotte Lewy Gossels, was desperate to get her sons out of Berlin. She somehow managed to secure visas for her boys from the French Embassy and they were sent by train to Quincy sous Sénart, twenty miles southeast of Paris, along with thirty-eight other Jewish children. There they were the "guests" of a French count and his wife, a Russian Jew, at the Château de Quincy that had served as a finishing school for White Russian teenage girls, whose parents had fled the Bolshevik takeover of Russia. After the Germans over-ran northern France in June 1940 and almost killed them during the battle of Fontainebleau, the Gossels brothers spent three months in an orphanage outside of Paris. In January 1941, the brothers were placed in the Château de Chabannes, a home for children run by Oeuvre de Secours aux Enfants, a French Jewish humanitarian organization in the unoccupied zone of France. The tiny hamlet of Chabannes was located near Vichy in central France. An award-winning documentary film, *The Children of Chabannes*, produced and directed by Peter's daughter, Lisa Gossels, and Dean Wetherell in 1999, picks up the story there.

Peter's mother and grandmother were murdered by the Nazis, as were many other members of his family.

The Château de Chabannes sheltered approximately one hundred Jew-ish children at any given time arriving from Germany, France, Poland, and Austria, who were protected by a staff of counselors led by its director, Félix Chevrier, and the local populace, all of whom were non-Jews. The children learned to speak French and attended the local school, which was conducted by two schoolteachers, the sisters Reine and Renee Paillassou. They also learned basic survival skills. Peter remembers how proud he was to receive two blankets donated to the orphanage by the American Friends Service Committee. And thanks to the assistance of the Quakers and Eleanor Roo-sevelt, who obtained visas for them (she asked the State Department for ten thousand; she got two hundred), Peter and Werner were among the lucky ones to be rescued and brought to the United States in 1941. The rest of the children who had been at Chabannes were hidden in private French homes, joined the French Resistance, or, when the Nazis could find them, sent to concentration camps.

The Gossels boys were placed with separate foster families in Brookline, Massachusetts. Peter went to Boston Latin and on scholarship to Harvard College and Harvard Law School. Werner went to Brookline High School and had to "settle" for Yale (a little tease between brothers). After serving in the

US Army during the Korean War, Peter returned to Boston in 1956 to look for a job. Unfortunately, Boston law firms in the fifties hired very few Jews. With no money and none of the connections many of his friends could call on, Peter had to make his own way. His first job was at the law firm of Sullivan and Worcester where he trained as a trial lawyer.

He started a family with his wife, Nancy, and they put their roots down in Wayland, a suburban town west of Boston. Their daughter Lisa is an Emmy Award–winning filmmaker; their daughter Amy works as an independent casting director, producer, and teacher; and their son, Daniel, serves as a managing director of Mesa Global, an investment bank in New York City where he and his sisters now live.

From 1965 to 1972, Peter was a partner in the firm of Zelman, Gossels, and Alexander. During this period, Peter worked with soon-to-be-governor Michael Dukakis to develop and enact the first system of no-fault automobile insurance protection in the country. In 1972 he joined the Boston law firm of Weston Patrick, P.A. where he practices in a wide variety of legal specialties to this day—litigation, real estate law, family law, school law and special education, municipal law, corporate and business law, and more. "I deal with people and the problems they bring. Helping people, solving problems keeps me alert and alive. The law is not all fun and games, of course; it's demanding, and to stay on the cutting edge is a challenge. I've been practicing for fifty-six years, but last year was the best year I ever had!" His influence within the legal profession is strong. A Master of the Superior Court, he helped persuade the Boston Bar Association to study ways to make the Massachusetts court system more accessible, less costly and time-consuming, and to adopt changes recommended in the report he coauthored in 2005. He is also a frequent contributor of articles on a variety of professional issues to the *Massachusetts Lawyers Weekly*.

Putting down roots meant contributing his time and expertise to the community. Peter served on the Town of Wayland's Finance Committee for two years and was Town Counsel for eleven years before being elected moderator of the town meeting. And, extraordinarily (to my mind), Peter served as moderator for thirty years! In my town, citizen self-government is *representative*; approximately two hundred elected members can discuss and vote on articles. In contrast, Wayland has an *open* town meeting, so one or two thousand residents or more can weigh in on every article. To manage the process and give everyone a reasonable opportunity to be heard, Peter developed a *Moderator's*

Handbook, laying out, for the first time, the rules and regulations that govern town meetings; he introduced separate microphones for "pro" and "con" voices, thus producing more civilized debates; he instituted time limits on the debates; and he implemented the first system of electronic voting to be used at a New England town meeting.

Yet another form of civic engagement is his family's commitment to public education in Wayland. Nancy and Peter Gossels contributed to a fund for Excellence in the Public Schools, originally funded by his brother, Werner, and his wife, Elaine, to provide money for extra educational opportunities. In addition, the two couples created the Gossels Fund for Human Dignity.

Putting down roots also meant participating in a local congregation. Although proud of their religious identity, the Gossels found going to the synagogue was like going to a museum because the forms of prayer seemed ossified and lifeless. Peter and Nancy set out in 1980 to revitalize Reform Judaism and make the prayer book less male-dominated. As a result, the lay members of the congregation, led by the Gosselses and Joan S. Kaye, published an *egalitarian* prayer book, *Vetaher Libenu*, which features nonsexist, inclusive language; uses feminine and masculine pronouns to refer to God; and includes both the matriarchs and the patriarchs. It also featured many original poems by Nancy Lee Gossels. Thousands of copies have been sold all over the world to Christians as well as Jews. Nancy and Peter also led a team, including Harry Abadi, Gary Bean, and Ellen Zellner, who edited and published an egalitarian Machzor for Rosh Hashanah, and composed a siddur (prayer book) for weekday prayers titled *Canfey Hashachar* in 2003 and other prayer books. As a result, all prayer books published by the Reform Movement are now egalitarian and many conservative congregations have adopted the egalitarian language pioneered by Nancy, Peter, and Joan.

Defining all of the many leadership roles Peter has assumed over the years is his worldview as a lawyer. "I don't think of it as my career. It shapes my life, and it is what I am. If you have your health, you can earn a living and be active and involved with people and issues, and you can help change things for the better. If I didn't have enough clients to support myself, of course, I would have to retire; but so long as I can attract new clients, I will be able to continue my practice, contribute to my community and enjoy my life, because the challenge of work keeps me sharp, up-to-date and involved with the best and the brightest of my clients and colleagues."

Peter admits he wouldn't know what to do with himself if he retired. "When I meet retired people socially, I often find their conversation less interesting, less stimulating, because they tend to see the world as spectators; not as people who are engaged in making a difference. To be honest, it frightens me. I've seen too many people retire and die." While he gets no pressure from family and friends to stop working, Peter knows that Nancy would like him to do more traveling with her. They have already been to countries all over the world, including to France for a reunion of the surviving children of Chabannes and the elderly Paillassou sisters in 1996. Those heroic teachers and the director who risked their own lives to save the children of Chabannes have since been designated "Righteous among the Nations" at Yad Vashem in Jerusalem.

Uprooted from his first home some seventy-four years ago, Peter Gossels knows how fortunate he was to be able to build a successful life in America with a wonderful wife and family and a profession he loves. As Lisa Gossels described him in a 2009 interview for the journal *Pulse-Berlin*: "My father is someone who believes in being a productive member of society. His response to his own personal tragedy wasn't to feel sorry for himself or bitter, but to make family a priority, to embrace an inclusive and progressive form of Judaism, to be involved in social justice and cultural institutions, and to give back through philanthropy."

Peter Gossels's worldview as a lawyer shapes his life. Men like Peter seek to change things for the better. Sartre would call this an ethics of action and involvement. And I am also reminded of the practical advice proffered by the plain-spoken and (literally) straight-shooting Mormon cowboy who ran the working horse and cattle ranch in Arizona where I spent two glorious summers in the 1950s: "The one who puts the most into anything gets the most out of it in return.... Each day is a page in your life's storybook. Put something good in each day so when it is finished it will be good reading material with no regrets." I hope readers of *Men Still at Work* will agree that the men who shared pages from their personal and professional storybooks have provided good reading material. They are reaping what they have sown (to mix metaphors) and with luck and good health can continue to do so as long as they wish.

To be sure, working late can be taxing for men in their sixties, seventies, or eighties. With the exception of Jim Fannin, the historic preservationist and cemetery conservationist you met in chapter 6, and perhaps a few others, the older men I studied are engaged in professions that do not require heavy physical labor. Nonetheless, job-related travel, stress, and fatigue can be wearing, as can the stress associated with the various financial uncertainties caused by our still-ailing economy. A challenge for some is trying to achieve a salutary work-life balance that accommodates family and friends, plus time for home maintenance, recreation, fitness, and cultural and community/volunteering activities. And for others, delaying retirement avoids having to address a worrisome problem: What comes next? Whether they live to work *or* work to live—whatever their reasons—ever-increasing numbers of highly accomplished older men with stable, interesting professional jobs that pay relatively well are gladly continuing in the paid labor force, thus proving that work can certainly be an important part of successful aging. While many of their peers and men even younger have already retired, older men still at work are in the vanguard of a strengthening trend.

Notes

CHAPTER 1

1. Nelson D. Schwartz, "Recovery in U.S. Lifting Profits, Not Adding Jobs," *New York Times*, March 4, 2013, A1, A3.

2. Elizabeth F. Fideler, *Women Still at Work: Professionals over Sixty and on the Job* (Lanham, MD: Rowman & Littlefield, 2012).

3. Roy P. Clark, "Eugene Patterson, 89, Voice on Civil Rights, Dies," *Atlanta Journal-Constitution*, January 13, 2013. Retrieved April 15, 2013, from http://www.ajc.com.

4. Retrieved February 17, 2013, from http://www.npr.org/workinglate.

5. Gary Burtless, "The Impact of Population Aging and Delayed Retirement on Workforce Productivity," Chestnut Hill, MA: Center for Retirement Research at Boston College. Retrieved July 8, 2013, from http://crr.bc.edu.

6. Sarah S. Willie, *Acting Black: College, Identity, and the Performance of Race* (New York: Routledge, 2003), 167.

CHAPTER 2

1. Laura B. Shrestha and Elayne J. Heisler, "The Changing Demographic Profile of the United States." Congressional Research Service. No. 7-5700. RL32701. March 31, 2011, http://www.crs.gov.

2. Shrestha and Heisler, "The Changing Demographic Profile."

3. US Census Bureau News, "Older Americans Month: May 2013." CB13-FF.07. Washington, DC, March 7, 2013. Retrieved March 18, 2013, from http://www .census.gov/newsroom/releases/pdf/cb13ff-07_older2013.pdf.

4. Retrieved February 15, 2013, from http://www.fairfaxcountyeda.org.

5. Sara E. Rix, "Unemployment Rises for Older Workers." AARP Public Policy Institute, Fact Sheet 255. March 2012, http://www.aarp.org/ppi.

6. Federal Interagency Forum on Aging-Related Statistics, "Older Americans 2012: Key Indicators of Well-Being." Retrieved March 18, 2013, from http://www .AgingStats.gov/main_site/data/2012_documents/population.aspx.

7. MetLife Mature Market Institute, "Transitioning into Retirement: The MetLife Study of Baby Boomers at 65." Westport, CT, April 2012. Retrieved January 8, 2013, from http://www.metlife.com.

8. Paul Solman, "Manufacturer Vita Needle Finds Investment in Older Workers Turns a Big Profit." Retrieved January 4, 2013, from http://www.pbs.org/ newshour/bb/business/jan-june13/makingsense_01-02.html?print. In addition to the *PBS NewsHour* feature, anthropologist Caitrin Lynch wrote a book about the company titled *Retirement on the Line*. German and Dutch filmmakers have made documentaries about Vita.

9. David Hackett Fischer, *Growing Old in America* (New York: Oxford University Press, 1978).

10. Scott Bass, "From Retirement to 'Productive Aging' and Back to Work Again," in *Gerontology in the Era of the Third Age: Implications and Next Steps*. Dawn C. Carr and Kathrin Komp, eds. (New York: Springer, 2011), 169–89.

11. Gordon F. Shea and Adolf Haasen, *The Older Worker Advantage: Making the Most of Our Aging Workforce* (Westport, CT: Praeger, 2006).

12. Helen Harkness, *Don't Stop the Career Clock: Rejecting the Myths of Aging for a New Way to Work in the 21st Century* (Palo Alto, CA: Davies-Black Publishing, 1999).

13. Sara Lawrence-Lightfoot, *Exit: The Endings That Set Us Free* (New York: Farrar, Straus and Giroux, 2012).

14. Marc Freedman, *Encore: Finding Work That Matters in the Second Half of Life* (New York: PublicAffairs/Perseus Books, 2007).

15. William A. Sadler, *The Third Age: Six Principles of Growth and Renewal after Forty* (Cambridge, MA: Perseus Books, 2000).

16. Dawn C. Carr and Kathrin Komp, eds., *Gerontology in the Era of the Third Age: Implications and Next Steps* (New York: Springer, 2011); Peter Laslett, *A Fresh Map of Life: The Emergence of the Third Age* (London: Weidenfeld & Nicolson, 1989).

17. Phyllis Moen, "A Life-Course Approach to the Third Age," in *Gerontology in the Era of the Third Age: Implications and Next Steps*, Dawn C. Carr and Kathrin Komp, eds. (New York: Springer, 2011), 13–33.

18. Graham D. Rowles and Lydia K. Manning, "Experiencing the Third Age: The Perspective of Qualitative Inquiry," in *Gerontology in the Era of the Third Age: Implications and Next Steps*, Dawn C. Carr and Kathrin Komp, eds. (New York: Springer, 2011), 147–67.

19. ADEA applies to workers forty and older.

20. Scott Bass, "From Retirement to 'Productive Aging' and Back to Work Again," in *Gerontology in the Era of the Third Age: Implications and Next Steps*, Dawn C. Carr and Kathrin Komp, eds. (New York: Springer, 2011), 169–89.

21. George E. Vaillant, *Aging Well: Surprising Guideposts to a Happier Life from the Landmark Harvard Study of Adult Development* (Boston: Little, Brown, 2002), 5.

22. Vaillant, *Aging Well*, 305–6.

23. Robert Waldinger, MD, is now leading the study.

24. Vaillant, *Aging Well*, 222.

25. Vaillant, *Aging Well*, 223.

CHAPTER 3

1. Gay Talese, "The Crisis Manager." *The New Yorker*, September 24, 2012, 40–49.

2. John Wooden, *Wooden: A Lifetime of Observations and Reflections On and Off the Court*. http://www.goodreads.com.

3. At the end of September 2013, Bud Selig announced his retirement in June 2014.

4. Barbara Ehrenreich, *The Hearts of Men: American Dreams and the Flight from Commitment* (Garden City, NY: Anchor Press/Doubleday, 1983).

5. Gail Sheehy's widely read *Passages* books built upon Levinson's work.

6. Daniel J. Levinson et al. *The Seasons of a Man's Life* (New York: Ballantine Books, 1978).

7. Daniel J. Levinson and Judy D. Levinson, *The Seasons of a Woman's Life* (New York: Alfred A. Knopf, 1996).

8. Levinson and Levinson, *The Seasons of a Woman's Life*.

9. Gerardo Marti, Davidson College, associate professor and chair of sociology. Course Syllabus for Sociology of Work (2006). http://www.davidson.edu.

10. Rucha Bhate, "A Woman's Place? A Cross National Exploration of Gender Role Perspectives—Quick Insights." Boston College, Sloan Center on Aging and Work (November 2012). Retrieved November 27, 2012, from http://www.bc.edu/content/bc/research/agingandwork/archive_pubs/QI1.html.

11. Bhate, "A Woman's Place?"

12. Anne-Marie Slaughter, "Why Women Still Can't Have It All." *Atlantic Magazine* (July–August 2012). Retrieved December 13, 2012, from http://www.theatlantic.com/magazine/archive/2012/07/why-women-still-cant-have-it-all/309020.

13. Stephanie Coontz, "Why Gender Equality Stalled." *New York Times*, February 17, 2013, SR1, SR6–7.

14. Hanna Rosin, "Who Wears the Pants in This Economy?" *New York Times Magazine*, September 2, 2012, 22–29, 38.

15. John Gray, *Men Are from Mars, Women Are from Venus* (New York: Harper, 1992).

16. Gray, *Men Are from Mars*, 12.

17. Gray, *Men Are from Mars*, 9.

18. APA Center for Organizational Excellence, "Work-Life Fit and Enjoying What They Do Top the List of Reasons Why Employees Stay on the Job" (September 5, 2012). Retrieved March 4, 2013, from http://www.apaexcellence.org/resources/goodcompany/newsletter/article/391.

19. Andrew O'Hagan, "The Male Bond," *New York Times Style Magazine*, March 10, 2013, 86, 88.

20. Robert Bly, *Iron John: A Book about Men* (Reading, MA: Addison-Wesley, 1990).

21. Edward R. Barton, *Beyond Men Hugging Trees: A Qualitative Exploration of Men's Participation in Men's Peer Mutual Support Groups* (Saarbrucken, Germany: VDM Verlag Dr. Muller, 2011).

22. Edward R. Barton, "Experiencing My Mid-Life Crises and Afterward: Various Hermeneutical Analyses of Lived Experiences, Part 1," *International Journal of Self Help and Self Care* 2 (4) (2003–2004): 329–38.

23. Barton, "Experiencing My Mid-Life Crises and Afterward," 329–38.

24. Terry Jones, *The Elder Within: The Source of Mature Masculinity* (Wilsonville, OR: BookPartners, 2001); Terry Jones, *Elder: A Spiritual Alternative to Being Elderly* (Portland, OR: Elderhood Institute Books, 2006).

25. Bly, *Iron John*; Joseph Campbell and Bill Moyers, *The Power of Myth* (New York: Anchor Books, 1991); John. H. Lee, *The Flying Boy: Healing the Wounded Man* (Deerfield Beach, FL: Health Communications, 1989).

26. Edward R. Barton, ed., *Mythopoetic Perspectives of Men's Healing Work: An Anthology for Therapists and Others* (Westport, CT: Bergin and Garvey, 2000).

27. Edward R. Barton, "Early History of the Changing Men Collections," *Journal of Men's Health and Gender* 3 (2), (June 2006): 213–14.

28. Rick Broniec, *A Passionate Life: 7 Steps for Reclaiming a Passionate, Purposeful and Joyful Life* (Greenwood, WI: Rick Broniec, 2012).

29. Ellen Cole and Mary Gergen, eds., *Retiring but Not Shy* (Chagrin Falls, OH: Taos Institute, 2012).

CHAPTER 4

1. US Census Bureau News, "Older Americans Month: May 2013." CB13-FF.07. Washington, DC (March 7, 2013). Retrieved March 18, 2013, from http://www.census.gov/newsroom/releases/pdf/cb13ff-07_older2013.pdf.

2. Maria Heidkamp, "Older Workers, Rising Skill Requirements and the Need for a Re-envisioning of the Public Workforce System." Rutgers University, John J. Heldrich Center for Workforce Development, 2012, 5–6.

3. Heidkamp, "Older Workers," 5–6.

4. Mitra Toossi, "Projections of the Labor Force to 2050: A Visual Essay." US Bureau of Labor Statistics, *Monthly Labor Review* (October 2012), 3–16.

5. US Bureau of Labor Statistics. "National Hispanic Heritage Month." BLS Spotlight on Statistics (September 2012). Retrieved January 28, 2013, from http://www.bls.gov/spotlight/2012/hispanic_heritage.

6. APA Center for Organizational Excellence, "Work-Life Fit and Enjoying What They Do Top the List of Reasons Why Employees Stay on the Job" (September 5, 2012). Retrieved March 4, 2013, from http://www.apaexcellence.org/resources/goodcompany/newsletter/article/391.

7. The full retirement age for Social Security is sixty-five for people born in 1937 or earlier. For people born in 1938 or later, it increases gradually until it reaches sixty-seven for people born after 1959.

8. Mitra Toossi, "Employment Outlook: 2008–18: Labor Force Projections to 2018: Older Workers Staying More Active." US Bureau of Labor Statistics, *Monthly Labor Review* (November 2009).

9. Laura B. Shrestha and Elayne J. Heisler, "The Changing Demographic Profile of the United States." Congressional Research Service. No. 7-5700 (March 31, 2011). http://www.crs.gov, RL32701.

10. Lauren Weber, "Americans Rip Up Retirement Plans." *Wall Street Journal* (January 31, 2013). Retrieved February 1, 2013, from http://www.online.wsj.com.

11. MetLife, "10th Annual Study of Employee Benefits Trends: Seeing Opportunity in Shifting Tides" (New York: MetLife, 2012). Retrieved December 27, 2012, from http://www.metlife.com.

12. Weber, "Americans Rip Up Retirement Plans."

13. Aegon, "The Changing Face of Retirement: The Aegon Retirement Readiness Survey 2012." The Hague, Netherlands: Aegon Group. (2012). Retrieved March 8, 2013, from http://www.aegon.com.

14. Alicia H. Munnell and Steven A. Sass, *Working Longer: The Solution to the Retirement Income Challenge* (Washington, DC: Brookings Institution Press, 2008).

15. Eduardo Porter, "The Payoff in Delaying Retirement," *New York Times*, March 6, 2013, B1, B5.

16. Kyoko Hasegawa, "Retirees Still Seeking Work," *Japan Times*. Retrieved August 1, 2012, from http://www.japantimes.co.jp.

17. Annet de Lange, "Sustaining an Aging Workforce." AGEnda, Aging and Work Blog. Chestnut Hill, MA: Sloan Center on Aging and Work, January 23, 2013, http://www.agingandwork.bc.edu/blog/2013/01.

18. Suzanne Daley and Nicholas Kulish, "Germany Fights Population Drop: Takes Steps to Avoid a Shortage of Labor," *New York Times*, August 14, 2013, A1, A6.

19. Ministry of Labour, Luxembourg, "Luxembourg 2020." National Reform Program for the Grand Duchy of Luxembourg under the Europe 2020 Strategy. The European Semester (April 2011). Retrieved November 15, 2012, from http://ec.europa.eu/europe2020/pdf/nrp/nrp_luxembourg_en.pdf. Also see http://www.noagesite.com.

20. Australian Workplace Innovation and Social Research Centre. Retrieved December 10, 2012, from http://agingandwork.bc.edu/blog/a-20-year-view-of-the-labor-force.

21. Catherine Rampell, "U.S. Adds 171,000 Jobs, More Than Estimated," *New York Times*, November 3, 2012, B1, B2.

22. According to the Economic Policy Institute's 2012 analysis of "The State of Working America," at the end of 2011, 10 million jobs were needed to return to the pre-recession unemployment rate. At the rate jobs were being created during the first six months of 2012, the target would not be reached before 2020.

23. Adapted from Economic Policy Institute, "Unemployment Rate, by Gender and Education, 2000–2011," *The State of Working America*, 12th ed. (Washington, DC: Economic Policy Institute, 2012). Retrieved February 11, 2013, from http://www.stateofworkingamerica.org/jobs/table5.4.

24. Adapted from Economic Policy Institute, "Unemployment Rate, by Education, Race and Ethnicity, 2000–2011," *The State of Working America*, 12th ed. (Washington, DC: Economic Policy Institute, 2012). Retrieved February 11, 2013, from http://www.stateofworkingamerica.org/jobs/table5.3.

25. Jennifer Medina, "Long-Term Jobless Regroup to Fight the Odds," *New York Times*, August 17, 2012, A1, A3.

26. Chelsey Dulaney, "Older Workers Face a Tougher Road," *Charlotte Observer*, August 21, 2012. Retrieved September 12, 2012, from http://www.timesnews.net/article/9050726/older-workers-face-a-tougher-road.

27. Megan Woolhouse, "Retirees Lend Their Expertise," *Boston Globe*, January 31, 2013, B5, B7.

28. Catherine Rampell, "A Sharp Drop in Job Growth Sows Concern," *New York Times*, April 6, 2013, A1, A3.

29. Sara E. Rix, "The Employment Situation, January 2013: Jobs Added to the Economy but Unemployment for Older Workers Holds Fast," AARP Public Policy Institute, Fact Sheet 277. Washington, DC (February 2013). Retrieved February 28, 2013, from http://www.aarp.org/research.

30. Gary Koenig and Lina Walker, "The New Reality: Important Facts about America's Seniors." AARP Public Policy Institute, Fact Sheet 230. Washington, DC (June 2011). Retrieved February 28, 2013, from http://www.aarp.org/research.

31. US Census Bureau News, "Older Americans Month: May 2013." CB13-FF.07. Washington, DC (March 7, 2013). Retrieved March 18, 2013, from http://www .census.gov/newsroom/releases/pdf/cb13ff-07_older2013.pdf.

32. Catherine Rampell, "Big Income Losses Hit Those near Retirement," *New York Times*, August 24, 2012, B1–B2.

33. Annie Lowery and Catherine Rampell, "Jobless, and Hopeless, in America," *New York Times*, November 2, 2012, B1, B2.

34. Megan Woolhouse, "Time Is Not in Their Side," *Boston Globe*, March 25, 2013, A1, A10.

35. Woolhouse, "Time Is Not in Their Side," A1, A10.

36. Sara E. Rix, "The Employment Situation, January 2013: Jobs Added to the Economy but Unemployment for Older Workers Holds Fast," AARP Public Policy Institute, Fact Sheet 277, Washington, DC (February 2013), page 3. Retrieved February 28, 2013, from http://www.aarp.org/research.

37. Helen Dennis, "The Older Entrepreneur," Sloan Center on Aging and Work. AGEnda, Aging and Work Blog. Chestnut Hill, MA: Boston College (November 14, 2012). http://agingandwork.bc.edu/blog/the-older-entrepreneur.

CHAPTER 5

1. Federal Interagency Forum on Aging-Related Statistics, "Older Americans 2012: Key Indicators of Well-Being." Retrieved March 18, 2013, from http://www .AgingStats.gov/main_site/data/2012_documents/population.aspx.

2. US Department of Education, National Center for Educational Statistics, 2012. Retrieved March 14, 2013, from http://nces.ed.gov/fastfacts/display.asp?id=27.

3. Jennifer C. Day, "Health Data from the Census Bureau: People," US Department of Commerce, State Data Center Annual Meeting, October 17, 2012.

4. Affordable Care Act.

5. Personal income from work does not include Social Security benefits a man may be receiving.

6. Gary Burtless, "The Impact of Population Aging and Delayed Retirement on Workforce Productivity." Table 4 (Earned income measured in constant 2010 dollars). (Chestnut Hill, MA: Center for Retirement Research at Boston College, 2013). Retrieved July 8, 2013, from http://crr.bc.edu.

7. According to the Social Security Administration, median annual income for married couples and nonmarried persons age sixty-five or older *increased markedly* between 1962 and 2010. After adjusting for inflation, median income for married couples in 2010 was $44,718, which was 115 percent greater than in 1962 when it was $20,759. For nonmarried persons, the increase was 112 percent ($17,261 in 2010 compared with $8,159 in 1962). At the other extreme are poor Americans. Overall, 9 percent of Americans sixty-five or older are poor (having income *below* the poverty line) and nearly 6 percent are *near* poor (having income greater than or equal to the poverty line and less than 125 percent of the poverty line). Married persons are much better off—4.2 percent are poor and 3.1 percent are near poor. Nonmarried women and minorities had the highest poverty rates in 2010, ranging from 15.8 percent to 18 percent. Social Security Administration, "Fast Facts and Figures about Social Security, 2012." SSA Publication No. 13-11785 (Washington, DC: Social Security Administration, August 2012).

8. Ricardo Alonso-Zaldivar, "Report: US Health Care System Wastes $750 Billion a Year." Associated Press, September 6, 2012. Retrieved September 6, 2012, from http://enews.earthlink.net/channel/news/print?guid=20120906/fdb50296-b1c3 -43dd-9cff-d8.

9. As reported by the AAUW, a woman working full time earns on average 82 percent of what a man earns, and an unexplained pay gap of 7 percent exists even when women and men have the same level of education and the same occupation. Retrieved March 15, 2013, from http://www.aauw.org/files/2013/02/graduating-to -a-pay-gap.

10. Renee Davidson, "Graduating to a Pay Gap," *AAUW Outlook* (Winter 2013): 8–11. AAUW acknowledges that women tend to choose lower-paying career fields than men (education and social sciences versus engineering and computer science).

After AAUW controlled for factors that affect earnings, such as type of university, grades, major, hours worked, career field, type of job, job sector, a pay gap remains. (Italics added.)

11. Anne-Marie Slaughter, "Yes, You Can." *New York Times Sunday Book Review*, March 7, 2013. Retrieved March 28, 2013, from http://www.nytimes.com.

12. James Allworth, "It's Not Women Who Should Lean In; It's Men Who Should Step Back." *HBR* Blog Network (April 8, 2013).

13. The US Census Bureau defines current dollars as income (unadjusted for inflation) in the year in which a person, household, or family receives it.

14. George E. Vaillant, *Aging Well: Surprising Guideposts to a Happier Life from the Landmark Harvard Study of Adult Development* (Boston: Little, Brown, 2002), 25.

15. Vaillant, *Aging Well*, 305–6.

16. Vaillant, *Aging Well*, 291.

CHAPTER 6

1. US Bureau of Labor Statistics, "Occupational Employment Statistics (OES) Highlights" (December 2010). Retrieved March 21, 2013, from http://www.bls.gov.

2. US Bureau of Labor Statistics, "Occupational Employment Statistics (OES) Highlights."

3. US Census Bureau News, "Older Americans Month: May 2013." CB13-FF.07. Washington, DC (March 7, 2013). Retrieved March 18, 2013, from http://www.census.gov/newsroom/releases/pdf/cb13ff-07_older2013.pdf.

4. Steven Greenhouse, "The Job You Make: Older Workers Mine Their Skills and Connections to Go Their Own Way," *New York Times*, March 4, 2010, Retirement Section, F1, F8.

5. Sylvania was an electronics manufacturer that became GTE Sylvania and later merged with Verizon.

6. Norbert Wiener was a brilliant American mathematician and professor at MIT. Wiener is regarded as the originator of *cybernetics*, which he defined as the study of control and communication in the animal and the machine, a formalization of the notion of feedback, with many implications for engineering, systems control, computer science, biology, philosophy, and the organization of society.

7. Steven Greenhouse, "In and Out, Off and On," *New York Times*, March 13, 2013, Retirement Section, F1–F2.

8. Greenhouse, "In and Out, Off and On," F1–F2.

CHAPTER 7

1. Society for Human Resource Management, "2012 Employee Job Satisfaction and Engagement: How Employees Are Dealing with Uncertainty" (Alexandria, VA: Society for Human Resource Management, 2012). Retrieved March 25, 2013, from http://www.shrm.org.

2. Jane Kramer, "A Fork of One's Own," *New Yorker*, March 18, 2013, 74–80.

3. Sunhwa Lee and Lois Shaw, *Gender and Economic Security in Retirement* (Washington, DC: Institute for Women's Policy Research, 2003), D456.

4. Society for Human Resource Management, "2012 Employee Benefits" (Alexandria, VA: Society for Human Resource Management, 2012). Retrieved March 18, 2013, from http://www.shrm.org/research/surveyfindings/articles/documents/2012_empbenefits_report.pdf.

CHAPTER 8

1. Bahá'ís embrace certain fundamental principles. They include the elimination of all forms of prejudice; full equality between the sexes; recognition of the essential oneness of the world's great religions; the elimination of extremes of poverty and wealth; universal education; the harmony of science and religion; a sustainable balance between nature and technology; and the establishment of a world federal system, based on collective security and the oneness of humanity. See http://www.bahai.org.

2. Completed and dedicated in the early 1950s, the graceful temple is capped by a dome rising twenty stories above beautifully landscaped grounds.

3. Ram Dass, "Conscious Connections and Aging" excerpt from *Still Here: Embracing Aging, Changing, and Dying* (2013). Retrieved April 21, 2013, from http://www.ramdass.org/RD/open-heart-extra.

CHAPTER 9

1. US Bureau of Labor Statistics. "Volunteering in the United States: 2012." Economic News Release USDL-13-0285. Washington, DC, February 22, 2013.

2. Jennn Fusion, "What Is the Target Market for Fitness Gyms?" 2010. Retrieved April 10, 2013, from http://smallbusiness.chron.com/target-market-fitness-gyms -3354.html.

3. Theresa M. Harrison, Sandra Weintraub, M.-Marsel Mesulam, and Emily Rogalski, "Superior Memory and Higher Cortical Volumes in Unusually Successful Cognitive Aging," *Journal of the International Neuropsychological Society* 18, no. 6 (November 2012): 1081–85.

CHAPTER 10

1. Mitra Toossi, "Employment Outlook: 2008–18: Labor Force Projections to 2018: Older Workers Staying More Active," US Bureau of Labor Statistics, *Monthly Labor Review* (November 2009).

2. Sindya Bhanoo, "Ants Become Job-Hoppers as They Age," *New York Times*, April 30, 2013, D6.

3. Rachel Reilly, "You Aren't the Only One to Think about Switching Careers . . . Ants Change Jobs as They Grow Older," April 19, 2013. Retrieved May 3, 2013, from http://www.dailymail.co.uk/sciencetech/article-2311688/ANTS-change-job -grow-older-scientists-discover.html.

4. John Gray, *Men Are from Mars, Women Are from Venus* (New York: Harper, 1992).

5. Gary E. Kessler, *Voices of Wisdom*, 7th ed. (Belmont, CA: Cengage Learning, 2010).

Bibliography

Aegon. "The Changing Face of Retirement: The Aegon Retirement Readiness Survey 2012." The Hague, Netherlands: Aegon Group, 2012. Retrieved March 8, 2013, from http://www.aegon.com.

Allworth, James. "It's Not Women Who Should Lean In; It's Men Who Should Step Back." *HBR* Blog Network, April 8, 2013.

Alonso-Zaldivar, Ricardo. "Report: US Health Care System Wastes $750 Billion a Year." Associated Press, September 6, 2012. Retrieved September 6, 2012, from http://enews.earthlink.net/channel/news/print?guid=20120906/fdb50296-b1c3 -43dd-9cff-d8.

APA Center for Organizational Excellence. "Work-Life Fit and Enjoying What They Do Top the List of Reasons Why Employees Stay on the Job," September 5, 2012. Retrieved March 4, 2013, from http://www.apaexcellence.org/resources/ goodcompany/newsletter/article/391.

Australian Workplace Innovation and Social Research Centre. Retrieved December 10, 2012, from http://agingandwork.bc.edu/blog/a-20-year-view-of-the-labor -force.

Barton, Edward R. *Beyond Men Hugging Trees: A Qualitative Exploration of Men's Participation in Men's Peer Mutual Support Groups*. Saarbrucken, Germany: VDM Verlag Dr. Muller, 2011.

———. "Early History of the Changing Men Collections." *Journal of Men's Health and Gender* 3, no. 2 (June 2006): 213–14.

———. "Experiencing My Mid-Life Crises and Afterward: Various Hermeneutical Analyses of Lived Experiences, Part 1." *International Journal of Self Help and Self Care* 2, no. 4 (2003–2004): 329–38.

———, ed. *Mythopoetic Perspectives of Men's Healing Work: An Anthology for Therapists and Others.* Westport, CT: Bergin and Garvey, 2000.

Bass, Scott. "From Retirement to 'Productive Aging' and Back to Work Again." In *Gerontology in the Era of the Third Age: Implications and Next Steps,* 169–89. Dawn C. Carr and Kathrin Komp, eds. New York: Springer, 2011.

Bhate, Rucha. "A Woman's Place? A Cross National Exploration of Gender Role Perspectives—Quick Insights." Boston College, Sloan Center on Aging and Work, November 2012. Retrieved November 27, 2012, from http://www.bc.edu/research/agingandwork/archive_pubs/QI1.html.

Bly, Robert. *Iron John: A Book about Men.* Reading, MA: Addison-Wesley, 1990.

Broniec, Rick. *A Passionate Life: 7 Steps for Reclaiming a Passionate, Purposeful and Joyful Life.* Greenwood, WI: Rick Broniec, 2012.

Burtless, Gary. "The Impact of Population Aging and Delayed Retirement on Workforce Productivity." Chestnut Hill, MA: Center for Retirement Research at Boston College, 2013. Retrieved July 8, 2013, from http://crr.bc.edu.

Campbell, Joseph, and Bill Moyers. *The Power of Myth.* New York: Anchor Books, 1991.

Carr, Dawn C., and Kathrin Komp, eds. *Gerontology in the Era of the Third Age: Implications and Next Steps.* New York: Springer, 2011.

Chagall, Marc. "Marc Chagall Quotes." Artquotes.Net, November 29, 2007, http://www.artquotes.net/masters/chagall_quotes.htm.

Clark, Roy P. "Eugene Patterson, 89, Voice on Civil Rights, Dies." *Atlanta Journal-Constitution,* January 13, 2013. Retrieved April 15, 2013, from http://www.ajc.com.

Cole, Ellen, and Mary Gergen, eds. *Retiring But Not Shy.* Chagrin Falls, OH: Taos Institute, 2012.

Coontz, Stephanie. "Why Gender Equality Stalled." *New York Times,* February 17, 2013, SR1, SR6–7.

Daley, Suzanne, and Nicholas Kulish. "Germany Fights Population Drop: Takes Steps to Avoid a Shortage of Labor." *New York Times*, August 14, 2013, A1, A6.

Dass, Ram. "Conscious Connections and Aging" excerpt from *Still Here: Embracing Aging, Changing, and Dying*, 2013. Retrieved April 21, 2013, from http://www.ramdass.org/RD/open-heart-extra.

Davidson, Renee. "Graduating to a Pay Gap." *AAUW Outlook*, Winter 2013, 8–11.

Day, Jennifer C. "Health Data from the Census Bureau: People." US Department of Commerce. State Data Center Annual Meeting, October 17, 2012.

De Lange, Annet. "Sustaining an Aging Workforce." AGEnda, Aging and Work Blog. Chestnut Hill, MA: Boston College, Sloan Center on Aging and Work, January 23, 2013. http://www.agingandwork.bc.edu/blog/2013/01.

Dennis, Helen. "The Older Entrepreneur." AGEnda, Aging and Work Blog. Chestnut Hill, MA: Boston College, Sloan Center on Aging and Work, November 14, 2012. http://agingandwork.bc.edu/blog/the-older-entrepreneur.

Dubus, Andre, III. *Townie: A Memoir*. New York: Norton, 2011.

Dulaney, Chelsey. "Older Workers Face a Tougher Road." *Charlotte Observer*, August 21, 2012. Retrieved September 12, 2012, from http://www.timesnews.net/article/9050726/older-workers-face-a-tougher-road.

Economic Policy Institute. "Labor Force Participation Rate, by Age and Gender, 1959–2011." *The State of Working America*, 12th ed. Washington, DC: Economic Policy Institute, 2012. Retrieved February 11, 2013, from http://www.stateofworkingamerica.org/jobs/figure5L.

——. "Unemployment Rate, by Gender and Education, 2000–2011." *The State of Working America*, 12th ed. Washington, DC: Economic Policy Institute, 2012. Retrieved February 11, 2013, from http://www.stateofworkingamerica.org/jobs/table5.4.

——. "Unemployment Rate, by Education, Race and Ethnicity, 2000–2011." *The State of Working America*, 12th ed. Washington, DC: Economic Policy Institute, 2012. Retrieved February 11, 2013, from http://www.stateofworkingamerica.org/jobs/table5.3.

Ehrenreich, Barbara. *The Hearts of Men: American Dreams and the Flight from Commitment*. Garden City, NY: Anchor Press/Doubleday, 1983.

Federal Interagency Forum on Aging-Related Statistics. "Older Americans 2012: Key Indicators of Well-Being," 2012. Retrieved March 18, 2013, from http://www.AgingStats.gov/main_site/data/2012_documents/population.aspx.

Fideler, Elizabeth F. *Women Still at Work: Professionals over Sixty and on the Job.* Lanham, MD: Rowman & Littlefield, 2012.

Fischer, David Hackett. *Growing Old in America.* New York: Oxford University Press, 1978.

Freedman, Marc. *Encore: Finding Work That Matters in the Second Half of Life.* New York: PublicAffairs/Perseus Books, 2007.

Fusion, Jennn. "What Is the Target Market for Fitness Gyms?" 2010. Retrieved April 10, 2013, from http://smallbusiness.chron.com/target-market-fitness-gyms-3354.html.

Gray, John. *Men Are from Mars, Women Are from Venus.* New York: Harper, 1992.

Greenhouse, Steven. "The Job You Make: Older Workers Mine Their Skills and Connections to Go Their Own Way." *New York Times,* March 4, 2010, Retirement Section, F1, F8.

———. "In and Out, Off and On." *New York Times,* March 13, 2013, Retirement Section, F1–F2.

Harkness, Helen. *Don't Stop the Career Clock: Rejecting the Myths of Aging for a New Way to Work in the 21st Century.* Palo Alto, CA: Davies-Black Publishing, 1999.

Harrison, Theresa M., Sandra Weintraub, M.-Marsel Mesulam, and Emily Rogalski. "Superior Memory and Higher Cortical Volumes in Unusually Successful Cognitive Aging." *Journal of the International Neuropsychological Society* 18, no. 6 (November 2012): 1081–85.

Hasegawa, Kyoko. "Retirees Still Seeking Work." *Japan Times,* July 24, 2012. Retrieved August 1, 2012, from http://www.japantimes.co.jp.

Heidkamp, Maria. "Older Workers, Rising Skill Requirements and the Need for a Re-envisioning of the Public Workforce System." Rutgers University, John J. Heldrich Center for Workforce Development, 2012, 5–6.

Jones, Terry. *Elder: A Spiritual Alternative to Being Elderly.* Portland, OR: Elderhood Institute Books, 2006.

———. *The Elder Within: The Source of Mature Masculinity.* Wilsonville, OR: BookPartners, 2001.

Kessler, Gary E. *Voices of Wisdom,* 7th ed. Belmont, CA: Cengage Learning, 2010.

Koenig, Gary, and Lina Walker. "The New Reality: Important Facts about America's Seniors." AARP Public Policy Institute, Fact Sheet 230, June 2011. Washington, DC. Retrieved February 28, 2013, from http://www.aarp.org/research.

Kramer, Jane. "A Fork of One's Own." *New Yorker,* March 18, 2013, 74–80.

Laslett, Peter. *A Fresh Map of Life: The Emergence of the Third Age.* London: Weidenfeld and Nicolson, 1989.

Lawrence-Lightfoot, Sara. *Exit: The Endings That Set Us Free.* New York: Farrar, Straus and Giroux, 2012.

Lee, John H. *The Flying Boy: Healing the Wounded Man.* Deerfield Beach, FL: Health Communications, 1989.

Lee, Sunhwa, and Lois Shaw. "Gender and Economic Security in Retirement." Washington, DC: Institute for Women's Policy Research, 2003, D456.

Levinson, Daniel J., et al. *The Seasons of a Man's Life.* New York: Ballantine Books, 1978.

Levinson, Daniel J., and Judy D. Levinson. *The Seasons of a Woman's Life.* New York: Alfred A. Knopf, 1996.

Lowery, Annie, and Catherine Rampell. "Jobless, and Hopeless, in America." *New York Times,* November 2, 2012, B1, B2.

Marti, Gerardo. Davidson College Associate Professor and Chair of Sociology. Course syllabus for Sociology of Work, 2006. http://www.davidson.edu.

McDougall, Christopher. *Born to Run: A Hidden Tribe, Superathletes, and the Greatest Race the World Has Never Seen.* New York: Vintage Books, 2009.

Medina, Jennifer. "Long-Term Jobless Regroup to Fight the Odds." *New York Times,* August 17, 2012, A1, A3.

MetLife. "10th Annual Study of Employee Benefits Trends: Seeing Opportunity in Shifting Tides." New York: MetLife, 2012. Retrieved December 27, 2012, from http://www.metlife.com.

MetLife Mature Market Institute. "Transitioning into Retirement: The MetLife
     Study of Baby Boomers at 65." Westport, CT, April 2012. Retrieved January 8,
     2013, from http://www.metlife.com.

Ministry of Labour, Luxembourg. "Luxembourg 2020." National Reform Program
     for the Grand Duchy of Luxembourg under the Europe 2020 Strategy. The
     European Semester, April 2011. Retrieved November 15, 2012, from http://
     ec.europa.eu/europe2020/pdf/nrp/nrp_luxembourg_en.pdf.

Moen, Phyllis. "A Life-Course Approach to the Third Age." In *Gerontology in the
     Era of the Third Age: Implications and Next Steps*, 13–33. Dawn C. Carr and
     Kathrin Komp, eds. New York: Springer, 2011.

Munnell, Alicia H., and Steven A. Sass. *Working Longer: The Solution to the
     Retirement Income Challenge*. Washington, DC: Brookings Institution Press, 2008.

O'Hagan, Andrew. "The Male Bond." *New York Times Style Magazine*, March 10,
     2013, 86, 88.

Porter, Eduardo. "The Payoff in Delaying Retirement." *New York Times*, March 6,
     2013, B1, B5.

Rampell, Catherine. "Big Income Losses Hit Those Near Retirement." *New York
     Times*, August 24, 2012, B1–B2.

———. "A Sharp Drop in Job Growth Sows Concern." *New York Times*, April 6,
     2013, A1, A3.

———. "U.S. Adds 171,000 Jobs, More Than Estimated." *New York Times*, November
     3, 2012, B1, B2.

Reilly, Rachel. "You Aren't the Only One to Think about Switching Careers . . . Ants
     Change Jobs as They Grow Older." April 19, 2013. Retrieved May 3, 2013, from
     http://www.dailymail.co.uk/sciencetech/article-2311688/ANTS-change-job-grow
     -older-scientists-discover.html.

Rix, Sara E. "The Employment Situation, January 2013: Jobs Added to the Economy
     but Unemployment for Older Workers Holds Fast." AARP Public Policy Institute,
     Fact Sheet 277. Washington, DC, February 2013. Retrieved February 28, 2013,
     from http://www.aarp.org/research.

———. "Unemployment Rises for Older Workers, March 2012." AARP Public Policy
     Institute, Fact Sheet 255, March 2012. http://www.aarp.org/ppi.

Rosin, Hanna. "Who Wears the Pants in This Economy?" *New York Times Magazine*, September 2, 2012, 22–29, 38.

Rowles, Graham D., and Lydia K. Manning. "Experiencing the Third Age: The Perspective of Qualitative Inquiry." In *Gerontology in the Era of the Third Age: Implications and Next Steps*, 147–67. Dawn C. Carr and Kathrin Komp, eds. New York: Springer, 2011.

Sadler, William A. *The Third Age: Six Principles of Growth and Renewal after Forty.* Cambridge, MA: Perseus Books, 2000.

Schwartz, Nelson D. "Recovery in U.S. Lifting Profits, Not Adding Jobs." *New York Times*, March 4, 2013, A1, A3.

Shea, Gordon F., and Adolf Haasen. *The Older Worker Advantage: Making the Most of Our Aging Workforce.* Westport, CT: Praeger, 2006.

Shrestha, Laura B., and Elayne J. Heisler. "The Changing Demographic Profile of the United States." Congressional Research Service. No. 7-5700, RL32701. March 31, 2011, http://www.crs.gov.

Slaughter, Anne-Marie. "Why Women Still Can't Have It All." *Atlantic Magazine*, July–August 2012. Retrieved December 13, 2012, from http://www.theatlantic.com/magazine/archive/2012/07/why-women-still-cant-have-it-all/309020.

Slaughter, Anne-Marie. "Yes, You Can." *New York Times Sunday Book Review*, March 7, 2013. Retrieved March 28, 2013, from http://www.nytimes.com.

Social Security Administration. "Fast Facts and Figures about Social Security, 2012." SSA Publication No. 13-11785. Washington, DC: Social Security Administration, August 2012.

Society for Human Resource Management. "2012 Employee Benefits." Alexandria, VA: Society for Human Resource Management, 2012. Retrieved March 18, 2013, from http://www.shrm.org/research/surveyfindings/articles/documents/2012_empbenefits_report.pdf.

———. "2012 Employee Job Satisfaction and Engagement: How Employees Are Dealing with Uncertainty." Alexandria, VA: Society for Human Resource Management, 2012. Retrieved March 25, 2013, from http://www.shrm.org.

Solman, Paul. "Manufacturer Vita Needle Finds Investment in Older Workers Turns a Big Profit." Retrieved January 4, 2013, from http://www.pbs.org/newshour/bb/business/jan-june13/makingsense_01-02.html?print.

Talese, Gay. "The Crisis Manager." *New Yorker*, September 24, 2012, 40–49.

Toossi, Mitra. "Employment Outlook: 2008–18: Labor Force Projections to 2018: Older Workers Staying More Active." US Bureau of Labor Statistics, *Monthly Labor Review*, November 2009, 30–51.

———. "Projections of the Labor Force to 2050: A Visual Essay." US Bureau of Labor Statistics, *Monthly Labor Review*, October 2012, 3–16.

US Bureau of Labor Statistics. "National Hispanic Heritage Month." BLS Spotlight on Statistics, September 2012. Retrieved January 28, 2013, from http://www.bls .gov/spotlight/2012/hispanic_heritage.

———. "Occupational Employment Statistics (OES) Highlights," December 2010. Retrieved March 21, 2013, from http://www.bls.gov.

———. "Volunteering in the United States—2012." Economic News Release USDL-13-0285. Washington, DC, February 22, 2013.

US Census Bureau News. "Older Americans Month: May 2013." CB13-FF.07. Washington, DC, March 7, 2013. Retrieved March 18, 2013, from http:// www.census.gov/newsroom/releases/pdf/cb13ff-07_older2013.pdf.

US Department of Education. National Center for Educational Statistics, 2012. Retrieved March 14, 2013, from http://nces.ed.gov/fastfacts/display.asp?id=27.

Vaillant, George E. *Aging Well: Surprising Guideposts to a Happier Life from the Landmark Harvard Study of Adult Development*. Boston: Little, Brown, 2002.

Weber, Lauren. "Americans Rip Up Retirement Plans." *Wall Street Journal*, January 31, 2013. Retrieved February 1, 2013, from http://www.online.wsj.com.

Willie, Sarah. S. *Acting Black: College, Identity, and the Performance of Race*. New York: Routledge, 2003.

Wooden, John. *Wooden: A Lifetime of Observations and Reflections On and Off the Court*. http://www.goodreads.com.

Woolhouse, Megan. "Retirees Lend Their Expertise." *Boston Globe*, January 31, 2013, B5, B7.

———. "Time Is Not on Their Side." *Boston Globe*, March 25, 2013, A1, A10.

Discussion Questions

Why are professionals remaining in their career jobs longer than in the past? What are the advantages to the older individual of continued participation in the labor force? What are the advantages to society?

"Job satisfaction" can have multiple meanings for older workers. Which do you prefer?

In what ways do the work life stories in *Men Still at Work* differ from the stories of older working women you know? In what ways are they similar?

Traditionally, a male was head of household and his career came first. With dramatic changes in gender roles in recent decades, men and women are expected to share responsibility for family care and for earning money. Discuss contemporary gender role perspectives with respect to work and how they differ from the past.

Achieving and maintaining work-life balance has become more challenging for men and women. Should company policies address this problem, and, if so, how?

Many older men can point to at least one person who influenced their career choice, perhaps a parent, grandparent, family friend, professor, or boss who provided encouragement or acted as a role model. Did you have a mentor at any point along your early or later career path and, if so, how important was the advice you were given?

Older men cite various reasons for continuing in the paid workforce past the conventional age of retirement. Often they believe "your job defines who you are," and they are fearful of losing their professional identity. Sometimes they fear boredom and an atrophied intellect if they stop working. What factors influence your thinking about retirement?

To what extent does/did your decision about retirement depend on the state of the economy?

If a man's work role shapes the organization of his life, what happens when he becomes unemployed? When he retires?

Why is *un*retiring becoming more commonplace?

Why is the number of older self-employed people increasing?

It is hard to pin down the definition of "older," especially when applied to the "older worker." If eighty is the new seventy, seventy is the new sixty, and so on, what does "older" mean? One study says that men consider themselves old at seventy-seven on average and women say they are not old until eighty. Why do you think that is?

Pejoratives directed at older men and women, such as "over the hill" and "no spring chicken," persist. How prevalent is age stereotyping today—in society in general and in the workplace in particular? Have you experienced it?

The AAUW's research on the gender pay gap finds that college-educated women experience inequity from the first paycheck through to retirement. Older women who stay in the workforce are more concerned about financial pressures than men are. Is this because men tend to choose higher-paying occupations or are there other reasons?

Men hold the majority of top jobs in the United States. Do you think the relative scarcity of women in top jobs is due to a lack of ambition, a lack of support, or something else?

Corporate law firms commonly mandate retirement for older attorneys who have reached a designated age. Do you think this kind of policy is reasonable?

Why do older men and women get so much satisfaction from mentoring early careerists?

What motivates older working men and women to perform unpaid volunteer work?

Technological literacy is essential to performing a significant number of job functions today, and technological change is proceeding apace. Are you comfortable with new technologies—at work? elsewhere? Why are some older men and women eager to acquire new skills and others are not?

Reading is the number one leisure activity among the older men and women discussed in *Men Still at Work* and *Women Still at Work*. Some belong to book groups in libraries, bookstores, and private homes. Why do you think book groups are proliferating?

Psychiatrist George Vaillant says that "successful aging is not an oxymoron." Do you agree? If so, how can aging be "successful?"

Index

About the Author

Elizabeth F. Fideler, EdD, is a research fellow at the Sloan Center on Aging and Work at Boston College. She received a doctorate in administration, planning, and social policy from Harvard University. Dr. Fideler has written and presented extensively on aspects of K–12 teacher development and university teaching and learning. Prior to becoming a research fellow at the Sloan Center, she conducted research projects at Education Development Center, Inc. Her current research and writing interests focus on older women and men who choose to continue in the paid workforce beyond conventional retirement age. *Men Still at Work* follows the book *Women Still at Work* (2012). Dr. Fideler can be reached at lizpaulfideler@mindspring.com and on Facebook.

main

JUL 2 2 2014

04/08/2014 $36.00

WITHDRAWN